Gumbo for the Soul

A volume in
Contemporary Perspectives on Multicultural Gifted Education
Donna Y. Ford and Malik S. Henfield *Series Editors*

Gumbo for the Soul

Males of Color Share Their Stories, Meditations, Affirmations, and Inspirations

edited by

Brian L. Wright
University of Memphis

Lucian Yates, III
Kentucky State University

Nathaniel Bryan
Miami University

Michael A. Robinson
Forest Of The Rain Productions

Christopher J. P. Sewell
Williams College

Kianga Thomas
Norfolk State University

INFORMATION AGE PUBLISHING, INC.
Charlotte, NC • www.infoagepub.com

Library of Congress Cataloging-in-Publication Data

A CIP record for this book is available from the Library of Congress
http://www.loc.gov

ISBN: 978-1-64113-564-1 (Paperback)
978-1-64113-565-8 (Hardcover)
978-1-64113-566-5 (ebook)

Copyright © 2019 Information Age Publishing Inc.

All rights reserved. No part of this publication may be reproduced, stored in a retrieval system, or transmitted, in any form or by any means, electronic, mechanical, photocopying, microfilming, recording or otherwise, without written permission from the publisher.

Printed in the United States of America

CONTENTS

Acknowledgments vii
Introduction.. ix

SECTION I
FAMILIAL IMPACT ON EDUCATION

1 Pushing for a Better Life.. 3
  Wil Greer

2 Choices 7
  George Suttles

3 Black Boy Rising 11
  Larry J. Walker

4 My Son Has a Purpose Too: A Father's Story of Autism 17
  George E. Stewart II

5 Where the Waters Met: A Story of Friendship, Brotherhood,
  and Service... 21
  Robert Mays

6 Freedom of Forgiveness 25
  Zaccheus L. Moss

7 I Might Cry, But I'll Get There 29
  MarQo D. Patton

8   Personal Agency: An Under-Discussed Factor for Successful
    Life Outcomes of Black Males 35
    Michael T. Owens

9   Still Standing: Bumps in the Road Along a Path
    to Greater Success 41
    Jason Rivera

10 Poverty and Education 47
    C. Sheldon Woods

11 The Destruction of Drugs 53
    Joel Bratton Jr.

SECTION II

INTERSECTIONS OF RACE, GENDER, AND SEXUALITY

12 From Unseen to Seen: The Power of Significant Others 59
    Derrick Robinson

13 One Hundred Percent Intelligent Black Child: Black and
    Exceptional in Mathematics 65
    Nickolaus A. Ortiz

14 Of Pain and Peach Fuzz: A Chief Equity Officer Rants 69
    John D. Marshall

15 Thank You So Much for Asking 75
    Darreon D. Greer Sr.

16 Things Fall Apart to Fall in Place 79
    Jajuan S. Johnson

17 The Menace of Immigrants: Reflections of Growing
    Up in Organisms Against My Development 83
    Oscar Espinoza-Parra

18 Be Yourself and the World Will Adjust 89
    Tyrone C. Hamler

19 Memoir of a Former Impostor 93
    C. Emmanuel Little

SECTION III

RACIAL DISCRIMINATION

20 What Was Intended for My Harm, God Intended for My Good: A Black Male Overcoming the Odds 101
Lucian Yates III

21 Coming Home: The Social and Educational Consequences of Being a Formerly Incarcerated Chicano Convict Criminologist 109
Oscar Fabian Soto

22 When I Woke Up to Being Black 115
Christopher J. P. Sewell

23 The Power of Forgiveness 119
Joseph Matthews

24 Stony the Road We Trod: Black Males Share Lived Experiences With Police Brutality 123
Antonio Ellis and Eddie Vanderhorst

25 The Race 129
Dwight Gordon II

26 A Black Man's Story of Empowerment: Why I Stopped Begging Whites to Accept My Blackness 133
Raymond Adams

27 The Emanuel Church Massacre and the School Across the Street: A Black Man's Narrative of Two Racialized Conflicts 139
Nathaniel Bryan

28 From Hopelessness to the Hallways of Higher Education 145
Lawrence Scott

29 To Leave or Not to Leave: That Was My Contemplation 149
Jamel Miller

SECTION IV
OVERCOMING NARRATIVE OF FAILURE

30 Becoming the Victor 157
Victor L. Powell

31 Overcoming the Obstacles and Breaking the Barriers................... 163
Jeremiah N. Taylor

32 Man Enough to Ask for Help: Overcoming a Learning
Disability and Family Issues 169
David C. Hughes

33 For Special Educators Who Have Considered Giving Up
When the Rainbow Is Enough: A Retrospective
and Prospective Essay on Being a Black Male
in Specialized Education 173
Brandon C. S. Wallace

34 Special Education to Higher Education: Speech Impediment
to a Degree in Speech Communications 179
Burgess Mitchell

35 From a Refugee Child to Success in America 185
Alex Sekwat

36 I Am Not Supposed to Be Here: Why Numbers Sometimes Lie....... 189
Stuart Rhoden

37 Social Capital and Its Impact on My Personal
and Academic Success.. 195
Solomon Tention

38 Nobody Told Me the Road Would Be Easy.. 203
Dante Pelzer

39 I'm Not My Chair... 207
Michael S. Washington

40 On Stuttering and Speech Impediments: Stepping Stones Not
Speed Bumps 211
Charles A. Barrett

41 Keeping My Head Above Water in a River of Whiteness................. 219
LaMarcus J. Hall

| 42 | Rising Above a Tracked System 225
Brian K. Williams

| 43 | Even Today I Remember the Pain 231
Gregory Washington

| 44 | The Test of a Man 237
Verontae Deams

| 45 | Rising Through the Concrete Like a Rose 241
Nathan Stephens

| 46 | Akoben: The Ancestors' Call 245
Mwalimu Donkor Issa Minors

SECTION V
SEXUAL AND SUBSTANCE ABUSE

| 47 | Forged by My Foundation 253
Michael A. Robinson

| 48 | Alone Was My Safe Place 261
Raphael Crawford

| 49 | Won't He Do It . . . : From Challenges to Triumphs 265
Derek Irvin

| 50 | From Victim to Victor: "I Don't Want to Play!" 269
Robert A. Massey

| 51 | Learning to Overcome Excessive Drinking 273
Charles Brown III

SECTION VI
EXPERIENCES IN HIGHER EDUCATION

| 52 | How Spirit and Soul Led Me to a Life as a Psychological Scientist 279
Brandon E. Gamble

| 53 | Do Not Apply to College 285
Eugene Pitchford III

54 Challenging Transitions: Reflecting Back, Projecting Forward 289
Brian A. Burt

Epilogue 295
About the Editors 299
About the Contributors... 301

ACKNOWLEDGMENTS

First and foremost, we wish to thank and praise Donna Y. Ford at The Ohio State University, for her vision to add a second *Gumbo for the Soul* book to give males of color space and place to share their counter stories in response to dominant narratives that too frequently frame males of color as a suspect, threatening, and malevolent. We also, acknowledge Malik S. Henfield (Dean of the School of Education at Loyola University Chicago) for his belief in this project.

Second, I, Brian, acknowledge my coeditors, Nathaniel Bryan, Christopher J. P. Sewell, Lucian Yates III, Mike Robinson, and Kianga Thomas who brought to this project a range of disciplinary perspectives, research interests, theoretical stances, life stages, and professional experiences that individually and collectively challenge the hegemonic ways of knowledge production, validation, and dissemination of narratives about men of color in society. Through the writing of their own stories and the careful review of the stories of the authors of this collection, they reinforced the legitimacy that our voices matter.

Third, a special thank you to our individual institutions, The University of Memphis, Miami University, Williams College, Tennessee State University, Forest Of The Rain Production, and Norfolk State University, respectively, for your support as well as space and time to write and complete this book. To our friends and families thank you for your unwavering support, encouragement, and belief in our intellectual ability to bring this book to fruition. To Jasmine Morton, thank you for your initial review of each manuscript to identify technical writing issues.

Fourth and final, my coeditors and I are grateful, appreciative of the authors who unselfishly shared their candid counter stories allowing themselves to be vulnerable in the pages of this book. Thank you for allowing us to learn from and with you. #*BrilliantMenOfColor*

INTRODUCTION

> *He's misunderstood, some say that He's up to no good around the neighborhood*
> *Well, for your information Alot of my brotha's got education*
> *Now check it*
> *You got your wall street brotha, Your blue collar brotha,*
> *Your down-for-whatever-chillin'-on-the-corner brotha*
> *Your talented brotha, and to everyone of ya'll behind bars*
> *You know that Angie loves ya, my my*
>
> —Stone, Saadiq, Lilly, Standridge, and Ozuna (2001)

The lyrics to the song "Brotha" sung by Angie Stone, specifically the verse above, is used to frame, describe, and explain the diverse lived experiences of males of color in society. Despite persistently negative stereotypes that suggest "he's up to no good around the neighborhood," this book, a companion to the Ford, David, Scott-Trotman, and Sealy-Ruiz (2017) *Gumbo for the Soul: Liberating Memoirs and Stories to Inspire Females of Color*, documents the trials, tribulations, and triumphs of men of color. The stories, meditations, affirmations, and inspirations serve as counter-narratives to the dominant-narratives, which are typically framed in terms of "problems" and "pathologies." Drawing on the work of Howard (2014), we focus on promises, potentials, and possibilities in the educational and social uplift of men of color. Collectively, this book pushes back against the primary ways in which the lives and experiences of men of color are framed—leaving them "broken," while ignoring the myriad existing institutional and structural factors that negatively shape our lives. Therefore, this edited book not only focuses on the critical academic, social, and environmental issues men of color face, but also the different paths they may have taken to circumvent institutional inequities and to achieve success.

In general, men of color, in the United States, face a number of critical academic, social, and environmental issues. These academic issues include, but are not limited to, disproportional rates of suspensions and expulsions, overrepresentation in special education programs, underrepresentation in gifted education, Advanced Placement or college-preparatory programs, excessively high dropout/pushout rates, and high incidence of stereotype threat (Ford, 2013). These academic disparities are inextricably linked to negative social and environmental outcomes. These include racial discrimination, high rates of unemployment, economic hardship, adverse health conditions, drug and alcohol abuse, negative media portrayal, and racial hate-crime violence, and police brutality (Wright, 2017).

While it is impossible to examine all of the institutional challenges facing men of color, this edited book documents the stories, meditations, affirmations, and inspirations of this diverse population. Moreover, this book offers counter stories authored by a new generation of men of color that brings attention to the myriad spaces and places that oppress, repress, objectify, and deny the strengths, assets, and more importantly, the humanity of men of color. Particular attention is given to stories that describe and explain trials, tribulations, and triumphs to validate, empower, and situate the cultural and personal identities of men of color who have successfully navigated and negotiated spaces within schools, family circles, and communities to maximize their promise, potential, and possibility.

Our hope is that all those who read this edited book would experience the ways in which the contributors who share their stories strategically and masterfully pivot from accumulated risk to resilience. These narratives and counter narratives are all lined up together in this edited book to become an indispensable statement for all to ponder, especially men of color, and at the same time, are testaments and pathways from despair to engagement and excellence. As the famous abolitionist Frederick Douglass once said, "it is easier to build strong children than to repair broken men" (Blow, 2014, p. 1). It is with this charge that the males of color share their stories in hopes of motivating, inspiring, and quite possibly saving a young man's life.

Why Gumbo for the Soul...

In the aforementioned spirit, and like its companion book, *Gumbo for the Soul: Liberating Memoirs and Stories to Inspire Females of Color* (Ford et al., 2017), the stories that comprise this series focuses on the impact—both the short- and long-term effects of rejection, loss, confusion, and pain. It is important that we acknowledge that not all men of color start from the same place. Many, as their stories will reveal have encountered a host of accumulated disadvantages brought about by a myriad of structural inequalities, historical exclusion of their racial-ethnic groups, poverty, racism, sexism, and a host of other emotionally and psychologically toxic realities. In the sections that follow we illuminate stories of risk, resiliency, and success that have too often been omitted from the narratives about males of color, especially Black and Latino males.

Our past and our future are intertwined. Each distinct memory becomes one life. In the words of Dr. Martin Luther King Jr. (1963):

> All men are caught in an inescapable network of mutuality, tied in a single garment of destiny. Whatever affects one directly, affects all indirectly. I can never be what I ought to be until you are what you ought to be, and you can never be what you ought to be until I am what I ought to be...(para. 4)

This is what drove the conceptualization of this edited book. The sharing of our stories echoes and illuminates the prophetic words of Dr. King—that our mutuality is indeed tied in a single garment of destiny albeit in different ways.

The authors assert that what once hurt, eventually heals, and the lesson (or lessons) to be learned becomes one with our soul and our spirit. Our experiences provide strength instead of destruction. Our great-grandfathers (great-grandmothers), grandfathers (grandmothers), fathers (mothers)—all men and women of power who came before us—were great descendants of the coastal lands of West Africa. They arrived in strange lands with their gumbo—their memories, rhythms, ingenuity, creativity, strength, and compassion. Their lived stories and conversation were recipes mixed with unique combinations of ingredients, dropped into the cast iron pot—stirred, dropped in, seasoned, dropped in, stirred again, and again, and again, until done. This gumbo is savory like the soul, carefully prepared, recipes rich with what our foremothers brought with them from their homeland. They brought the best of what they had to offer.

Gumbo has become a cornerstone of life in African-descended communities across the south and southwest spanning from South Carolina to Louisiana and Texas. Gumbo is a treasure...a reminder of the greatness that lived in the village in a time of strength and abundance...a reminder of the resilience and richness of our people over generations.

We must admit that there are a growing number of books on men of color, many of which have elicited their voices and perspectives. However, this book—a collection of memoirs—places the lived realities and experiences of men of color from varying age groups, socioeconomic backgrounds, professional experiences, and walks of life in conversations with each other and is shared to inspire and motivate readers, regardless of societal status. What these men have in common, though, is their drive to tell their story. Stories of pain, discovery, strength, and stories of beginnings. Many of the experiences, as difficult as they may have been, made the men who they are today. Telling these stories to a new generation will empower and encourage them in their experiences no matter how troubling or challenging. These stories, like our forefathers and mothers offering their gumbo, present the best these men have to offer. These authors want the world to know that deep inside of each of us is a rich, vibrant, purposeful beginning. As our lives develop and we are "stirred and stirred again," like gumbo, our experiences begin to shape who we are and who we become. When the stirring is complete, a comforting meal—one that says no matter what has gone into the dish, it's going to be amazingly magnificent!!

Methodology

In the spirit of gumbo and the African tradition of storytelling, we see each chapter contributor as a griot—an African term meaning "storyteller." Griots were known for passing down African wisdom, folktales, myths, and stories from one generation to another. As such, each contributing man of color becomes a griot who passes along his personal story of struggle and triumph, which coalesces with other stories of men of color to push against what Bryan (2017) considers "intergenerational legacies of negative views of [men of color]" (p. 326). In so doing, we utilize a storytelling and/or counter-storytelling methodology. Drawing on the academic scholarship of critical race scholars (Cook, 2013; Milner, 2010; Solórzano & Yosso, 2001), we define storytelling as a way people of color express and share knowledge of their lived experiences and realities in their own way; whereas counter storytelling serves to challenge dominant narratives about people of color, which are often untrue and dehumanizing. As stated earlier, the voices of males of color are often silenced and relegated to the margins. Such marginalization gives credence to dominant stories and narratives that position men of color as pathological, culturally deprived, and deficient—to suggest the least. The idea of storytelling and counter storytelling in this book is consistent with other books on Black males (Howard, 2014; Warren, 2017) that have elicited their voices and experiences. We desire to build on these works by following this trend.

Organization of the Book

We are very proud to be the keepers of these rich gumbo recipes. They represent and challenge particular hegemonic ways of sharing stories and knowledge production. The dissemination of these stories and/or counter stories serve as validation and also a form of currency and legitimacy of what it means to move through this world in Black and Brown bodies. Whereas the gumbo companion book is organized by contributing author's last names, this collection of inspirational stories, meditations, affirmations, and inspirations is organized by six themes to help males of color live out their destiny and become the boys to men they were born to be. The six themes are as follows:

Section I: Familial Impact on Education
Section II: Intersections of Race, Gender, and Sexuality
Section III: Racial Discrimination
Section IV: Overcoming Narrative of Failure
Section V: Sexual and Substance Abuse
Section VI: Experiences in Higher Education

Each theme represents a section of the book, and each section commences with a brief introduction followed by a series of stories crafted by contributors. The brief section introductions serve to provide theoretical framing of the stories that follow. At the end of each narrative, contributing authors have provided recommendations to encourage the next generation of men of color to persist in a world where Black and Brown lives are undervalued. As it is our desire to make this book accessible to men of color regardless of age, background, and/or experiences and other marginalized populations beyond academia, we find this way of organizing the book palatable to multiple audiences including academicians and non-academicians.

CONCLUSION

In conclusion, the authors hope these stories will inspire and motivate men of color to trust their experiences—whether good or bad—to help them become boys to men. Our belonging, being, and becoming means that after all that life has thrown our way, we are strong, purposeful, resilient, and powerful people who are a great treasure to a world that sometimes rejects and ignores our existence. We are indeed the embodiment of *Gumbo for the Soul: Males of Color Share Their Stories, Mediation, Affirmations, and Inspirations.*

REFERENCES

Blow, C. M. (2014, February 28). Fathers' and brothers' keepers. *The New York Times*, pp. 1–4.
Bryan, N. (2017). White teacher's role in sustaining the school-to-prison pipeline: Recommendations for Teacher Education. *Urban Review, 2,* 326–345.

Cook, D. A. (2013). Blurring the boundaries: The mechanics of creating composite characters. In M. Lynn & A. D. Dixson (Eds.), *Handbook of Critical Race Theory in Education*. New York, NY: Routledge.

Ford, D. Y. (2013). *Recruiting and retaining culturally different students in gifted education*. Waco, TX: Prufrock Press.

Ford, D. Y., David, J. L., Scott-Trotman, M., & Sealy-Ruiz, Y. (2017). *Gumbo for the soul: Liberating memoirs and stories to inspire females of color*. Charlotte, NC: Information Age.

Howard, T. C. (2014). *Black male(d): Peril and promise in the education of African American males*. New York, NY: Teachers College Press.

King, M. L., Jr., (1963). Letter from Birmingham jail. *Liberation, 8*(4), 10–16.

Milner, H. R. (2010). *Start where you are but don't stay there: Understanding diversity*. Cambridge, MA: Harvard Education Press.

Solórzano, D., & Yosso, T. (2001). Critical race and LatCrit theory and method: Counterstorytelling. *Qualitative Studies in Education, 14*(4), 471–495.

Stone, A., Saadiq, R., Lilly, H., Standridge, G., & Ozuna, R.C. (2001). *Brotha* [Recorded by Angie Stone]. On Mahogany Soul. New York, NY: J Records LLC.

Warren, C. (2017). Urban preparation: Young Black men moving from Chicago's Southside to success in higher education. Cambridge, MA: Harvard Education Press.

Wright, B. L. (2017). Five wise men: African American males using urban critical literacy to negotiate and navigate home and school in an urban setting. *Urban Education*, 1–33. doi:10.1177/0042085917690203\

SECTION I

FAMILIAL IMPACT ON EDUCATION

Although families of color are often constructed as disinterested and uninvolved in the educational process of their children, they have always played an important role in it. That is, despite facing racial discrimination and other forms of opposition, families of color have used their cultural and social capital to ensure the educational needs and desires of their children were met. In her work on segregated Black schools in the South, Siddle Walker (1996) documented how Black families were instrumental in collecting funds to establish Black schools, supporting their children in secondary schools by attending PTA meetings and other school-related functions, encouraging their children to pursue higher education, and providing resources to ensure they were well taken care of when they attended post-secondary institutions. The same is true in Latino communities. Documenting what he conceptualizes as family-based college-going capital of Latino (and Black) males, Carey (2016) noted how Latino families supported their sons during post-secondary schooling by inspiring them and providing essential resources to ensure college success.

It is also important to note that in communities of color, the idea of family goes beyond individuals who are biologically-related. In other words, fictive kin or extended family members who are not biologically related often play a significant role in supporting and having an impact on the education of children of color, particularly boys (Fordham, 1996; Milton-Williams, 2018). Drawing on Fordham's (1996) conception of fictive kinship networks, Cook (2013) highlighted the roles Black teachers and community members played in the ins and outs of schooling survival of Black children in post-Katrina New Orleans. Similarly, Milton-Williams (2018) documents how Black female teachers served as fictive kin in a middle school setting to support the academic and social needs of Black boys (and girls) who often faced challenges in schools and communities.

In this section of the book, we highlight stories of men of color who share the importance of familial impact on their education. These stories serve as counternarratives which contest the idea that Black and other families of color are disinterested and uninvolved and/or do not care about the educational experiences of their Black and Brown sons. Particularly notable within these narratives are ways contributing authors highlight influential family members and fictive kin who played major roles in their personal success and uplift. While some of the contributing authors may express regret of fathers and other family members who were not actively involved in their lives and faced particular institutional challenges (e.g., prison, drugs) which negatively impacted their personal and familial lives, we encourage readers not to see such critiques as vilifying fathers and other family members but see it as critique of institutions and systems which perpetuate societal issues in the lives of these men. According to Blow (2015), fathers of color, particularly Black fathers are more actively involved in the lives of their children than White fathers.

REFERENCES

Blow, D. M. (2015, June 8). Black dads are doing best of all. *The New York Times*. Retrieved from https://www.nytimes.com/2015/06/08/opinion/charles-blow-black-dads-are-doing-the-best-of-all.html

Carey, R. (2016). "Keep that in mind…You're gonna go to college": Family influence on the college-going processes of Black and Latino high school boys. *The Urban Review, 48*(5), 718–742.

Cook, D. A. (2013). Blurring the boundaries: The mechanics of creating composite characters. In M. Lynn & A. D. Dixson (Eds.), *Handbook of Critical Race Theory in Education*. New York, NY: Routledge.

Fordham, S. (1996). *Blacked out: Dilemmas of race, identity, success at capital high*. Chicago, IL: University of Chicago Press.

Milton-Williams, T. (2018). Strategies for culturally relevant caring in middle level classrooms from the community experiences and life histories of Black middle level teachers. *Research in Middle Level Education, 41*(6), 1–13.

Mosher, J. J. (2013). *Fathers' involvement with their children: United States, 2006–2010*. National Health Statistics Reports; no 71. Hyattsville, MD: National Center for Health Statistics.

Siddle Walker, V. (1996). *Their highest potential: An African American school community in the segregated south*. Chapel Hill: The University of North Carolina Press.

CHAPTER 1

PUSHING FOR A BETTER LIFE

Wil Greer

There are three aspects of my childhood that definitely impacted my school success: being an avid reader; watching my mother, aunts, and uncles turn to drugs and be sent to jail or prison; and believing that a college education was consonant with a better life. My mother gave birth to me at 19. She was a community college student at the time but dropped out shortly after I was conceived. Fortunately, she loved books and made sure I did as well. I gravitated toward books on Black history, and remember receiving praise for my early elementary school reports on Malcolm X and the Rev. Dr. Martin Luther King Jr. Having books in the house was crucial, because it never allowed me to voice that I was bored without my mother quickly directing me to "read a book." She and I played board games, math games, and worked out word problems on a chalkboard she kept in our hall closet as well. My mother was by far my best teacher.

However, when I was about six she became addicted to crack cocaine. In fact, of my mother's eight brothers and sisters, six of them had an addiction to either crack, heroin, or phencyclidine (PCP), and all but one of them did time in either jail or prison. Though much of my childhood blends, there are clear cut points that stand out as demarcation lines: the period before my mother was on drugs, the period during, and the period after, when she remarkably got sober and stayed clean.

Before the drugs, my mother and I lived a stable life in a two-bedroom townhouse in San Mateo, a small city in Northern California, just below San Francisco and right across the Bay Bridge from Oakland. Afterwards, we moved back to San Bernardino, a Southern California town about 30 minutes east of Los Angeles County (I was born in San Bernardino but moved as a toddler and have most of my earliest childhood memories in San Mateo). There, I lived with just about everyone in my family, usually for short bouts at a time: with my great Uncle Leon in his one-bedroom apartment, with my Aunt Del and her family in their apartment, with my otherwise absent biological father at his parent's house, and occasionally with my Uncle Ronny in his car.

At this time, school seemed optional. While my mother was on drugs, which was only for a few years or so, I attended perhaps half a dozen elementary schools. All of them were in urban areas and were attended primarily by Black and Latinx children living in poverty. An adult in my family usually made sure that I was enrolled, but my attendance was irregular, and I was often disengaged. Nothing we did in class seemed important or as if it had implications for my life. One of the lessons that I learned during this period was that there was only accountability for class disruption and misbehavior, not for failing to excel academically. This meant homework was also optional. After all, my teacher's response to fighting, horseplay, off-task talk, or class clowning was always swift and stern. There was not a time, it seemed, when I engaged in these behaviors and failed to be talked to harshly and given a consequence, including suspension.

On the other hand, not having my homework, missing a class assignment, or earning a low score on a test yielded far less concern from my teachers, if any. Those behaviors were more readily accepted and were met with no consequences or even a serious talking to. From what I could gather, controlling kids' behavior was the primary purpose of school. Teaching and learning, at least at the schools I attended, were definitely secondary. Other than for the free lunches, I saw no point in going, or in playing the game.

Despite being disengaged at school, I still believed in the concept of education. Even at an early age I came to see it as a tool that could be used to greatly improve one's life. I knew the story of how Frederick Douglass learned to read as a young man, then started studying the abolitionist movement, and soon decided that he would simply no longer be enslaved. I knew about how the civil rights and Black power movements were largely built on a detailed knowledge of the legal system. And, more contemporarily, I knew that the family on *The Cosby Show* was, without a doubt, the most beautiful, affirming, and shining example of what Black families could look, sound, and be like, if its patriarchs and matriarchs made education a priority and set the standard for their children.

The contrast between the Huxtables and my family was not lost on me. Cliff and Clair lived in a nice, clean, well-manicured house; we lived in small, crowded apartments with roaches. They had upstanding careers as a physician and an attorney; people in my family were often unemployed, underemployed, or participated in illegal economies, always at the cost of their freedom. Their children went to Princeton University, New York University, and Hillman College (a fictitious historically Black college); with the exception of one of my aunts who lived several states away, no one in my family had graduated from or even attended college. At 7 years old I knew I wanted a better life, like the Huxtable's, and that education would be one of the key factors. I just had no idea how to secure it.

A HAND UP

With considerable effort and determination, my mother was able to get clean and remain sober for the rest of her life—a feat that has always made me extremely proud of her. I moved back with her just before fifth grade. She now had a man in her life that she would marry, and who became the consistent father figure I desperately needed. They built a solid, working class life together. She took a job as an office manager for a local construction business, and he worked as a maintenance man.

The stability and family support I now had led to great improvements in my school attendance and behavior. However, I was still not academically engaged, and had no serious plans for my future. By the end of middle school, many of my friends were turning to gangs, and by the end of high school some had been killed. I simply wanted to finish school alive, drug free, and not in jail. This made high school bittersweet, however. While some students were taking honors and advanced placement courses for college, I had consistently opted for the easiest way out and the least challenging classes possible. As a result, when it was senior year, and some of my classmates were receiving university acceptance letters, I had to face the haunting, anxiety-inducing reality that graduating from high school might be my highest academic achievement. I would not reach my dream of living like the Huxtables.

Thank God the local community college offered me a hand up (not a handout, as I had to do the work, study hard, and stay motivated to succeed). During the summer after graduating from high school I made an unplanned visit to the San Bernardino Valley College (SBVC) campus. I was amazed at how quick and easy it was to register and become a college student. In the time it might take to watch a movie, I was registered, secured a date for the placement test, and completed financial aid paperwork.

Sometime after my first year at SBVC God intervened again. My car had broken down, I lost one of my two jobs, and was struggling to pay rent in an apartment I was sharing with two friends. For a moment, I thought it would be easier to dropout of school and find additional work. Fortunately, I came to my senses. I swallowed my pride, moved back home with my parents, got a bus pass, learned which transfers I needed to make the near-two-hour bus ride to and from SBVC (by car, this was but a 15-minute drive from my mom's house), and re-enrolled after missing one semester. During the semester that I returned, I had a chance encounter with Joyce Higashida, a transfer coordinator from the University of California, Riverside (UCR). Joyce looked over my transcripts, outlined several courses that I needed to take to transfer to UCR, and gifted me with a blueprint for getting to the next level.

After adding the courses Joyce recommended and completing two marathon semesters in the spring and summer, I was a junior at UCR. It was there that I decided to become a teacher. I made the dean's list during several quarters and graduated with a joint degree in sociology and ethnic studies. After graduating from UCR, I enrolled at California State University, San Bernardino (CSUSB) to earn my teaching credential. Five years later I went back to CSUSB and earned a master's in educational administration. A few years after that, wanting to further study ways to improve the kinds of urban schools that I attended as a child, I enrolled in Claremont Graduate University's educational leadership PhD program. Defending my dissertation and earning a PhD has been one of my most meaningful, joyous professional accomplishments. Given where I started, it still feels surreal when someone calls me "Doctor."

Yet, I am convinced that none of this would have happened if I did not (a) have what scholars Donna Ford and Gilman Whiting have termed *a scholar identity*, and (b) if I did not desperately want a better life and believe that education could help me get it. Because I was already an avid reader and had some academic skills, what I eventually learned in college was that if I kept myself motivated and improved my study habits, I could actually be a great student. That helped me take responsibility for my success. Wanting a better life was critical as well. I was tired of roaches! More importantly, I had seen enough examples of brilliant, talented people who, with no formal education, were depressed, turned to drugs, and could only participate in illegal economies. This created a cycle wherein they would go to jail, get out, do the same things, and go back to jail. I wanted more than that. If you are a young person reading this, I pray that you find your Huxtable family goal, stay motivated, and stay focused on one day being a college graduate. This formula has consistently worked well for our people, and it can work for you too.

CHAPTER 2

CHOICES

George Suttles

My father was born in the 1950s and grew up in New York City, spending most of his childhood running the streets of Harlem and the Bronx. He was a tall, lanky, charismatic man who had his first child at 17 years old. He was high school educated. He worked several jobs over the course of his lifetime, none with any professional career trajectory. My mother was also born in the 1950s, although she spent her early years living in North Carolina, she grew up in Bedford Stuyvesant (Bed Stuy), Brooklyn. She was also high school educated. My mother was able to secure several secretarial jobs until she landed at a prestigious law firm where she would stay for 30-plus years before retiring. My mother was, and still is, the bedrock of our family; one of the wisest, most compassionate, and selfless people I will ever know.

My father met my mother in the 1970s. After a stint hustling and running the streets, I believe my mother's love and belief in him sharpened his focus and he was ready to start a family and be a husband and father. My father, when he was present and clear-minded, was a hard-working man who was a loving parent and devoted husband.

With that said, the hardest challenge I have had to face was my parent's divorce. Divorce in and of itself can have tremendous impact on a family, especially the children, but when you complicate it with drug addiction and violence, then you have a totally different situation.

When my father first began grappling with his addiction, it came on the heels of him losing his job. I cannot say for sure but reflecting on it now I imagine that issues of masculinity, specifically hitching his worth to employment and being able to provide for his family, played a big part in his emotional distress. At 14 years old, I had experienced my father as my coach, mentor, parental figure, and best friend. When I was younger and had days off from school, I would beg my mom to allow me to go to work with him. We woke up at 5:30 a.m. and we would drive through the city making payroll deliveries. Before we would hit the road, we would go to the bodega and get bacon, egg, and cheese sandwiches and he would get a small coffee, light and sweet. The sun would rise in the east on us, a loving father and his loyal son.

Looking back, I cannot really speak to how it made my sister and brother feel, but one thing I am glad for is that they didn't have to experience the decline of my father in real time with my level of understanding. Although I was the oldest child, I can't claim to have fully understood what was happening as a 14-year old but I knew that something was wrong. The only way I can explain it, or how I internalized it for years, was that my father was failing himself and his family, he gave up and I did not know why. For a long time I believed that he made a choice to walk away from us, to pursue drugs instead of loving his family. I now know that addiction is a sickness and because of that I have been able to understand and forgive him. This has allowed me to reflect on the whole man, and appreciate, accept, and see the better parts of my father in me. As an adult, it has also informed my public service. I currently sit on the board of Odyssey House, a community-based mental health and substance abuse clinic that offers individuals comprehensive, compassionate treatment with wraparound services to support them and their families.

At the same time that this was happening with my father, I was also starting a new chapter in my life. I had just started transitioning from attending a New York City public middle school to an elite private Ivy League preparatory school. The opportunity was made possible by the Albert G. Oliver Program, an academic enrichment and placement program that selects high achieving young people from New York City public middle schools and prepares them to enroll in the best private day and boarding high schools in the country. After intensive academic enrichment and several interviews, I was placed at the Dalton School, one of the best private high schools in New York City. As my home life became more and more turbulent, I ventured into the world of New York City elite private high schools.

This experience totally changed my personal, academic, and professional trajectory. Without the help of the Albert G. Oliver Program and the

Dalton School, I would not be where I am today. With that said, the Dalton experience also frustrated me and was fraught with its own obstacles. As I realized how privileged I was to be at Dalton, a very White, affluent space, resentment bubbled up inside of me. As I spent more time getting to know the school and the students, I grew frustrated and upset; I did not understand why we were receiving one type of education while the kids in my neighborhood and at my former middle school were receiving a far more inferior education. The Dalton School is a highly resourced institution, designed to support students and families, whereas the public middle school I attended was not. More so than a disparity, it was a fundamental and systemic inequity. I constantly questioned my place at the school. How could a young Black kid from Harlem, with an inferior educational background and a drug addicted father persist and graduate from Dalton . . . I wondered if the other kids had the same family issues, or if they even had issues at all. What I quickly discovered was that we all had issues, and in some weird way that was comforting to me. Affluence, race, and socioeconomic status may have manifested different types of issues, but fundamentally we all struggled with the same human condition. This realization was helpful because it allowed me to reach out for help within my new high school community. Instead of being embarrassed and ashamed of what was going on at home and letting my lack of academic confidence hinder me from seeking help, I made the choice to show my vulnerability. I sought help, I spoke with teachers and trusted advisors, and after initially lashing out, I exposed that I was hurting and needed support.

Despite contending with immense personal and cultural challenges and insecurities, I persisted and graduated from the Dalton School. I consider my high school experience truly exceptional and I am grateful for the opportunities, the friendships, and the community that the school afforded me. After graduating Dalton, I matriculated and received my undergraduate degree from Wesleyan University and later went on to pursue two graduate degrees. I continue to dedicate my entire professional career to helping others, with the hopes that my contribution creates opportunities for people who need them.

Here's what no one ever really explicitly tells you when you are young: life, or more precisely, navigating this life, is very, very, difficult. Humans are complex, flawed beings who are multidimensional, capable of equally amazing and terrible things. We should not only be compassionate and forgiving to others, but also to ourselves. More than anyone else, I have had to forgive myself for mistakes I have made; these many moments are always difficult, but ripe with growth.

I think the one thing we often take for granted is that although there are systemic and institutional barriers in our way, we also have choices. We may not be able to control some of our circumstances, but we can control, to a large degree, how we respond. When I think about the profound nature of choices, I mostly think about my mother. She had to make some tough choices. As a teenager she got pregnant and chose to give the child up for adoption. Years later, she chose to pursue a high school diploma and work to make a decent living. She chose to love my father until the choice became clear to separate from him. She chose to make a family. In fact, every day she actively chooses to love, cherish, and support us. All of these were, and continue to be, her choices.

I try to remember that there are things outside of my control, but having a choice is a blessing. Because of this, I often ask myself and others, "What choices are we making for ourselves...For our communities...For our friends and family...Are we choosing to speak out...To be silent... To work hard...To work together...Are we choosing to love...To accept... To hate...Are we choosing to create spaces or close doors..." What we choose, how we choose, and who we choose are important, and only we can know what choices will make us happy and what choices will constitute wise ones. Expanding the possibilities for ourselves means having more and more choices. The more choices we have, the more success we realize. The more success we realize, the more it becomes imperative that we create choices for others, reaching back to our communities. Choices are opportunities and opportunities are pathways to financial, emotional, spiritual, and physical health. This type of prosperity will hopefully lead us one step closer to justice, bring us together, and uplift our communities.

CHAPTER 3

BLACK BOY RISING

Larry J. Walker

Throughout my life, I had to navigate various challenges including being born to a teenage mother in Camden, New Jersey, which is currently one of the poorest cities in the nation (Kozol, 2012). My family was rooted in the Black church, which hardened the relationship between my mother and grandmother before and after my birth. Fortunately, the challenges didn't portend a dark future. However, throughout my childhood and adolescence I sought answers to the following questions: (a) "Why did my maternal grandparents have to mediate disagreements between my mother and stepfather..."; and (b) "Why did I struggle to stay focused in school..." In retrospect, I realize the support from my grandparents including instilling a strong moral foundation allowed me to find my place in the world. Without their investment I would have stumbled throughout life and faced a daunting future.

WHY FAMILY MATTERS

Historically, the Black community has forged strong familial relationships to survive the transatlantic slave trade, Jim Crow, among other challenges.

These bonds extend to other members of the community that allowed us to survive harrowing times. The trials can come from unpredictable events including job loss, a decline in health, or systemic issues that force us to recalibrate. For the Walker family, my mother's pregnancy and my subsequent birth created turmoil in a household led equally by my grandparents. Evelyn and Jacob Walker were pillars in the Black community, well respected, regularly attended church and committed to community service. Thus, the realization that their eldest daughter was pregnant created a very tense environment.

My mother and biological father had a tenuous relationship that quickly dissolved after my birth. While I have pleasant memories of my father, including going to museums and accompanying him to events, we have not talked in several years. For a long time, I carried an emptiness that could not be filled because of his persistent absence from my life. That feeling still slightly aches during moments of reflection. While I know how to reach him, I'm not ready to sit and review all of my accomplishments and missteps in life. His absence from my life is a wound that still has not fully healed. In retrospect, I realize my grandparents played a vital role ensuring I felt valued and loved. They both were critical to helping me develop important traits including a strong sense of spirituality and empathy.

Without my grandparents, I would have faced a harrowing journey that could have led me down a dangerous path. This could have included becoming a victim or victimizer that dramatically altered the trajectory of my life and/or members of the community. Similar to most Black families in the 1970s and 1980s, my grandparents provided emotional scaffolding that prepared me for more difficult times including witnessing intimate partner violence between my mother and stepfather.

Like most young mothers, the burden of parenting was difficult for my mother. Prior to marrying my stepfather, the Walkers (including aunts and uncles) supplemented my mother's inexperience as a parent by caring for me before, after school, and during weekends. After my mother married my stepfather and gave birth to my sister my life became more tumultuous. The violence I witnessed is difficult to comprehend and shaped but did not define me as a person. During this tough time, the lessons I learned in church while sitting on my grandmother's lap or attending Sunday school proved to be critical. For most of my life my grandparents were a calming force throughout my frenetic childhood.

I can recall my grandparents frantically racing in to save my sister and I during difficult times between my parents. Their commitment to protecting us while also helping the less fortunate influenced my belief in helping vulnerable groups. This includes my role on the board of directors for an organization that fights to prevent intimate partner violence. Periodically I would travel with my grandfather to drop off clothes and nonperishable items to nonprofit organizations and churches. His focus on community service influenced my decision to become an educator and fight for social justice issues.

After my parents divorced, my mother, sister, and I lived with my grandparents. The transition was seamless because we spent so much time visiting throughout the week. However, the constant turmoil and trauma from my experience took a toll on my academic performance. For example, I began to forge my mother's handwriting on progress reports, get in trouble for talking in school, and became a mediocre to below average student. My limited academic accomplishments would continue throughout high school. Later in life, I realized that my childhood dramatically impacted my view of school. My research on the experiences of traumatized children, adolescents, and adults highlights the struggles they encounter in school and later in life (Walker, 2015; Walker & Goings, 2017). Some traumatic experiences include witnessing violence or the retelling of violent or dangerous encounters.

Despite my troubles in school, my grandparents continued to be steadfast in their support. However, my grandfather believed in stern discipline and I frequently found myself in trouble. His approach was shared by my mother's new husband, which created an antagonistic relationship between he and I.

During middle school, my mother, new stepfather, sister, and I moved to Philadelphia, which placed me farther from my grandparents than any other time in my life. Although we were only separated by a bridge (Ben Franklin), I often yearned for their wisdom and constant assurance. I was grateful that the distance didn't keep me from visiting as often as possible. Unfortunately, living in a different location and attending a new school didn't prevent my stepfather and I from disagreeing on several issues; this contributed to feelings of alienation, which was reflected in my lackadaisical attitude towards school.

Similar to my time living in Camden, Evelyn and Jacob Walker provided me with solace every time I visited on weekends or during the summer. No matter the circumstances, I always felt welcomed. The lessons I learned talking to my grandparents regarding a myriad of issues proved critical to my long-term development. For instance, attending church every Sunday gave me purpose and shaped my morals and values. Watching my grandfather give to the less fortunate influenced my decision to become a teacher and work to address issues including food deserts, ensuring people have 21st century workforce skills, and ending intimate partner violence. Furthermore, their work ethic and ability to overcome obstacles taught me the importance of fortitude and hard work. Those important traits would help me navigate academic and personal challenges.

During my sophomore year of college, my grandfather died from complications from pneumonia. His death shattered my world, yet a conversation with my grandmother shortly after this tragedy proved to be a catalyst. She reminded me of all the lessons he tried to teach me and how it was my responsibility to uphold his legacy. This advice was important and gave me the impetus I needed to excel as an undergraduate. Years later I continued to utilize the same principles to overcome challenges, including the death of my grandmother, family, and friends.

TRIUMPH AND SUPPORTING THE NEXT GENERATION

In spite of the challenges I have encountered, the guidance from my grandparents was critical. They sheltered me throughout my turbulent childhood while creating a nurturing environment. Instilling a strong work ethic helped me complete my dissertation and navigate other challenges. Their investment contributed to my personal and professional success including:

- Working on Capitol Hill addressing issues that affect the lives of millions of Americans. Working as the senior staffer for a member of the Congressional Black Caucus was a tremendous experience. During my tenure, I applied skills learned from my grandparents including humility, work ethic, interpersonal skills, and leadership. Each skill served me well in an environment that requires long hours and an attention to detail.
- I have worked in PreK–20 settings mentoring children, adolescents, and adults. My interest in teaching grew from watching my grandparents volunteer during Sunday school, supporting members of the community, and their belief in education. Although neither of my grandparents attended college, they instilled the importance of helping others and exceeding expectations.

There are a few recommendations I would offer to individuals with similar experiences. While I am not an authority on life's challenges, I have encountered a number of barriers that nearly upended my future. We all need guidance during difficult times. Thus, I offer the following:

1. Relationships with family (including extended), friends, and others (e.g., mentors) are vital to long-term success. They can provide us with a respite when we have reached a difficult time in our lives. Depending on others when you cannot move forward is important. Secure relationships with dependable people are worth more than any form of currency.

2. My grandparents taught me that having a strong work ethic and commitment to equity is vital. This is particularly important for the Black community. We encounter significant racial barriers that impede our progress. However, historically, the community fought against racial injustice by collectively fighting to address specific goals. Today, we have to apply the same principles inside and outside of the workforce. Collaborating on economic, political, and social issues could create opportunities for the next generation. Ignoring the current political rhetoric could hamper efforts to eliminate systemic barriers.
3. Spirituality and religiosity continue to play an important role in the Black community. Faith in a higher power or philosophical belief has guided my decisions and hopes for the future. While some people may choose to center their beliefs in other areas, it is important to develop some sense of connectedness (e.g., meditation, etc.) to understand life's challenges.

REFERENCES

Kozol, J. (2012). *Savage inequalities: Children in America's schools.* New York, NY: Broadway Books.

Walker, L. (2015). *Trauma, environmental stressors, and the African-American college student: Research, practice, and HBCUs.* Philadelphia, PA: Penn Center for Minority Serving Institutions. Retrieved from https://cmsi.gse.upenn.edu/sites/default/files/Walker%20Research%20Brief%20%28final%29.pdf

Walker, L., & Goings, R. (2017). A dream deferred: How trauma impacts the academic achievement of African American youth. In N. Finigan-Carr (Ed.), *Linking health and education for African American students' success* (pp. 3–11). New York, NY: Routledge.

CHAPTER 4

MY SON HAS A PURPOSE TOO

A Father's Story of Autism

George E. Stewart II

September 16, 2010 was one of the happiest days of my life. It was the day that my son Landon was born. Before Landon, my wife and I had lost three children, each just weeks into my wife's pregnancy. Doctors said that if Landon could make it to 24 weeks, he would have a chance at life. However, in order for Landon to make it to 24 weeks, my wife would have to undergo a surgical procedure; the same procedure done when we lost our second child. So with losing three children, a 24 week hump we had to get over, and the uncertainty that this surgical procedure would even work, you can imagine how nervous my wife and I were throughout this pregnancy. But on September 16, 2010, after being in the womb for 38 weeks, my son had arrived.

A few months before Landon's first birthday, my wife and I noticed that he was not exhibiting "normal" baby behavior. Whenever my wife and I would try to gaze into our son's eyes, he would not reciprocate the gaze. He would look right past or over us. Truthfully, there was a time when we thought that Landon saw ghosts. Later, we found out that he was actually displaying an inability to make eye contact. Another thing my wife and I noticed was his lack of interest in things that children are typically interested in, such as appropriately playing with toys and playing with other children. The biggest thing my wife and I noticed in Landon was, by the time he turned a year old, he was not speaking at all and was not showing any signs of even trying to speak. With us both being educators, we knew something was not right. So after much research of these symptoms, my wife and I discovered a disorder called autism spectrum disorder (ASD). For those who don't know, autism is a developmental disorder that slightly or severely impairs someone's ability to communicate and interact with others in an appropriate way. After reading about autism for awhile, I had that "not my child" moment, but in the back of my mind I knew something was wrong. Knowing that something was wrong, I engaged in a discussion with my wife about having our son tested for autism, and before we gave denial any time to completely set in, that is exactly what we did.

After going through various tests, my son was diagnosed with autism at the age of two. As parents, you never want to receive any news about your child having problems, especially those in which there are no cures. When receiving such news, the first thing that you think about is your child and the difficulty they will have, as they progress through life. As a father of a child diagnosed with autism, I started to wonder if my son would ever have a chance to do things that many boys do, such as playing sports or being able to effectively engage in "guy talk." Then, the optimist in me said that the silver lining in Landon's diagnosis is that it was detected early, which was extremely beneficial for him.

Not too long after my son's diagnosis, my wife and I made a very bold move; a move that many people still question us to this very day. We moved from the economically rich city of Houston, TX back home to the economically strapped state of Mississippi; a move that we both prayed about and thought was in the best interest of Landon. This move seems, in large part, to be a success, as our family has really supported us and has really rallied around Landon. To watch him interact with his cousins as well as show affection toward not only his mom and I but his grandparents, aunts, and uncles gets me all emotional just thinking about it. Why would that make me emotional... Because many people diagnosed with autism typically don't show emotion or affection toward people.

As Landon's father, one of the things I want to do is be his voice at a time that he can't speak. I have developed a presentation titled, "How the Faith-Based Community Can Support the Autism Community." The purpose of this presentation is to educate church leaders on autism, share my story, and make suggestions on how the church can better serve families that deal with autism. As I read and talk with parents who are raising children with autism, I've discovered that many families simply don't attend church, because a lot of churches are not autism friendly, and this needs to change.

I've also co-organized a "Day of Support" for fathers raising children with special needs. Oftentimes, you hear of or read about mothers being the primary caretakers of the child with special needs. Through this event, I found that there are fathers out there who are on the passenger side, if not in the driver's seat of the caretaking responsibility. This event has proven to be very impactful but there needs to be more events like this, as there are more fathers out there taking on this role in places other than just my little corner of the world.

Many autism families, as I so affectionately like to call us, live inside of a bubble. It's because so many people don't understand our children. And sometimes, people are afraid of or simply don't want anything to do with things or people they don't understand. Sometimes autism families are embarrassed by the behaviors that the autistic child exhibits, and that causes the autism family to live inside a bubble. I can vividly recall times when I, along with my family, had to leave church early, exit a restaurant before we wanted to, or openly defend my child because of remarks made or looks given, because he was not displaying behavior that was considered the "norm." With that being said, there's a need to help move autism families beyond this bubble. There's a whole world out there, and I want, not just my family, but other autism families to enjoy it and for our children to thrive in it.

In the spirit of transparency, I have to say that raising a child with autism is tough. I've struggled emotionally and my faith has been tested. There were times I wanted to question God regarding Landon. There were times I blamed myself for Landon's condition. There were even times when the spirit of envy tried to take ahold of me. As a father, I saw other fathers engaging in sporting activities with their sons, meanwhile, my son is still learning basic life skills. Then I think, Landon could have very well not been here, which was pretty likely when I think about my fatherhood history. I've realized that Landon is nothing short of a miracle, and I thank God for every day that he's here.

So how is Landon today... He's progressing. He's 6 years old and still not talking, but every now and then he shows signs that he's trying. He still has crying fits and makes noises that attract strange looks when we are out in public, but not as often as before. His sleeping has gotten better, his eye contact is amazing, and he is showing slow but steady progress in school. Every positive report I get from his teachers and his therapists gives me more and more hope. I'm so looking forward to watching this little boy grow up. He may never score the game's winning touchdown or hit the game's winning shot and may never come to me with questions about a girl he has a crush on, but I know that what he will be able to do will simply amaze me.

Despite the many limitations that Landon has, he has a purpose. He has moved me from a "Why my son..." father to an inspired father, by watching his son move through life with a huge smile on his face. Despite those limitations, he's taught me how to love on a whole new level, and I would trade places with him in a heartbeat just to see the world as he sees it. As an educator, I'm often asked how I am so patient. Landon taught me! Most importantly, my faith has grown immensely just by watching what God is doing in his life. Landon's impact on people really moves me. Anyone who gets to know Landon falls in love with him. You get the feeling of being a better you from your time spent with him. What's awesome is he's only scratched the surface of the impact he will have on this world. His story has just begun, and I'm so blessed to have the opportunity to be right by his side, like the proud father I am, watching it unfold.

Since my son's diagnosis, I have added to the work I do. I've gone from school teacher to now teacher, author, youth and family advocate, and speaker. Through these roles, I'm dedicated to the academic, social, emotional, and spiritual development of children, the family, and the community at large. Sometimes, operating within these roles can be a lot, but if what I do opens up my son's world and the world of those like my son, I count it a blessing. Finally, my advice to fathers and families raising children with autism or any other disability would be lean on your support system, play an active role in your child's individualized education program (IEP) process, and advocate for the change that you want to see.

"Jesus answered, Neither hath this man sinned, nor his parents: but that the works of God should be made manifest in him" (John 9:3). It was this verse that made me realize that it is not my fault that my son has autism. I realized that through my son, God's work will be manifested. As I said, he has a purpose too.

CHAPTER 5

WHERE THE WATERS MET

A Story of Friendship, Brotherhood, and Service

Robert Mays

I am a trained social worker, serving my people in the urban environment. I love myself and I recognize the power I possess as well as my responsibility to society. However, I have not always been in this place of evolving crystallization. My journey of self-awareness has been one of pain and hurt, but also filled with promise and amazing opportunity. On this spiritual journey we call life, the only constant is change, with the variables being the people we encounter within certain phases. Some people we counter we wish we'd never met, some taught us the lessons we needed, and others came into our lives for a period of time to complete a specific task. Their exits, as much as their entry can be swift, but each one contains answers guiding us to who we are called to be.

My gratitude will always be present for my village, to have people who support you and care, is of great value. My parents provided my brothers and me with a solid foundation of love and a safe secure place to call home. However, even amongst their greatness, their humanity is salient, and I understand why a village is needed—for they could not provide me with everything I needed. At a young age, I recognized I was perceptive, intuitive, and could examine situations keeping specific details in context. My parents did not shut these things down in as much as they tried to streamline them to fit cultural norms. So, navigating who I was to adhere to cultural norms was challenging because I thought I needed to change or shrink myself to fit. Never evoking the totality of myself just those parts which were either lauded or deemed worthy by others. I opted to rely on my intellect.

Hence the entrance of Rudy into my life. I met Rudy when I was 22 years old, during the first year of my master's in social work program. He was the security guard in the apartment complex in which I lived. One day, I was leaving my field placement in West Baltimore waiting at the bus stop and he yelled out the car at me, "Get in!" I looked at him perplexed because I did not recognize him and only knew him in passing; so, I ignored him, as I was comfortable with waiting for the bus. He yelled out the car once again, "C'mon and get in!" It was at that time I recognized his presence, pronounced and secure, and so I proceeded to get into the car. He would later say, he noticed me waiting at the bus stop previously and said anyone who could wait at the bus stop and walk through Baltimore city without fear was a special person; he actually called me a "hoodrat." From that moment, Rudy and I would develop a relationship mirroring one of father and son, but it became much deeper than that, as we were friends.

Our friendship was a peculiar one because we both thought each other was annoying and we verbalized this to one another; but it was all love. I thought he could be stubborn and ornery; he would follow up and say I came off as a "know it all." I was a recent Temple University graduate, with a robust Africana studies background and involved in community work; "woke" was not even the word to describe my stance. In contrast, Rudy was ex-military, where he honorably served in the U.S. Navy for 25 years straight out of high school. He traveled all over the world and knew about cultures that most people had no clue existed. He had lived the bulk of his life having been married, with three children and the most recent additions of his family included his grandchildren. Methodical, he was old fashion, and the world was his classroom. He was well versed in music and loved to learn, so our natural desire for understanding people and hunger for knowledge linked us.

We would often converse on issues within the Black community, war, music, relationship dynamics, and issues regarding our most downtrodden and ostracized people. We'd go back and forth as that was our norm. One time, we were having a discussion with another group of people, and he scolded, something he had never done before. I tried to interject, to explain myself, and he shut me down again. I was embarrassed and really upset because I was not finished with my thought and I thought to myself, "Why would you do this to me..." I didn't speak to him for several days and on the last day of my silent protest, I walked past the office hoping he wouldn't see me. He saw me and said come here, and out of respect, I stubbornly went inside. I crossed the threshold and he instantly hugged me, stating, "I love you. I also know you love yourself, I just want you to love yourself more," he released me and I retreated to my home.

When we discussed the incident, he explained how I should never let anyone or anything "shake my foundation." He further went on to comment on my talents and the light I contained for others. In that moment, I realized he was attempting to rebuild what had been chipped off of me, resetting how I saw myself and my interactions with the world. I do not have anything to prove to anyone for I am enough, and my presence alone should speak volumes. That's the basis of loving yourself: releasing that which does not serve you well and adhering to the patterns guiding you towards wholeness versus destruction. That was the one time we ever truly "bumped heads" but the challenge to grow and be better never stopped.

To delve deeper into one's self is difficult especially originating from an African diasporic culture where the notion of anything regarding self is seen as sacrilege. The premise is the community pours into you and you pour into others, which works in a spiritually grounded, loved filled system and society; unfortunately, the reality is quite the opposite. Being a Black boy transitioning into manhood is difficult, especially when you recognize the dehumanizing nature of society. I was given values and ways to exist, which were mostly "good," but it still left me with no room for expression. I wonder how many other young Black boys recognize their individuality and creativity yet are forced to shrink themselves into a box. Even amongst those who are "successful," I question what was lost in the process to arrive "there"... What good is perseverance and being the best, or being "twice as good" if I am in pieces by the time I reap the harvest from my labor... The feeling of always doing, always performing, and always giving left me feeling abused and discarded. I don't think men communicate or feel comfortable stating those realities because it challenges the schema of their masculinity. In my opinion, many men will suppress these thoughts and feelings or transpose them into some other socially acceptable way to cope, or just survive. For many men, this can either appear as hyper-vigilance or forcible solitude. These things we need to critically reflect on to challenge if what we accept is really of any benefit.

Even after I moved to Washington, DC to begin my career, my friendship with Rudy remained the same as we communicated regularly. By this time, I had even developed a relationship with his wife, who would send me food and nurtured me as if I was her own. But shortly after my move, Rudy became ill and spent much of the next 14 months in and out of the hospital. I visited only, after his wife called stating, "Rudy is asking for you." I did not want to go and I was completely uneasy about it. I had recently experienced another great loss and the stress of a new job made going to the hospital difficult, but I went anyway, and learned he was supposed to be discharged soon. I took the whole day off and spent hours with him; and I did for him what he had done for me on multiple occasions; I took care of him. I made sure he had his food, told him to stop being mean and ornery to the staff, and enjoyed his company. I am grateful I pushed past my own discomfort because he was never discharged. Instead, within 6 days, he passed away. I believe he waited to see me, and my act of kindness was one of the last things he needed to give him peace. I am in the beginning of my journey of service, he had done his life's work. I wholeheartedly believe I was one of his last assignments on this earth.

To quote one of my favorite artists, Erykah Badu: "Pack light...love can make it better...and let it go" (Young et al., 2000). We don't often hear stories regarding healthy Black male relationships or the spontaneity of Black brotherhood. My encounter with Rudy changed my life and altered how I viewed relationships across my life. He taught me how to live with purpose and intent. I am humbled and honored to have received such a blessing and I hope I continue to make my "guru of all knowledge" proud.

As Black men, young and old, we must be honest about who we are and our origins. When we figure it out, we must release the segments which caused us to be us and to be compartmentalized. We silo and stagger ourselves because that is how we were instructed to survive, not to mention there is honor attached to the struggle and brokenness. I believe there is more to life and I accept the challenge of something new. For your ability to free yourself from your own limitations will cause thousands more to follow suit. How we act, think, and project does not solely impact us but those around us, even those from afar. Understanding that principle and implementing it into our daily lives is how we build young men and create a nation.

REFERENCE

Young, A. R., Bailey, B. A., Longmiles, C. A., Hayes, I., Hale, N. D., & Brown, Jr., R. E. (2000). *Bag lady*. [Recorded by Erykah Badu, 1998]. On Mama's Gun. New York, NY: Electric Lady Studios/Motown.

CHAPTER 6

FREEDOM OF FORGIVENESS

Zaccheus L. Moss

The first memory of my father was not picture perfect but the image and sound is still present over 30 years later. Imagine an impressionable young man like any other son who thinks his father is a superhero, police officer, or the boss. Unfortunately for me, my father was MIA by his own mission in life. This absence certainly was not a military leave of absence but was a personal leave of inaction in my life.

I remember my mom telling me, "Son, there is your father." I was so excited because this to my best recollection was my first interaction with my father, at least that I was aware of. I was overjoyed because this was my dad. Little did I know, that even though I carried his last name, I represented a living art exhibit of an ordained pastor's mistake. Despite my excitement and anticipation of this meeting with destiny, the words he said to me were, "Hey, boy!" Not, "Hello son." No, "I love you" or "I missed you." No hug like the great movie scenes I had watched of a loving father and a son. What a let down! The family portrait in my eyes was shattered into a million pieces with fragments etched into my memory bank.

I was crushed as the tears flowed down my cheeks only to be consoled by the one constant in my life, my mom. Growing up, I was teased as being a change-of-life child, because of my mother's age, but truthfully, meeting my father was a life changing moment. I wondered were it not for meeting my father for the first time, would I have felt better if I held onto the fantasy of the knight in shining armor slaying the dragon? Maybe it would have been better if this meeting never happened and this painful real life episode of "The Facts of Life" (a 1980s sitcom) would not be in reruns in my mind.

Little did I know that seeds of frustration, anger, and pain were planted in the fertile soil of my mind that day. It was painful each time I saw fathers and sons enjoying a strong relationship, knowing that I was not as fortunate. I would often wish I carried another last name and that my father was someone else. After all, who wouldn't desire to have a son that loved everything about life, food, football, and faith... is there anything else better than the image of a father and son representing the future, reflecting the past, and connecting in the present.

Despite the absence of my father, I was blessed to have my grandfather in the home with me. His presence was the strength and stability that helped me but still was not the filler for the empty place that often plagued me daily as a painful reminder. It was not reasonable for me to believe my grandfather would play catch, go fishing, and ride bikes when a walking cane was a standard part of his wardrobe. While others may have been with their fathers, I was lucky to spend time with my mother, but this son, needed the same person that caused the most pain to rescue him.

As time passed, I found myself struggling to do the most basic tasks that a son would learn from watching his father. For me, it was like I was on the Earth as an apprentice but my instructor on manhood, my biological father, was not present but in a far galaxy. The inner window panes on the building of my life became darkened by the inward struggles that mounted up by blocking a once bright looking glass of great expectations. I can remember the misplaced anger being fired from my mouth like a machine gun striking the innocent victim (my mom) each time the adolescent mishandled situations based on misplaced emotions without knowledge of proper restraint.

As the anger for my father grew, and I adjusted to the reality that my father was not going to be a visible part of my life, I noticed that a will to make things happen for myself was being developed. I began to notice that suddenly things that I would strive for was done as a way of saying to my father, I made it without you. The accomplishments I took pride in and wanted to seemingly throw in my father's face (despite the distance of his presence in my life) included getting a high school diploma while living 2 years alone as my mother dealt with her mental illnesses, getting my license with little drivers education training, and graduating from college and securing a career. Of course, it was only in my mind that this game of proverbial dodgeball of sorts took place because the intended target was not present instead, a painful wall was there.

I later realized that my negative emotions were transformed and became my motivation to make my father proud but my pride, anger, and naivety would not allow me to admit that at the time. I would give speeches in church and score a touchdown, make a tackle, or make good grades and secretly think to myself, dad, are you proud of me. I found myself just wanting to hear the words from my father, "Good job son, I am proud of you." I listened only to hear silence for words that never came to me as a young son.

I remember the moment as it is forever etched in my life that the silence of a hospital room, would unlocked the Pandora's box of my life. My mom, as my brother and I were sitting in her hospital room, as she sat at death's door steps, spoke her last words to a hurting son, "Have you talked to your father..." It was as if time stood still and all the pain of 20 plus years were in this moment opened up and only my mom and God knew its contents. I responded, as a momma's boy and not as the angry son who hid the past pain and I said, "No, but I will."

In a very short time after my mother's death, I was awakened in the morning to my tears and I cried to God please don't let my father die before I am able to talk to him. I immediately made a trip to see my father. We had never held a conversation longer than 30-minutes my entire life. However, this time, we spoke for over 2 hours and I learned who he was but most importantly, I now had my identity of who I am.

My father and I embraced and the cold and callous heart of a son was warmed and refreshed by my father whose absence affected both our lives. My father died at 90 years old, less than a year after our meeting, but our relationship was repaired. At an appreciation service my father called my name and said, "This is my son" and I was able to say, "My dad invited me and I am here for my dad." This was the proudest moment of my life, simply because publicly my father acknowledged me.

Little did I know that my father's presence in my life carried with it the key to my identity that my inability to forgive, kept it locked up. Until I forgave my father, both our lives and true destiny were MIA while our relationship was like a POW, simple prisoners of a war of reputation and pride.

I was able to beat the odds by not succumbing to the path of joining a gang, selling or becoming addicted to drugs, not become a teenage father, and not becoming a negative statistic despite many opportunities. Despite my father's absence in my life, I make it my purpose to be a positive example of fatherhood for fathers and sons. While I do not have children of my own, I have become a community father to sons and future fathers through sharing my story of the freedom of forgiveness. While only fatherhood can remove a child imprisoned by the solitary confinement of anger and resentment, only a hurting son holds the pardon for an absentee father.

My first piece of advice is that a son whose father has been absent, to let go of the anger by forgiving their father and transferring the negative energy in the direction of something positive. If possible, look to repair the relationship with their father and then, be to their own children the kind of father they missed in their life. My second piece of advice, for the father missing in action, the best course of action is to make every effort to become a bridge that reconnects the islands of the child and father and if necessary, be willing to "swim" the entire distance for the sake of the relationship.

    I would not trade the year that I was able to spend with my father for anything in the world because often the pain of regret hurts more than the pain of abandonment. I never asked my father why he was not a part of my life but truthfully, I realized that every aspect of my life he was and will always be a part of. It's awesome to know that the key not only to my freedom was in forgiving my father, but also in my father forgiving himself. Until men choose to forgive fathers that have been absent from their lives, they will remain "imprisoned" by anger while wearing a painful "state issued jumpsuit" as a reminder of a painful childhood with no chance of parole.

CHAPTER 7

I MIGHT CRY, BUT I'LL GET THERE

MarQo D. Patton

Growing up in Dayton, Ohio, I recall many struggles in my life and in those who lived around me. I was not a stranger to gunshots and sirens, growing up in Trotwood and especially when I lived with my grandparents for a few months, on the west side of Dayton. Constantly moving around with my mother, I ended up attending 12 different schools before I landed in high school. We also hit a rough time in our life and were homeless for over a year, moving from three different homeless shelters, from New York to Ohio. While my mother never lived a dangerous or scandalous life in front of me, we struggled for financial stability and lacked opportunities for growth. When my mom found a decent job (moving to Columbus, Ohio) and I began attended a public magnet high school (CAHS IB Magnet), my life changed. It was at this point that I bought into the power of education and faith to help me see greater than what I could see as a Black young man living in poverty.

The road always looked long, arduous, scary and uncertain, but I reasoned years ago that if rising above those struggles were to break me down, I would be okay. I reasoned that I might cry, but I won't quit...I will get to that expected place, that I hear God's Word describe (Jeremiah 29:11, NIV). I knew that I was becoming accustomed to discipline, wisdom, and knowledge in ways that was going to be challenging. I knew that I would travel a road that I had not seen traveled in my family, and that journey would be a lonely one. While I did not know ultimately how God would seek to use me, my life experiences have taught me that I came into this world built for the struggle. Even though I only wanted to become a singer, God was showing me that there was more in me to offer to his people.

The choices we make, the people with whom we interface, and even our self-perception are influenced through the standards by which we choose to live our lives. Those standards, or codes, may change and bend along with the experiences we face, with the tides of societal norms, or through our own spiritual compass, but there are certain views that govern those codes. These views are the lens with which we see the world. With reflection, these revelations can be powerful. In the next few moments, I discuss ethical behavior, through my experience. I hope you gain a perspective that can help you through tough stages in your life, realizing that we heal by our words and actions towards each other. This chapter is written through a look at worldview, motivations growing up, and the processes and experiences that led me to accepting an identity as an educator that I did not initially see coming. Operating in purpose did not come easily; on the contrary, it came through personal convictions, studying the Word of God, and through the process of simple reflection, education, and God's grace through moments of doubt and faithlessness.

WORLDVIEW

During my adolescent years, I got the chance to see "church" on many levels, and not just in the actual buildings—I began to see God in my daily walk. I soon realized that God was truly my Father, in the absence of my biological father, by whom I was never raised. God began to speak to me; and in many ways, I was naïve when He would speak, thinking it was just some higher, inner man, that I could choose to listen to (or not). It was through his voice that I would weigh all the affairs of men. Even though I was reluctant at times, hearing God's voice remained consistent throughout my life.

I do not know how I developed the confidence of knowing that God speaks, except by reading his Word and growing up, making mistakes, and relying on the wisdom of God through experience. In reference to mistakes, for instance, I recall times of feeling intense guilt. This one particular time, I was really beating myself up over something I had done, then I heard his voice speaking to me so clearly and it asked me how dare I act as if his grace wasn't sufficient for me. That spoke a lot to me about how this God which people speak of really desires to know us and love us into all truth and fullness of purpose. It is his faithfulness, not ours, that compels us to want to please God through our mindset, words, and actions—or ethical behavior.

According to an ethics professor at Abilene Christian University, Randy Harris, our worldview impacts our ethical behavior. I believe that our ethical behavior is what ultimately helps us to win in this journey called life. And I am convinced that my worldview of being a believer greatly influences my aspirations and my choices, especially during difficulties. Even as an academic, I am not convinced that the creator's voice had less of an influence on my ethical philosophy than any other aspect of my life. For example, when pursuing my doctoral degree, there were many times I questioned my involvement in education—in a seemingly rigid and crooked system that places unfair demands on underserved populations. I questioned whether it was wise to take up this endeavor when I still was not sure of my path of impact. However, it was through this process that my concept of purpose and leadership was challenged the most.

While I do not profess to be a superhuman, or possess any power higher than the next man, that still, small voice continued to lead me. Like Harris, my views closely reflect a pluralistic deontologist approach, an approach which reasons with right and wrong. Also, like Harris, my ethical philosophy is shaped by the teachings of the Bible. It is the philosophy of *cruciformity*—an acceptance of committing, and at times re-committing, to the story and examples of Christ (particularly through the lens of the Beatitudes; Matthew 5–7, NIV)—that I am convicted, challenged, and ultimately made into a better leader. So, if I had any advice following the iteration of my life's journey, it would be rooted in the concept of cruciformity.

MOTIVATIONS

As described through my Christian worldview, I believe that God uses various experiences through our lives to motivate change in us. These collective circumstances are what I consider motivations. These are the factors that have shaped my ethical philosophy and why I behave the way that I do. Being a young, Black male, it might come as no surprise that my life has been met with hard times, especially in my youth. I have dealt with many challenges related to poverty and instability but grew up with a rich Christian background. Coming from a family of modest preachers, and from a single-parent household, God was a source of strength and hope. Similarly, education was uniquely my hope, particularly coming from modest opportunities of educational success evident in my family. While faith and education were anchors of hope, growing up with challenges were motivating factors.

My childhood shaped me, but leaving home put the growth to the test. Like many of the anecdotal experiences and research in this collection, our motivators tend to be things beyond which we can control—how we were raised, our experiences growing up, our racial, regional, and socio-economic backgrounds, and spiritual convictions. For me, however, it was an acknowledgement of my responsibility in this journey that provided a sense of purpose and peace with the struggle. I consider this *the process*. For those who dare to dream, in spite of failed circumstances and past attempts, understanding the process becomes a demonstrated tool of faith. I think so highly of this stage of the journey, that I argue that honest, consistent, and fair reflection on one's process will lead to one's calling.

THE PROCESS

While growing up presented many challenges, the biggest leap of faith occurred for me when I decided to leave my family and attend college, two states away. Attending Fisk University, confident that I needed to move away and trust God, opened me up to experiences that challenged my identity and character. I was prepared intellectually, so struggling academically was not my story in college. As a student and young professional, I did well because after living in instability and being homeless as a kid, I vowed that I would work super hard in high school so I could go to college. I certainly bought into the "make 1,000,000 dollars more in your lifetime narrative." And while I did not struggle academically, God blessed me throughout my high school experiences with a great school and mentors that "met me" where my single mother could not.

As a young man, however, I was not as clear about my purpose and of my identity as a believer, leader, and musician. I decided to attend Fisk University to study music business and found myself teaching and tutoring when I wasn't in class or traveling as a Fisk Jubilee Singer®. As a young college kid working out my identity and purpose, God still chose to speak to me, and in times of testing he would teach me through my experiences. While high school was much more of an academic and self-awareness struggle, college was socially and professionally rigorous, the work that students did was on a higher level and in direct preparation for their respective careers; both of which required ethical decision making, and, like a child, I had to rely on Father God for wisdom, and many times, grace and mercy. What I did not realize was how God was setting me up for relationships after Fisk. I thought that I would be a singer who would live up to the conformations of becoming a household name. These factors motivated me to be what I thought was simply singing inspirational soul music. That did not happen immediately after graduation, the Spring of 2011—an opportunity to teach was now on my radar as the next, best opportunity to give back and to figure out what I wanted to do.

I trained to become an educator through the Teach for America (TFA) corps in Mississippi during the Summer of 2011. I found myself walking to my dorm site, burning profusely in the Mississippi heat that I had never experienced before. My morning routine consisted of waking up early between the hours of 4:00–5:00 a.m., eating breakfast, and grabbing lunch within 30 minutes, to be ready to catch the bus to my school site. We began learning the first week about what we needed before starting our first teaching exercises with students (the 5 weeks following); I would then go home after classes were over, heading straight to dinner, and then to learning and planning sessions. Then I would come back to the dorm after the sun went down, plan some more until late in the evening, sometimes early morning, and do it all over again for 6 days at a time. This was all new to me and was like drinking a hydrant load of information through a straw. This educational baptism by fire, nostalgically, was something with which I was all too familiar, reflecting on my high school days, when I was first exposed to consistent high academic expectations. If this is what the world of work looks like, however, then I knew for sure that I'd be serving tables, passing out my mixtape to people I met. I knew I wanted to be a singer, and I also knew I did not want to be poor like I was before. I felt a bit powerless at that point, and for the next few years of my start as an adult, I actually felt like I made a mistake, along the process.

As I trained for my first job, as a teacher, I felt mingled feelings of excitement, nervousness, cluelessness, and doubt. I was not a stranger to hard things, I just did not know where all of this was leading the singer who just wanted to sing. God whispered in my ears, pretty early on, that I was to learn and do my best for Him. . .not for anyone or any organization. In a sense, God was using my TFA experience to prepare me for where he was leading me. And where I am today shows evidence that God was my guide because I still do not feel sure, or totally sold that education is my profession (in the way we currently revere and respect it). Yet, I have seen the grace that God has given me with students, colleagues, and parents in my 10 years of teaching.

To this day, I tell everyone that I am graced to serve—students, colleagues, supervisors, family, community, media, and so on—that teaching is ministry to me; which carries a similarly challenging responsibility. This motivation has led to an interestingly curious life, teaching teenagers in my areas of interest and expertise—the music business. The experiences that taught me—in the classroom, on-the-job training, and in real life—have truly prepared me to realize and achieve my dreams, in a much richer way. This required just the right amount of ethics, and God's intervention. In other words, I had to buy into certain principles to endure and to remain teachable, in spite of the many lessons I learned. It is hard to get to this stage in reflecting on the process if one finds it difficult to rise above their challenges. Until challenges become motivations, you will not choose to do the hard stuff through the process that will lead you to your purpose or calling.

REFLECTION

Take time to ponder why it is important to identify whether the concept of a worldview works for you. What is your worldview and how does it impact your personal and professional life... Give some thought to motivations. Do you think it is true that what doesn't kill you makes you stronger... Motivations have provided countless powerful lessons for me.

Reflect on the role of faith in your life. "Does it pay to apply faith to one's purpose in life..." "Is that, alone, enough..." Our life must be purposeful, "What does *the process* mean to you..." Like me, "How can you learn from being more reflective of your life and the decisions you make..." And lastly, "How does the concept of cruciformity impact a believer's life goals..." "Are we called to leadership, as believers, over our own desires..."

CHAPTER 8

PERSONAL AGENCY

An Under-Discussed Factor for Successful Life Outcomes of Black Males

Michael T. Owens

I should be in jail. I should be poorly educated. I should also have multiple kids from multiple women. I should be dead—at least these are the primary outcomes society, research, and statistics promulgate about Black men. Well, I've never been in jail. I'm well educated. The only children I have are from my wife. And most importantly, I'm alive. However, I realize that one poor decision or a "wrong-place-wrong-time" situation could have drastically altered my life's course. Occasionally, I stop to ponder how I avoided many of the pitfalls plaguing Black men. I attribute it to my family and other positive influences (teachers, mentors, church, community organizations, etc.). But I also recognize my own role and refusal to become another gloomy statistic. Family dynamics certainly play significant roles in the lives of children, but too much emphasis is placed on family structure and not enough on personal agency. Personal motivation has an equal, if not greater influence on life outcomes.

BACKGROUND

My background isn't much different from many other Black men. I've had significant exposure to violence, drugs, and crime. I've benefited from various forms of government assistance. I've had to deal with racism, discrimination, and bigotry. I've also had unwarranted run-ins with the police. And yes, I'm the product of a teenage mother.

When I was born, my parents were barely old enough to drive and too young to vote. In today's pop culture, *16 and Pregnant* and *Teen Mom* are reality shows, but for Ma it was just reality—no lights, no cameras, no syndicated reruns. Like many young Black mothers, mine was uncertain about the future, but fully committed to raising a child despite being forever tied to a "baby's daddy." Conversely, like many Black fathers mine was scared out of his mind, unwilling to accept the responsibilities of fatherhood. He went his way. Ma went hers.

My family consisted of female kin networks: my grandma, mother, two aunts, and a female cousin a year younger than me. I was, of course, the only male. While my mother and grandmother were at work, my aunts sat around drinking, playing cards, and smoking weed with their friends. At the time, their hoodlum male friends were my main exposure to Black men—my father wasn't around and my cousin's father was in prison. Taking all of this into consideration, society provided me a ready-made list of excuses in case I "failed" in life. By chance if I had fallen by the wayside, social scholars would immediately point to my family makeup. They would argue I was destined for deviancy mainly because I was born to a young, unmarried Black woman. They might theorize that my nontraditional family increased my susceptibility to waywardness or that, as a single mother, Ma was incapable of effective parenting. None of these notions accurately depicted my family. Sarkisian and Gerstel (2004) noted that researchers routinely focus on perceived weaknesses of Black families often characterizing them as disorganized, deficient, and dysfunctional. I'd argue that *every* family, regardless of race, experiences disorganization and dysfunctions. The key is how effectively an individual navigates this environment. A major flaw in these deficit-based approaches is that they fail to sufficiently account for a child's personal willpower and drive; instead, they place virtually all the focus on the parents. Ultimately, individuals have the strongest control over their life trajectories, regardless of a one or two parent upbringing.

MARRIAGE MERRY-GO-ROUND

Ma caught the eye of a tall, slender deejay while hanging out at a bar with friends. Two weeks later, they were living together. Six weeks after that, they were married. Instantly, I went from a single-parent home to a two-parent home. I now had a father whom I called "dad" rather than "stepdad."

Dad offered a male perspective of life that I hadn't experienced. I remember when he started a lawn business with a beat-up truck and a used lawnmower. I was just a scrawny, little kid, but I wanted to help. One humid morning, we stood at the entrance of an affluent subdivision. It was Dad's first major customer and the largest chunk of his income.

"What do you want me to do..." I asked, leaning on the side of the truck.

"If you see a weed, pull it." He was already sweating; moisture had formed around the neck of his t-shirt. He walked to a nearby hibiscus flower bed, pointed to a weed sprouting from the mulch. "See, grab it by the root and pull it up."

He left to do another task and I started on mine, but I got bored quickly. *These are just weeds,* I thought. I did the job half-heartedly, thinking it didn't matter if I missed a few here and there.

A few weeks later, while driving back to the subdivision, Dad said he received some complaints about the weeds. As a man taking great pride in his work, he wasn't pleased. "These people pay us good money to do a job," he said. "If you're not gonna do it right, then I'll stop bringing you with me." Not only had I jeopardized our family's livelihood but I also let him down. I had let Ma down before but disappointing Dad just seemed different. In only a few words, he reinforced the importance of responsibility, accountability, and work ethic.

My quality of life definitely improved after Ma and Dad married. I left the all-female, drug, and alcohol-filled environment at Grandma's and moved into a balanced male–female home where we attended church regularly. We lived in a better neighborhood; had cars, electronics, and pets among other things. Even at a young age, I knew that having a father was a big deal in the Black community. With two parents at home, I was statistically projected to have a higher probability of life success—but it wasn't guaranteed. My life would be whatever I made it.

Eighteen months later, my parents drifted apart. Ma worked all day but stayed focused on being a wife and mother. In between work and deejaying in seedy nightclubs, Dad tried to be a husband and father. His schedule and recreational drug use proved too much for Ma. They divorced.

Now what... My life up to that point consisted of a single-parent household, two-parent household, and now a divorced-single parent household. In the blink of an eye, I was back at Grandma's—back to the booze, weed, and sporadic church attendance.

Ma continued to plant within me seeds of knowledge, independence, and achievement. However, despite her efforts, I had behavioral problems in school. I was always one of the smallest kids, but I always had the biggest mouth. My disposition understandably led to fights, frequent trips to the principal's office, and scathing letters from teachers. However, nothing deterred me. I did what I wanted and simply accepted the consequences. Ma told my teachers that her divorce probably caused my unruliness. As a perceptive and opportunistic kid, I began using this excuse to justify my poor behavior.

About a year later, Dad's lifestyle changed for the better. He stopped deejaying, smoking, and drinking. He even enrolled in college. Now he was truly ready to be the strong man that Ma and I needed. As a result, my parents remarried each other (and have remained married for nearly 30 years); and Dad legally adopted me, officially giving me his last name. I felt like I had a real family; like those in television sitcoms.

I remained the resident smart mouth throughout elementary school and much of middle school; two parents, one parent, married, divorced—it didn't matter. In my young mind, the attention I received as class clown outweighed the punishments at home. I was entering a stage of life where opinions of peers had a stronger impact than my parents' desires.

A TURNING POINT

My seventh grade English teacher suggested I move up to his advanced class. I declined. I was fine hanging with the homies in the regular class, acting uninterested while privately acing all the tests. Geography class was no different until I wrote an essay for extra credit. When it was all said and done, I had a 100% average and immediately became a class legend. My geography teacher showered me with praises because in her years of teaching, no student had ever earned a perfect average. I downplayed the achievement. "It's only because I did extra credit," I told her. She obviously saw past my excuse. Similar to my English teacher, she asked that I consider moving to the advanced class. I declined again. Besides, I knew the fellas would surely hit me with the "You actin' White" spiel. My geography teacher pushed back and literally forced me to switch classes.

When I arrived in the advanced class, my classmates were familiar with my story. Consequently, they all expected me to perform at a high academic level. This was a different type of pressure because I was accustomed to getting rewarded for deviant behaviors. But in this class, I gained respect by participating and knowing the answers to questions. What a concept! *I'm just as smart as these White kids,* I thought to myself. This new confidence translated into popularity—the ultimate form of acceptance at that age. When I reached high school, no one had to twist my arm to take honors classes. High academic achievement became an expectation. When I decided on my own to do better, things changed.

Though I come from what scholars would deem a fragmented or disrupted family background, I still received the guidance, life lessons, and support needed for success. But it was up to me to decide exactly what to do with it. My words of wisdom for young men of color...

1. Race nor background determines success or failure in life—you do.
2. If you don't know where you want to go in life, any road will take you there.
3. Pray.

REFERENCES

Sarkisian, N., & Gerstel, N. (2004). Kin support among Blacks and Whites: Race and family organization. *American Sociological Review, 69*(6), 812–837.

CHAPTER 9

STILL STANDING

Bumps in the Road Along a Path to Greater Success

Jason Rivera

I took a deep breath, took in my surroundings one last time, and quietly said goodbye. It would be the last time in my grandmother's house; the last time I would sit at the kitchen table late at night with a warm ham and cheese sandwich and chocolate milk; the last time I would hear my brother's jovial laughter; and the last time, as a child, that I would be able to call somewhere home. At 13, I was a homeless orphan—abandoned by my drug-addicted mother and rejected by both my maternal and paternal grandparents. Admittedly, I was a difficult child. Growing up in an environment where physical, sexual, and mental abuses were commonplace took its toll on me. I quickly became the "angry kid with a chip on his shoulder." I developed a thick-skinned exterior that I carefully crafted to protect myself.

Growing up, my life felt like a perpetual landslide, with obstacle upon obstacle overwhelming me. At 13, being confronted with the reality of becoming homeless seemed trivial in comparison to some of the experiences

I had in my childhood. Still, my personal challenges gave rise to a determination to persevere.

I learned, at an early age, that school was my sanctuary. It was, in every real sense, the only stability my childhood offered. Amid the brick and mortar, and the waxed floors and wooden desks, I unknowingly became the architect of a pseudo-family. I found in my teachers, pseudo-parents, and in my counselors, relatives that I could go to for a hug or a kind word. My friends became siblings and our daily transgressions would help to distract me from the real-life horrors of my world.

In school, I shined. I developed a passion for learning and yearned to read books. I started writing short stories and eventually developed into a poet. In time, I found success in my academics that helped me to map a way out of my personal nightmares. I slowly began to understand that going to college was my way out. Yet, reality continued to remind me that school, in many respects, was a luxury that I might not be able to afford.

When I turned 15, I ran out of options. No longer able to continue living with friends, I dropped out of school and found a job at a neighborhood mom-and-pop restaurant bussing tables. I made just enough money to rent a room and was able to eat when I worked. I felt like a fish trying to swim upstream, pushing against the current, and hoping for an unlikely outcome. I wanted desperately to continue in school but didn't think it was a possibility.

Then, I received a surprise visit from Dr. Enid Margolies, the assistant principal for guidance at the high school I no longer attended. Even now, I don't know how Doc, as I came to affectionately call her, knew where to find me. Fortunately, she developed a plan for me to return to school. She was passionate about my success, showing me love and compassion at a time when I felt most abandoned.

Quickly, Doc taught me to understand that the obstacles in my life were merely bumps in the road along a path to greater success. I channeled my anger into my academics, but my prolonged absences affected my grade point average, making college seem even less likely in my immediate future. Still, with Doc's guidance, I applied to 12 residential colleges in hopes that I would be accepted to one. Slowly, acceptance letter after acceptance letter arrived. In total, I was accepted to nine schools, and decided on Manhattanville College, a small, liberal arts school in Purchase, New York.

Manhattanville College, set on a beautiful campus in an affluent suburban community, offered me more than I could have imagined. Although tragedy continued to follow me, I refused to allow it to define me. In my first semester, my mother died of kidney failure due to complications related to HIV. I helped bury her, but returned back home, to Manhattanville, shortly after the funeral services to resume my studies. When I returned, I was greeted with an array of supports and services that allowed for a seamless return.

Manhattanville offered me a sound educational experience and helped to broaden my appreciation of—and perspective on—the role institutions of higher learning play in developing our nation. I learned how to think critically, to analyze situations objectively, to question with integrity, and to freely engage in academic discourse. Moreover, I developed into a strong leader, ultimately becoming the first openly gay, Latino, student government president.

In 1997, I graduated college and embarked on a mission to find my professional calling. On September 11, 2001, that was all interrupted when two airplanes barreled into the Twin Towers. Following the tragic events that would change so many lives, I deeply understood that my success could only be measured by how large or small my contributions would be to the greater society. Moreover, my drive to succeed was no longer about how to transform my life into something more positive, but instead a desire to help transform the lives of others. I felt an overwhelming responsibility to do something more meaningful and decided to become a New York City public school teacher.

Becoming a classroom teacher was a natural fit. Being with students, guiding them through the rigors of the learning process, and understanding and valuing their multiple intelligences, awakened a passion inside of me which helped me discover that teaching was more than a choice—it was a calling. I realized that I connected with students in urban settings, and pursued positions in schools located in inner cities that were designated "hard-to-staff." After a few years of teaching, I started to understand how teachers collide with the "system." I began to question how I might be able to have a greater impact. I knew, from personal experiences, that students educated in large public schools could easily become marginalized within educational systems attempting to teach large masses.

Following my professional instincts, I would deviate from the curriculum, because I understood that to help my students achieve success would require greater instructional support. I knew that my students needed intense, guided, and well-planned opportunities to make real connections to abstract concepts. I became much less concerned with how well a student performed on standardized exams, and much more interested in their ability to absorb information, synthesize it, and then attempt to apply it to an activity, assessment, or discussion.

My master's program taught me to become a reflective professional. I would journal about lessons, experiences with students, and my growing frustration with the system. In the 6 years I remained in the classroom, I witnessed teaching moving further and further away from the students and becoming more about legislation and standardized exams. While schools publicly declared lofty mission statements about developing critical thinkers and community service-oriented citizens, they focused, very directly, on preparing students for standardized exams, which would not only determine a school's "grade," but also decide whether administrators and teachers would receive financial bonuses. I became disheartened by the system, and quickly felt my passion for teaching waning. I soon discovered that to have a greater impact, I had to shift my focus from teaching children to training teachers. Consequently, I left the classroom and transitioned back into higher education administration.

As a child, education was a road map that helped lead me to a stable, more productive life. As an adult, education has become a vehicle that has allowed me to guide others down a similar path. Today, I am fortunate that I am able to continue to use education as a tool to transform my life and the lives of those I am fortunate enough to impact.

My lived experiences have taught me many valuable lessons that have certainly informed the ways in which I move in the world; lessons that surely can benefit others. For example, I learned that in life we will encounter what might seem like insurmountable obstacles. We can overcome those obstacles through the love, care, and support of others. But, we have to be willing to seek help and listen to advice when it is given. I know that in my life, I overcame every obstacle I encountered because there were people in my life that loved and cared for me. Doc was one of those special people. After she helped me graduate high school, Doc became my foster mother. She attended every family day gathering when I was in college, was at all of my graduations from high school through my PhD, and she provided me with unconditional love, care, and support for over 30 years. Who is your Doc... Who helps you to remain hopeful in the face of adversity... Do not be afraid to reach out to that person to ask for help. Most importantly, be open to the advice and willing to do things that might make you uncomfortable in order to persevere.

In closing, my life experiences may sound harrowing and perhaps they were, but I overcame every obstacle because there were people in my life that loved and cared for me. I went from being a child who loved school to a homeless high school dropout to the first in my family to graduate college and obtain a PhD. If I can do it, so can you! So, stay the course, continue to navigate the bumps in the road along your path to greater success by finding your inner strength, and tapping into those that love and care for you as you continue to strive toward your successes.

As you move forward, here is some valuable advice:

- Seeking help and support are signs of strength and intelligence!
- Spend time reflecting on who you are at your core, which can be achieved through mindfulness and getting comfortable in your own skin. Reflect on the obstacles you have had to overcome in your life—and yes, we all have things we have had to overcome. How did

you do it... What enabled you to persevere... Answering these two questions will help you develop a deeper understanding of who you are and how you can leverage your inner-strength.
- Remember to try your very best, but to be gentle with yourself—success comes with hard work and continuous effort!

CHAPTER 10

POVERTY AND EDUCATION

C. Sheldon Woods

As I look back on my 20 plus years in academia, I reflect on my childhood of poverty and the impact it has had on my life. I grew up raised by a single mother who worked up to three jobs to make ends meet. I was born in the Third Ward section of Houston, an inner-city neighborhood where the odds were against an African-American male child. According to the statistics, I had a better chance of dying due to violence or ending up in prison than I did of going to college. This was evident every day when I stepped out my front door. I frequently walked over dried blood on the sidewalk from altercations the previous night. Hearing gunshots did not startle me. Seeing police tape and crime scenes were regular topics of discussion over meals. Violence and death were so common that it seemed to be the norm to me as a child. The community was, and still is, surrounded by several universities, yet most youth in my neighborhood could tell you more about what occurred in the state penitentiary located hours away, while having no knowledge about the institutions of higher education in and around their neighborhood. This environment coupled with a fierce determination to escape the chains of poverty started me on a path that would lead me to a full scholarship to pay for my undergraduate degree and a full fellowship that would pay for my graduate education. This ultimately resulted in me earning a PhD at the age of 25 and becoming an assistant professor at the age of 26.

My childhood, was a kaleidoscope of experiences, both good and bad. The circumstances surrounding my birth did not give me a good start. I was the product of an extramarital affair. My father wanted nothing to do with me. He did not even want his name on my birth certificate. This would result in lots of rumors and cruel remarks from neighbors. Most of these were made behind my mother's back.

I did not know I was poor until I started school. Up until then, I was only exposed to the poverty in my neighborhood. So, I never gave it much thought. My first-grade year, I was bused to a school in a White upper middle-class neighborhood. I was amazed by the houses that I saw from the bus window. These homes were drastically different from mine. More than that, many of my classmates had two parents that seemed to take an equal interest in their education and seemed to be wearing the best in style and designer clothing. My clothes were clean and matched, but nothing about them was in style or designer. In fact, my teacher informed me that I dressed and behaved like an old man. This would not have been a shock to her if she understood my circumstances. My mother worked long hours and often would not get home until 11:00 p.m. While she was working I was being watched by my grandmother or some other senior citizen.

School was where I had an experience that would prove to be pivotal in my life. I was an average student and struggled with spelling. I had been placed in a class for students who were considered low achieving. Our teacher was harsh and took every opportunity to let us know that we were the low achieving class. She told me that I was "plumb dumb and would never amount to anything in life." These words would haunt me for a very long time and cut through my spirit like a dagger. Later in life, I would learn to use these words as motivation to succeed.

I continued to be bused to schools outside of my neighborhood. In middle school, my self-esteem was very low. It was reflected in my grades. I was being picked on by kids at school because of where I lived and the clothes I wore. It did not help that I was a late bloomer and puberty was not kind to me. I so badly wanted to fit in, but I was an unpopular outsider. My mother accepted my mediocre grades as long as, I was well behaved in school my grades did not seem to matter.

For high school, my mother decided I should attend the local Black high school. This was an eye-opening experience for me. I was still poor, but it was not the topic of conversation every day. I felt like I was a part of something. My self-esteem improved. I was even identified as exceptional in science and was moved to an honors science course. That first report card, I received 5 As and a C. I was shocked. I had never received an A in anything but PE. This event changed my mother's attitude about school success. She did not say anything about the As, but she did ask me several times why I got the C. She then informed me that from now on she would not accept anything less than As from me.

The following year I was bused to a school for computer technology. The good grades continued. In fact, I started excelling in school. I was picked on still because of my clothes and my lack of resources. But by then my attitude had changed. When I was picked on, I used the anger I felt as motivation to be better than my tormentors. When people picked on my clothes, I studied harder with the belief that someday in the future, I would get a good job and be able to dress how I wanted, eat what I wanted, live where I wanted, and travel.

As I neared the completion of high school; I was thinking about universities. Initially, my mother was shocked that I wanted to go to college. I had visions of going to an Ivy League school and was visited by a couple of recruiters from some of those schools. My mother quickly put a damper on those dreams by telling me that those schools did not want any N-word there. This crushed my heart and made me even more determined to leave home and go away to college. Despite this setback, I did apply to local colleges and I received several scholarship offers. At my mother's request, I accepted a full scholarship to an HBCU nearby as a pre-med major. I tried to take full advantage of all the academic resources laid out in front of me. I joined study groups, attended summer programs, and spoke to former students to get advice on studying for my classes. Before my senior year, I decided that I did not want to go to medical school, that I wanted to attend graduate school instead. My mother was horrified and gave me such grief. She asked if I planned to drive a cab with my PhD. I was torn. I knew what I wanted to do but not how to do it. However, I eventually figured out how to pursue my graduate school goals. I relied on advice from my undergraduate advisor. He informed me to apply to doctoral programs. If I was successful in the program, I would earn a PhD. If I was not successful, the school would give me a master's degree as a consolation gift. Based on *this* bad advice, I started applying to PhD programs my senior year. I received numerous rejection letters.

I graduated with a Bachelor of Science in biology and had no clue what I was going to do when the fall started. One day, while home from work, I received a phone call offering a fellowship to work on a PhD at a school that I had never heard of or applied to. I was told if I was interested I would have to complete the application and return it quickly because school was starting in 2 weeks. Soon I was on a bus traveling to a place I had never seen to do what I am now told is impossible. The bad advice would partially pay off.

After an initial crisis of confidence, I excelled in my program. I was initially told by my first academic advisor, that because I attended an HBCU, that the As and Bs that I got there would be like Bs and Cs at this larger

White school. This rattled my confidence. And indeed, the very first class I attended was a biochemistry class. The professor gave a quiz the first day of class. All I could do was put my name on it. I was overwhelmed. The second day of class he gave a similar quiz and informed the class if we could not pass this quiz we would not pass the course and should drop the class while there was still time. When it was time to turn in my blank quiz, I walked to the front of the room passed the professor's desk and out the front door to the Registrar's office to drop the class. I started thinking the advisor was correct about my academic abilities.

The next class I took was something that I had never heard of before. It was plant disease diagnosis. This sounded like I was in for more trouble. I did not know that plants contracted diseases. To my surprise, this urban kid who had never been around crops before excelled in this class. I often did not know the name of the crops I was examining but I could easily identify the pathogen. I did so well in this class that I was approached by the professor the following year and asked to be her teaching assistant. I successfully completed my degree plan and received my PhD with an emphasis in science curriculum at the age of 25.

The poor kid from the hood had managed to do something that no one in his family had accomplished. Now all I had to do was get a job to avoid becoming a cab driver. I got a job as an assistant professor at a large private Midwestern university at the age of 26. I would learn so much there. The politics of academia can be brutal. I was denied tenure at this institution and thought that my time in academia was over. I did apply for jobs at other locations and to my surprise received several offers. I have been at my current institution for 14 years. I am tenured and trying to make a difference in the lives of young people.

I have learned several lessons over the course of this journey. If I could speak to my younger self this is what I would say:

1. The circumstances surrounding your birth do not determine your future.
2. Know that being poor and struggling can be a benefit depending on your outlook. Use it as motivation to get ahead. It is your strength and will that makes you appreciate future successes.
3. Education is the key to a better future. Don't let anyone steal that from you. People will tease you and call you a nerd and accuse you of trying to be White. Reject this sentiment. Don't equate intelligence with Whiteness.
4. Be prepared to take advantage when opportunities come your way. Do not let fear rule your life. When opportunity comes, grab it and learn from the experience.

5. Failure can be motivation to learn and do better. Do not let mistakes define or limit your future. Learn from them, never repeat them, and move on.
6. Your loved ones may say the most hurtful things to you. It is not from a place of hatred. It is out of fear for you and their own shortcomings and not being able to express their true feelings.
7. Most importantly, stay focused. Keep your eyes on your goals and you will be successful. You will surpass those who made fun of your circumstances.
8. There is nothing wrong with HBCUs. They are fine institutions preparing productive citizens.
9. Develop a mantra for success. My mantra was influenced by my teacher telling me I was plumb dumb. My mantra became: "She is wrong about me." That became my motivation whenever I had academic struggles. The desire to prove her wrong has been a powerful motivation.
10. Lastly, no matter how painful or embarrassing, never forget where you come from. All those experiences shape you. They also serve as benchmarks to help you measure your progress. I once had a student of color, trying to get a pass on an assignment, tell me that I forgot where I came from. My thought at the time was no, I remember it well and I remember how hard I had to work to get where I am today.

CHAPTER 11

THE DESTRUCTION OF DRUGS

Joel Bratton Jr.

A large portion of my journey into manhood took place in the early '80s through the mid-'90s, during the drug epidemic era in Baltimore, particularly West Baltimore where I resided. There was a staunch belief that the CIA infiltrated drugs in the Black and Hispanic communities; especially, crack cocaine which spread quickly across the country (Bourgois, 1996). The urban landscape was changing and instead of Black males going to college, they were on the street corners selling dope. The pipeline to prison saga was in existence and becoming kind of normalcy in the urban community. The homicide rate doubled amongst Black males 14–17, while the homicide rate in general, remained steady amongst 25-year olds and older (Cooper & Smith, 2011).

Growing up, I witnessed a lot of my relatives and friends enduring hardships, such as financial instability, unemployment, and health issues resulting from drugs and alcohol abuse. During those times, it seemed like I was far removed from that harsh reality because they did not directly impact me. I would quickly learn how close the drug game would hit home.

In 1984, during my freshman year of college, I experienced a traumatic incident relating to drugs. I was finishing up my fall semester of college and was eager to come home for winter break. I was even more excited that my cousin, Robert "Manny" Brown, was coming home from the U.S. Navy for the holidays. We decided to meet at Givenchy/Pascale's, a club in Baltimore owned by Edward R. "Slim" Butler, a known drug kingpin. Initially, I was going to meet Manny at his home where my aunt, Linda Jordan, uncle, Charles Jordan aka Squeaky, and cousin, Lisa Brown resided. I decided not to come over to the house because the club was closer to me. They lived in the county and I resided in the city, so I went directly to the club.

Once Manny arrived at the club it was complete excitement amongst the two of us. The drinks were flowing, the conversation was sensational, and the DJ was jamming on the 1s and 2s. When the club closed, we talked about what we were going to do over the break and said our goodbyes. Upon returning to my mother's house I noticed she wasn't home. Completely unaware of anything that happened, I saw a note on the table for me to come to Sinai Hospital. Not knowing what was going on I rushed out the door. When I finally saw my mother, she was overwhelmed with grief. She tried to explain as best she could due to the circumstances that my uncle and cousin were killed execution style and that my aunt Linda was shot and survived.

Throughout the remainder of the morning so much was going through my mind and I hadn't quite processed the ordeal. It was hard seeing my grandmother, Christine Jordan experiencing the loss of her only son. To say that I was completely devastated would be an understatement. I was in total shock and disbelief that someone had cowardly caused harm to members of my family.

We tried desperately to find reasons why someone in our family would be killed in such a violent way. It bothered me that my uncle's involvement in the drug game may have led to his death. But what was most disturbing is that whoever committed this crime, also murdered my cousin, Lisa who did not have any role in criminal activities. The only surviving person that fateful night was my aunt Linda. She was able to escape with a single gunshot and minor injuries.

Questions void of answers led me to my own conclusions about what happened that night. Due to the heinous nature of the crime, I thought my uncle may have been targeted. There were certain details of that night that just did not add up for me and did not make sense. We later found out that there was $15,000 in the house that was not taken by the perpetrators and there were no drugs present. So many different scenarios raced through my mind. The more I thought about the situation, I came to the conclusion that my uncle was set up by someone and perhaps it got complicated because my aunt and cousin were home. I also thought that my aunt may have had something to do with the situation. She stayed in the streets, meaning she always associated with drug dealers, hustlers, and criminals. My uncle spent time in federal prison for drugs and lived the street life of a drug kingpin, which may answer how the two met.

I continued to struggle with the death of my uncle and cousin. This ordeal happened when I was in my first year of college. I was home for the semester break trying to study for my midterm exams. I tried to block the death out of my mind, but it continued to cloud my thought process. I would leave home to go to Coppin State College library to study, but the concentration level was not there. I was having a hard time focusing.

As my winter break was coming to an end, I prepared myself mentally to return to school. I drove back to school with several of my friends from Baltimore. The drive was difficult because so much was racing through my mind. I started getting emotional because my uncle and I had gotten closer over the years. Since my father was not present in my life the way he should have been, I looked to my Uncle Charles and other male relatives as father figures. My family has always been a close-knit unit and his death was a tremendous loss.

Moreover, I was concerned about my grandmother. Although she seemed to handle my uncle's death the best way she knew how, I knew the pain rippled through her. As a spiritual person with a strong family support, my grandmother endured in her own way. She was so strong about the whole ordeal. It seemed that she knew this day would come to fruition. It was like she was expecting this to happen because of the lifestyle my uncle lived.

I was worried about her because she was older and not in the best health, but I was equally concerned about my mother's pain. Out of the three surviving siblings, it seemed that all the pressure was on my mother. One sister was a functioning addict and another sister had 11 children and deteriorating health. My mother was faced with a lot of family challenges that she had to endure and did her best to raise her two children, my sister and me.

During the funeral arrangements, there was an outpouring of support and grief from friends, relatives, and associates of my uncle. Most of the bereaved participated in the same lifestyle that ended my uncle's life. In addition, it was hard for many of my cousin's friends who attended Woodlawn High School in Baltimore County. Lisa was a very popular young lady who had a beautiful smile and always dressed fashionably. During the viewing, many of her friends ascended onto Nutter's Funeral home in West Baltimore. It was sad to see so many of her friends being consoled by one another. It seemed her death had a dire effect on everyone; particularly, those that were close to her and our family.

This ordeal seemed to serve as a wakeup call for me. It was a clear and painful reminder that dealing drugs and using alcohol had an effect on not just people in my family, but many of my friends with whom I associated. Most of my friends came from single parent households primarily run by their mothers. The unfortunate reality is that most of my friends didn't have to indulge in illegal activities or use any form of drugs and alcohol. Peer pressure was the main reason they indulged in illegal activity. My friend's parents afforded them the best resources that should have swayed them away from illicit activities, which included attending top schools, providing financial stability, and obtaining opportunities for a better life.

My mother played an important instrumental role in my life to keep me on the right path. She was spiritually grounded and provided a solid foundation. She made sure we attended church regularly and strongly encouraged me to incorporate God into my life. My mother also exposed me to the finer things in life. Attending Broadway musicals, plays, cultural events, and traveling to different U.S. cities, allowed us to expand our vision beyond the streets of Baltimore. My mom preached education early on and she remained involved throughout my academic career. She made sure that I excelled academically and had the resources to succeed. I participated in athletics and earned a college scholarship. I also had family members making sure I didn't indulge in negative behavior.

After my uncle was killed, it was hard for me to concentrate on school when I returned. The thought of my uncle's death overwhelmed me to the point I wanted to drop out. There was a period where I wasn't attending classes and completing assignments. I just completely withdrew from the things that normally kept me afloat. However, the support from family members and friends provided me with a constant reminder about my life's purpose, particularly as it related to my education. The next semester I joined a fraternity which played an important role in my development and afforded me the opportunity to heal my wounds and understand my purpose of life. I was surrounded with like-minded men who lived the same cardinal principles in which I believed; manhood, scholarship, perseverance, and uplift. Therefore, if I had to advise anyone who experienced a similar ordeal, I would encourage you to have faith in God, be selective of your friends, and choose associates that have similar goals and encourage you to do well in life. Take stock in your associates, remove any toxicity that stunts your progress, and seek out mentors that can guide you. Lastly, stay away from drugs and alcohol as they can often cloud your judgement.

REFERENCES

Bourgois, P. (1996). In search of masculinity: Violence, respect and sexuality among Puerto Rican crack dealers in East Harlem. *The British Journal of Criminology, 36*(3), 412–427.

Cooper, A., & Smith, E. L. (2011). *Homicide trends in the United States, 1980–2008: Annual Rates for 2009 and 2010—U.S. Department of Justice.* Washington, DC: Office of Justice Programs, Bureau of Justice Statistics.

SECTION II

INTERSECTIONS OF RACE, GENDER, AND SEXUALITY

Contrary to popular belief, men of color are not all the same (Harper, 2015; Howard, 2014; Johnson, 2013). In others words, they have social identities which differentiate them from other males of color. These social identities include but are not limited to varying expressions of Blackness and Brownness (i.e., biraciality), the fluidity of gender, and various expressions of sexual identities. Originally coined to describe the experiences of women of color, Crenshaw (1991) introduced the term *intersectionality* to describe how women of color experience oppression at the intersections of race, gender, social class, and other forms of subordination. In recent research studies, scholars (Howard, 2014; Warren, 2017) have taken up the notion of intersectionality to describe the experiences of Black males. In his book, *Black Male(d): Peril and Promise in the Education of African American males*, Howard (2014) documented the school-going experiences of Black males in urban schools finding that their experiences had been replete with issues of institutional racism causing them to underperform in every academic area. Furthermore, as one of his recommendations, Howard suggested that educational scholars and others who study Black and other men of color should use intersectionality to better understand their lives. Following that recommendation, Warren (2017) investigated the schooling and college-going experiences of Black males who attended Urban Prep Academy on the Chicago's South side, using critical race theory (CRT) and precisely intersectionality to bring attention to the need to better examine practices of all male schools, which serve Black male students. Scholars have also used CRT, specifically intersectionality, to explore Black males in higher education spaces (see Harper, 2015; Johnson, 2013). For example, using autoethnography, Johnson (2013) documented his racialized experiences being profiled on a predominantly White campus in the Midwest.

While these studies are notable and have helped us to better understand the experiences of Black males, undertheorized in these empirical studies are those which investigate the intersections of race and sexuality, particularly the experiences of men of color who may self-identify as queer. As there is a growing body of work on men of color who are queer, this idea is not to suggest that scholars have not explored men of color who are queer. However, what this idea suggests is that more studies applying an intersectionality perspective on men of color who self-identify as queer are needed and essential to understanding all men of color.

In Section II, we center Crenshaw's (1991) conception of intersectionality. Contributing authors shared narratives about what it means to live at the intersection of being men of color. In the same manner we contend that men of color are all different, we acknowledge that each story, narrative, and/or counter narrative is different, but provides insight regarding the lived experiences and realities of being men of color in America. We encourage readers to take an intersectional gaze as they acknowledge, value, and learn about the mosaic of differences existing among men of color.

REFERENCES

Crenshaw, K. (1991). Mapping the margins: Intersectionality, identity politics, and violence against women of Color. *Stanford Law Review, 43*(6), 1241–1299.

Harper, S. (2015). Black male college achievers and resistant responses to racist stereotypes at predominantly white colleges and universities. *Harvard Educational Review*, 85(4), 646–674.

Howard, T. C. (2014). *Black male(d): Peril and promise in the education of African American males.* New York, NY: Teachers College Press.

Johnson, R. (2013). Black and male on campus: An autoethnographic account. *Journal of African American Males in Education*, 4(2), 103–123.

Warren, C. (2017). Urban Preparation: Young Black men moving from Chicago's Southside to success in higher education. Cambridge, MA: Harvard Education Press.

CHAPTER 12

FROM UNSEEN TO SEEN
The Power of Significant Others

Derrick Robinson

My neighborhoods were challenging. They were isolated and isolating. I lived in three of the four roughest neighborhoods in my area: (a) Southern Manor apartments, (b) Janna Lee Apartments, and (c) Gum Springs Apartments. My mom and I finally settled in Gum Springs when I entered fifth grade. To the outside world, we were unseen, voiceless, and neglected. I developed a core group of friends there: Kirk, nicknamed *Spike*; Karston, nicknamed *Kooley*; Mike, nicknamed *Old Face*; and Reggie, nicknamed *Lil' Reg*. We formed a singing group and did talent shows at school and in the community recreation center, called *The Gym*. However, our divide began around middle school. Spike, Kooley, and Mike began the dropping out process around the seventh grade. It started with skipping a day, then two, then a week, and more. By ninth grade, it was clear that we were not the same anymore. I became invisible to my core friends.

NINTH GRADE

Entering West Potomac High School in 1985 was a challenge. It was a new high school that combined two high schools into one. The school was predominantly White, with most of its Black students coming from four neighborhoods. If *race-based tracking* in education were a good thing, West Potomac High School would be award-winning. Being placed on the *good* side of tracking meant rarely having classes with neighborhood friends. It physically felt like we parted ways at the bus and rejoined at the end of the school day. In my classes, I was one of no more than four Black students in a class, and I did not know them. They knew I was from Gum Springs and I carried an *I'm tough, so leave me alone* look that haunts me to this day. It took years for those Black kids to really *see* me. I was just that kid in classrooms where I didn't belong.

My freshman year was pretty much a blur. Between increasing strains with my core friends and the passing of my grandmother, I was pretty much a strong *C* student. I recall one incident that slightly woke me up. In ninth grade biology class, my lab partner, Yonas, an Ethiopian kid, was tasked to do a urinalysis, which would require one of us to submit a urine sample. Yonas decided to purchase apple juice from a vending machine and use that as our sample. Our teacher found out eventually and scolded us. Yonas laughed and walked off. As I attempted to do the same, the teacher grabbed me by the arm and said, "Why do you Black people always settle for mediocrity..." I didn't respond. Truthfully, I did not know what *mediocrity* meant. I gathered that it wasn't good and I had no answer. I later discovered what mediocrity meant and it forced me to seriously think about myself as a student.

TENTH GRADE

Sophomore year, I became more serious about school. I had my first and only Black teacher during my K–12 experience. Mr. McGuire was my English teacher. My laziness bothered him, and he began to talk very frequently with my mom. He also challenged me to be a better student. He made us all, even the White kids, read *Native Son*. It was the first book that I had ever completed. In Bigger Thomas, the main character, I saw my friends and me. Like Bigger, our circumstances always put us one step away from trouble.

Mr. McGuire, along with a small group of Black teachers, led a visit to Virginia State University, a Historically Black College and University (HBCU). Although I wasn't supposed to go, Mr. McGuire made provisions for me. Seeing Black college students having fun, talking about the future, and not fighting or doing things I was used to seeing when large groups gathered, excited me. I daydreamed all the way home. I visualized myself on a college campus. I came home and told my mom, "I'm going to college!" She smiled and replied, "We already know that!"

In the neighborhood, problems with my friends increased. Guns and drug dealing entered the friendship. Washington, DC in the late 1980s was very challenging and our neighborhood, always labeled as dangerous, was not immune. Being in school every day meant I wasn't a part of the crew anymore. I would normally catch up with them after school, primarily at the gym. In those moments, we were fine. Eventually, however, they would have to go somewhere and wouldn't include me. Also, another friend, Tim, joined the crew. He was not a bad person, but he would do anything someone told him to do, which made him dangerous. By December, we had reached a point that exploded into a very violent fight. According to the rumors that week, I was supposed to be getting jumped by my former friends. I knew they carried weapons, so I kept a hammer in my backpack every day. When we finally clashed at the school bus stop, Tim stepped forward with his hands in his pocket. I pulled out the hammer, charged at him, and we fought. My slipping on ice saved Tim's life, and my life too. As I sat with police, with Tim's blood all over my clothes, I had a moment to think forward on how college would get me out of this area for good. There I was alone again, essentially friendless, and navigating a negative portrayal of me as this incident reached school. For me, *Native Son* was becoming my life. I felt like I was spending most of my energy trying to escape trouble but was always one bad move away from trouble.

ELEVENTH GRADE

My sophomore year ended with improvements in my overall grades and a new network of friends. I was placed in an Advanced Placement (AP) United States History class, but was told that I was not an AP student. Mr. Hiller, the AP U.S. History teacher, was quick to inform me that, "You should not expect me to change what I am teaching to accommodate you. This is AP U.S. History and if you cannot get scheduled out of this course, you're gonna have to figure it out." I felt he truly resented my presence in his classroom. He gave two assignments in the first quarter. I missed one and got a 90 on the other. It was the first F grade in my life. I let him win! I became even angrier to prove that I can beat these AP students. Mr. McGuire and Mrs. Driggins, another Black teacher/mentor of mine, became the only people I could talk to about what I was feeling in his class. I was also the only Black student in that class, which became increasingly evident when Mr. Hiller, teaching about Harriet Beecher Stowe's *Uncle Tom's Cabin*, decided it appropriate to *act out* stereotypes of slaves for the class. The performance garnered a mixture of laughter and stares at me, a 15-year-old Black student trying to hold back tears. I still cannot articulate the anger and isolation of that moment. I was frozen.

Mr. McGuire and Mrs. Driggins guided me through that year and introduced me to the Black Cultural Alliance and Junior Toastmasters, where I would meet another Black teacher, Mrs. Graves. These organizations provided an outlet for strengthening my voice and occupying my time after school. I eventually became student president of each group. By the end of my junior year, I had received a gift from Mrs. Driggins. It was a copy of *Black Voices: An Anthology of Afro-American Literature* that would become my summer reading. I was finally being seen!

TWELFTH GRADE

Returning for my senior year, Mrs. Driggins handed me two college applications to Morehouse College and Hampton University. I gathered two other HBCU applications and scheduled a time to sit with my counselor, Mr. Meier. I was prepared to seek assistance in the application process. Instead, Mr. Meier informed me that I was not "college material" and would be better off seeking opportunities within the military. Within 2 weeks, Mr. Meier had scheduled for representatives from the U.S. Army to take me and three other students to their recruiting offices to take the Armed Services Vocational Aptitude Battery (ASVAB). I recall telling the recruiters, "I do not know why we're even doing this. I am going to college." Confused, it was Mr. McGuire and Mrs. Driggins that picked me up and still encouraged me to apply to college. On January 27, 1989, I received a letter of acceptance from Hampton University in the mail. Excited, I called my mother to tell her and she told me she would call right back. Unbeknownst to me, she called Morehouse College who informed her that I was accepted, and the letter would be sent the next week.

MY ADVICE

To the young person looking at me, please know three key things. First, choose yourself! There may be moments where it could be easy to join in on what your friends are doing. However, when you know it's wrong, you must be willing to stand alone. You may never be seen for who you really are by all people. Ultimately, my friends came back, and they respected me more for standing my ground. They finally saw me!

Second, seek and accept significant others! While I had parental support, it was Mr. McGuire, Mrs. Driggins, and others that went beyond their job to provide support and calm to me in times of crisis. Learn to listen to those that speak to your dreams. My significant others kept me focused on my goals, helped me overcome spirit-breaking teachers, and provided opportunities to do something different. They saw me!

Finally, open up and be seen! I wasted a lot of time appearing tough and distant. Getting involved in positive activities allowed people to see me in a better light and occupy my idle time. Opening up, getting involved, and seeing others allows you to be seen and valued for who you are. For me, after school activities helped me discover myself and be discovered by others.

CHAPTER 13

ONE HUNDRED PERCENT INTELLIGENT BLACK CHILD

Black and Exceptional in Mathematics

Nickolaus A. Ortiz

One of the earliest memories that I have in mathematics transpired after I enrolled in a predominantly White school in metro Atlanta. Though I had not dwelled on it much, this was the first time that my race had been made conspicuous and salient, at least as a personal revelation. I did not have any bad experiences in this class from what I can remember, but I do recall noticing that the students on this side of the city no longer looked like me.

During instruction, I found something remarkably fascinating about the numerical patterns involved in the memorization of the times tables. All throughout the year the class would practice these timed activities as a way to drill multiplication facts, and I remember practicing at home because I yearned for more stickers to place on our achievement board at the front of the room. Every time a student excelled on one of these timed tests, he or she would get a mastery sticker and would subsequently advance to the next level in the following week.

In the same year that Erykah Badu was nominated for best new artist at the Grammys, I was in competition for the smartest kid in this classroom. On our final day of class I had worked my way up to the 11s, but there was another student, a White female, who had convinced me that I was not yet on that level and still had to complete the 10s. Instead of wasting the time to check the display in front of the classroom, I took her word as law. Once again I had a perfect score on the test and I proceeded to take my star to the display at once; however, this time I had a different feeling once I arrived, one that was indignant and full of disappointment. There was already a star in the position that I had been told to place this new sticker; I realized that I had mastered the 10s on our previous assessment and was, in that moment, confronted with the doubt that another individual had about my mathematics feats.

I remember that my third-grade heart was broken, simply because I would never be able to prove that I had mastered the 11s now. I felt stripped of an accomplishment that was rightfully mine. When I questioned the girl in my class about her misinformed notions of my accomplishments, she offered a futile, melancholy apology that was about as effective as a Trump press conference.

In retrospect, this was the beginning of a reality that I would endure in most of my encounters with mathematics. There would be those who would doubt my brilliance in mathematics simply because, I speculate, I did not fit a preexisting depiction of the typical student who excels in the subject. I believe that oftentimes my love for mathematics is doubted and that I have essentially had to prove my ability to contend with others. My third-grade experience is the earliest portrayal of this idea that not everyone would help to nurture my love for mathematics.

What is interesting to me is that I cannot forsake the role that Black women have played in my life, especially as it pertains to embracing my giftedness in education, and within mathematics specifically. However, what precedes that part of my story is a perpetual battle with depression that has both high and low days. Throughout my years in K–12 education, I attended at least nine different schools. I believe this led to my reluctance to build relationships because I felt that I was going to lose all those friends in a matter of another year or two (this was a time before social media had become so popular and allowed individuals to maintain long distance friendships). Not only was I distraught about having to leave friends and was forced to cope with insatiable loneliness, I felt that it was only a matter of time until the other students would begin to taunt me. It never failed. Soon after I arrived to a new school, everyone would be fascinated with the new cute boy. Almost immediately, however, people would question my sexuality.

I realized at an early age that I did not necessarily present like a "typical" Black male. As many of my peers would point out, my mannerisms, speech, even interaction was not always consistent with their ideas of Black masculinity. Though a full discussion of this epiphany is justifiable, it is beyond the scope of the present chapter. The most significant point that this ridicule and bullying in my life shaped how much I chose to interact with others and how I chose to allow my intelligence to manifest within the mathematics classroom. I remember wanting as little attention as possible because responding in group problems or going to the board to share an alternative solution to our mathematics investigations would reveal the mannerisms that I tried so hard to conceal daily. Furthermore, because I felt that there was already too much focus on my orientation by the other students, I shied away from my supposed brilliance in mathematics; notwithstanding all other accusations, I did not want to *also* be perceived as a nerd.

Eighth grade prompted a new sense of direction and perspective for my life. I was now enrolled in school on the southside of Atlanta where the school population was predominantly Black and had an algebra teacher who also matched this demographic. I was enrolled in her gifted course where I was no longer underrepresented in class—Black students were the majority. One conversation that stood out to me about this class involved Mrs. Allen telling me that I was incredibly smart but that I only worked periodically. I remember even asking her to define the word, and she told me that I chose the moments in which I wanted to showcase my brilliance. Subconsciously, I was realizing that she had discovered my attempt to mask my intelligence, but she had no idea of why I chose to hide it.

Nevertheless, I needed Mrs. Allen. She showed me that living up to her expectations was much more valuable than my secret fear. My effort began to match her willingness to see the class succeed. I remember her holding Saturday sessions because she realized halfway through the year that she would not be able to cover all of the content that the curriculum required. I was at every one of those optional (but not so optional) class sessions. Additionally, I remember her words and her expectations as I boldly walked in front of the whole school to accept my mathematics award at the 8th grade honor ceremony. This was an obstacle that she helped me overcome; never before had my brilliance been nurtured in this way.

My freshman year found me in yet another school, this time on the eastside of Atlanta. My sophomore-level mathematics teacher observed my blossoming understanding of the subject and quickly began to show me tough love. After having an almost perfect grade in her class, she informed me that she was recommending me to enter the gifted level mathematics course in my junior year. I expressed to her that I was not ready and informed her that I had changed my schedule to enroll in the on-level course. Honestly, I was trying to abide by the rules of Black masculinity that I had internalized up to this point and at this new school, and mathematics was not what I perceived to be consistent with this image.

The next day, she presented me a new schedule; she had gone to my counselor to say that I was going to take that class whether I liked it or not. Again, there was power in the perceptions that these Black teachers held for my mathematics ability, despite my desire to suppress it or to give into my own doubt about being challenged. This same teacher was one who I needed in my senior year, not because I was struggling with mathematics necessarily, but because I had been having a series of disputes with my mother.

I walked into her classroom one afternoon while she was on planning—for those in education, they know most teachers cringe at the sight of a child on their planning period—but she welcomed me because she knew something was on my mind. I remember pouring my heart out to her in that moment and remembering that she did not have much to say. As I cried, I noticed that she had tears streaming down her face as well. Nevertheless, she provided words of encouragement that would allow me to push through not only the rigorous and stressful moments of Advanced Placement (AP) Calculus, but also the tense encounters that I was having with my mother.

To be honest, I do not believe I would have made it through my K–12 experience or exceeded the deficit notions about Black students' odds of achievement without the teachers described in this chapter. Expectations for Black masculinity (both implicit and explicit) would have circumvented my mathematics intelligence but thank God for the Black women in my life.

The first piece of advice that I would give to anyone who is masking their brilliance for any reason is to seek out your own mentors. Find someone who can play the role that these Black women played in my life. The second suggestion that I would offer is to find organizations or hobbies that allow you to exhibit your brilliance in atmospheres where you are comfortable. If it is a hindrance within one facet of your life, find an alternative one that will celebrate your gift. This might be through a club like 100 Black Men of Atlanta was for me. Lastly, I would say to find a friend in which you can confide. This friend may help you work through those fears or help to find the resources or persons who are more adept to providing that aid. Though my journey reflects myriad doubts and fears, I learned to define Blackness and masculinity on my own terms. Further, I take pride in knowing that I am a statistic of hope for other young brothers and a statistic of confusion for those who ever doubted my Blackness or masculinity from the onset.

CHAPTER 14

OF PAIN AND PEACH FUZZ

A Chief Equity Officer Rants

John D. Marshall

I remember how my father almost cried when my brother and I finally started getting noticeable hair on our faces. He made us shave our mustaches off. "Fellas, I do not want them thinking you are older than you are. I do not want them rushing you to manhood." He would always say partly in earnest and in part jest, "There's not much I can do about them treating you like a boy when you become a man, or them treating you like you are a man when you are a boy. But I can make you jive turkeys keep that peach fuzz off your faces for a little longer." My father was big, brilliant, and bold. If there was a fight that needed to happen, he would oblige. Be it via activism, debate, or a brawl, my father would engage if left with no choice. It was his hope that by shaving his sons' faces, the world might just see our faces for what they were: black, smooth, and young. It was his way of trying to keep us from the inevitable fight as long as possible. The internal and external fight/war that fathers and mothers cannot keep from entering their home when raising Black boys is what he was trying prevent. It was not the check-to-check financial station that we lived in that worried my father. It was that station that he knew the world would put me in soon enough that unnerved him.

James Baldwin, who my father said was, one of the greats in regards to illustrating the plight for Blacks in America said, "To be a Negro in this country and to be relatively conscious is to be in a rage almost all the time." My father believed that my poor black peach fuzz would quicken the looming racists to pass violent and vile judgement of me; thus, propelling me into a rage that he wanted to keep from me as long as possible. It is difficult to pinpoint the first moment that I became conscious and could no longer keep the intrusion of racism from placing me in a perpetual state of anger; however, I affirm that my understanding of the system and how it has inoculated many of us to believe that by and by everything will be alright, if we just keep picking the corporate cotton, has lead me to the following rant.

Throughout my professional career, I have been told by those that thought they were rendering sound advice that I should just do my job and ignore the mistreatment, move beyond what they say, and continue to do the so called good work I am doing as it relates to educational equity and advocacy for students and families of color. I have heard in abundance that if I just keep doing what I am doing and work like I have always worked, it should not matter what detractors, saboteurs, and sadists say or do. Beyond any doubt, I know that many of those that told me to keep doing what I am doing, truly had and have my best interest in mind.

As of late I have had a soul shattering melee with myself. I began to scrutinize my internal posture and question if just doing my job, as good as many say it is, is enough. Am I not in some fashion picking the corporate cotton of the majority if I just keep doing my job... I wonder how many times enslaved mothers told their enslaved sons and daughters to just keep picking. I wonder how the enslaved sons of enslaved fathers felt when they realized that the most painful whipping is not the lash but the lack of liberty. When the enslaved son realized that the noose may not be as bad as being the nincompoop (N-word). How did the enslaved son of the enslaved father feel when he witnessed the daily internal fight his father had in his soul—knowing he is a man while the external world tells him he is a mule. Every day he plowed, picked, pulled, and pushed. Every day he was plowed, picked, pulled, and pushed. He just kept doing his "job."

As the great grandson of an enslaved great grandfather, my wounds from mistreatment, worry, and fatigue barely patch the gashing wounds of the whip that swung across the south yesterday. The hymns of hope moaned by my kin are still the psalms I silently sing in the boardroom and bedroom. The (original) state song from which I hail chants the haunts of privilege. "The sun shines bright on my old Kentucky home. Tis summer the darkies are gay." Could it be that the author of the song saw my great grandfather appearing to ignore the atrocities and degradation by singing, agreeing, and picking... Not realizing that such compliance was to avoid getting red stripes on their midnight blue backs at the hands of Whites. The original American flag is flown on the flogged backs of Blacks.

The tightrope balancing act that I once considered "performing," found me questioning and worrying if I stage myself as being the "Angry Black man." Conversely, I remain steadfast that I would rather be the angry Black man than the compliant concubine of bigotry and racism. I have been told that my mannerisms should not spark their racism. That my intelligence should not shed light on their ignorance. That the inflections in my speech should not denounce their daggers. As a Black man, if I just do my job, and balance the beguiling behaviors of others, I may make it to the other side. Is there much difference from walking a tightrope and being hung by a rope... Yes! But the rope that hung my forefathers is now the rope that I am asked to walk. If I fall off —death.

Even in this chapter, I find myself almost disinclined to push each key wondering if this will be the behavior that puts another stripe on my back, another attempt at someone trying to whip me into "Toby," or if my fire singes them to firing (at) me. But the roots of righteousness are deep and the watchful bright eyes of my daughters dare me and drive me to be brave. My youngest did not get physically assaulted by a White child, because I am evangelizing the inequities of a system that is mistreating her and her brothers in vain. She was assaulted because, "Your daddy is making school unsafe." Beside the irony of the action and declaration, the White child has a parent that works in the same corporation where I work. One can only be lead to deduce that his action was a regurgitation of what he heard in his "big house"; and is in fact the heirloom of privilege that is still in mint condition.

I did not enlist. I was drafted into this war. I did not raise my hand. My hands were chained. I did not run away. I was torn away. I no longer have peach fuzz. I have coarse gray hair stained by underestimation and intrusion my father kept at bay for as long as he could. In turn, the most haunting parts of my trek, are still the facts that pattyrollers are hunting, and hoping, that curricular confederates and counterfeiters catch me. Access to the drinking gourd of freedom comes with staying on a rail that so many are afraid to get on. It comes with, deciphering and identifying microaggressions, committing to a compass that is off the beaten path but not void of beatings, seeing through faulty head nods, and trusting purpose of the plight, not the foes in the fight.

I harken to a time, when I thought that the system was broken. It was time that I believed that with the right systemic mechanics and architects, the system could be fixed in time. Lo the moment that I realized that the system is not broken; it is, in fact, a fine oiled locomotion that is doing exactly what it is designed to do. The designation of dividing, deluding, and derailing great grandchildren of slaves and the indigenous is the function of the train/system. *For those* whom it is was designed for, the system works. Thus, I ask myself, what kind of architect am I...Am I a missioned mechanic bent on bringing a system across the Jordan...

My affirmations and charge to continue comes when I ban with others that are also following the gourd. I look to men, like those reading this book to affirm that my aches, anxiety, and anger are warranted and shared. My joys and the road I trod is not in isolation but inspiration. Methinks that two sledgehammers and a heart can beat the machine. Methinks that the drinking gourd is still the morally true north. Be that star research, unity, self-defining, experience, faith, and/or hope, the system must be broken if not annihilated.

When my daughter got shoved to the ground, I saw in her a sense of understanding. Probably what my father saw in me when I realized why he wanted me to shave. Although her assault slit my poise and patience, what was clear was that my daughter had a life lesson whacked across her being that she is not unconditionally safe... She affirmed that if safety comes with silence and accepting the status quo, then that's not safety. She realized that although the sun may shine bright, there is an elephantine amount of struggle and catastrophe that must be brought to light. My daughter would not accept my apology. She looked at me very similar to how I imagine enslaved children looked at their enslaved parents and said, "You did nothing wrong. You are trying to make things better." The boy that lashed out at her freedom has yet to apologize.

As a chief equity officer in the field of public education, I would recommend for those reading this and are looking for advice the following:

1. Your drinking gourd is data. Use data to show others what you already know—we are mistreating children that have peach fuzz on their face. We are suspending as opposed to attending to children. Let the data guide you.
2. Staying true north is the only way to freedom. Concessions corrupt and keep all students from crossing the very guarded Mason Dixon line. Regardless of where you are and when you are called to speak, speak! Speak even when not spoken to. Speak at the risk of being muted, mutilated, and attacked.
3. Take it personal. Being told not to take it personal is the latest iteration of a pattyroller telling you to keep picking, pulling, working on this machine that has personally left you out. You must be vested in the emancipation of all students and families. This level of investment can only come when you are conscious and personally understand how this system is not broken at all and that it impacts your own emancipation.

Although stanzas to "My Old Kentucky Home" are now redux, there is still a bellowed belief that Black men should be happy in spite of the circumstance. I do not hate those that tell me to just keep doing what I am doing and ignore the spit of lies, the molesting of manhood, and the negative narrative. I simply cannot oil the system so that it can continue to run us over or underground.

Metaphorically the whip still swings. Literally our real job is to pick, pull, push up each other, and protect our peach fuzz as best we can.

CHAPTER 15

THANK YOU SO MUCH FOR ASKING

Darreon D. Greer Sr.

"I wouldn't be here if I couldn't be here." I recount numerous times I have heard one of my "big dog" mentors state this quote. This adage signifies the never-ending status of Black males not only in the academy, but all walks of life, having to doubly prove we are worthy to occupy whatever space we choose to occupy. For most males of color, "life ain't been no crystal stair" (Rampersad & Roessel, 1994, p. 30). The myriad academic, social, psychological, and environmental issues faced daily only explicate the reasons why so many Black males find themselves either kicked or pushed out of formal K–12 schooling, which often leads to a history of deviant acts or low quality of life. I second the notion that the historical and current academic disparities are inextricably linked to negative social and environmental outcomes. The cognitive as well as psychosocial factors that influence Black males to "do whatever it is that they do" or partake in whatever occupation they choose is often related to the way in which they were socialized. One must understand that Black males are born with the age-old adage that they were first born Black, and that they second were born male. This has often been touted as the already "2 strikes" out of 3 and you're out rule. In turn, this simply means that Black males are oftentimes brought into this world from a deficit perspective. The question then has to be raised, "What do Black men do to not only survive, but thrive in a society that has not always been so kind to them..." This chapter focuses on how racial socialization and grit are essential factors that any Black male must have in order to succeed in a society that was not necessarily designed for their success. Hence, the reason why I respond, "Thank you for asking."

RACIAL SOCIALIZATION

"Thank you so much for asking" allows me the humble opportunity to share how I, as a Black male in society, was racially socialized to achieve the success that I have thus far. I believe I was put here to make a difference in this world. This is undoubtedly due to how I was raised by my mother, father, and beloved grandparents. It was instilled in me at a young age that my education was important for upward social mobility. My grandmother and grandfather, not having a high school diploma, had no working knowledge of the concept of upward social mobility. More importantly, what they did have was a love for God like no other, first, a love for each other, second, and an unconditional love for their 12 children and almost 40 grandchildren. This did not seem like a huge family to us, as people would always call us. It was a norm for us, as this is what we knew. We had each other and that is all we felt that mattered. As my grandmother and grandfather had their PhD in hard work and common sense, my mother Ruth went on to become what I have coined for at least the past decade, the "Maya Angelou" of my community. A product of the integration of school systems, especially in the Deep South in the 1960s and 1970s, my mother graduated high school and went on to our main public Historically Black College and University of our state, the University of Arkansas at Pine Bluff. She became a certified teacher by the age of 24, and soon after had my older sister. My childhood at this time is one that I remember to be happy and serene. My mother had moved back home next to her parents and I began kindergarten at Anna Strong Elementary School. How I was socialized and raised is an experience that I would not hesitate to do all over again. When one is socialized with unconditional love and compassion, they are given a chance to succeed in an environment that is conducive for such. Being socialized to know that God is my savior and that education is the greatest vehicle to my success were the two keys to life taught to me by my family. I am forever indebted to my mother and family for this. Blessed that my teachers usually took a keen liking to me, I believe this stemmed from the intelligence bestowed upon me by my mother and the grace shown me by my grandparents.

In the rural areas of America, when Black elders called or referred to a youth as smart, they were often speaking in not just academic terms. In all honesty,

I did not mind washing the dishes or cutting the yard without any reluctance. My great grandmother, born in 1902, would sit across from the kitchen as I cleaned it after another gracious meal, probably cooked with love by grandmother. She would look at me with such a look of approval and say the words, "You smart ain't you boy." While I was an academic in school, my beloved great grandmother meant that I had the mind to clean and help the family out. This look of approval from the matriarch of our family instilled a sense of pride in me that I carry with me every day of my life. That look she gave me is etched in my mind forever, as it makes me smile even while I write this.

One thing that is missing today in the racial socialization of our Black children is the love and guidance once readily available from matriarchs and patriarchs of our families and communities. One can have hope when he or she feels they have the ones who they love most in their corner, no matter how much they mess up or stray away. Coming from a predominantly Black neighborhood, church, school, and social environment, for as long as I can remember, I was made to feel as if I mattered and that God loves me, no matter what. My mother and family were and continue to be what a lot of Black folk call the-bomb.com. I could not ask for another set of human beings to assist in molding and making me the man I am today, which is a husband, father, doctoral candidate, and most importantly a child of God.

GRIT: DO YOU HAVE IT...

Grit, coined in the research literature by Duckworth, Peterson, Matthews, and Kelly (2007), is the perseverance and passion for long-term goals. Grit entails working strenuously toward challenges, maintaining effort and interest over years despite failure, adversity, and plateaus in progress. The gritty individual approaches achievement as a marathon; his or her advantage is stamina (Duckworth, Peterson, Matthews, & Kelly, 2007). Black males must possess this heavily researched construct of grit. It is imperative for their very survival. The myriad obstacles faced daily, juxtaposed with the covert and overt discrimination and racism that is still experienced in today's society, causes many Black males to do as I heard my elders always state, "fall by the wayside." The old proverb does reveal, "Until the lions have their own historians, the history of the hunt will always glorify the hunter." I am thankful that I am asked to share my inspiration for the grit I sustained not to quit when everything around me suggested that I would never make it. The love and all around, support from my family and community put me in a position to not even know that we were broke folk. Gaining full-paid scholarships to the second largest university in my state, Arkansas State University, was an amazing thing for me. Faced with a bevy of obstacles that I believe were meant to make me give up on the promise of obtaining my undergraduate degree, I am forever grateful to say that by the grace of God,

I obtained it. I had not a clue at this juncture of my life what a construct such as grit meant, however, I do believe I possessed it and did not know it. Through many dangers, toils, and snares, I was blessed to graduate college at the age of 21 and still in my right mind. I experienced life in a way that made a good portion of Black males around me either quit college, never go, settle for menial jobs, or be lost to detriment such as prison or the grave. How I was racially socialized by my family and social environment has been paramount to my success. Must any Black male possess an inner drive to succeed, despite his racial socialization or upbringing... The commonsense answer is yes... However, his family and community must set the impetus or the environment for him to be great. As I aspire to become what I don't see in my everyday walk, which is a Black male licensed psychologist, I will forever be indebted to the family and community who loved me unconditionally, and instilled in me the resilience and grit to succeed, by any means necessary. In our journey for success, we as Black males are never truly asked how it is we navigate the historical and current roadblocks that attempt to thwart our becoming great. I am humbled by the fact that I am able to share with you how a praying and educated family socialized me to know that my Black is beautiful and that I am worth it.

WORDS TO GROWN ON...

We will all face the natural vicissitudes of life, or better yet the fiery trials that are inevitable. The number one piece of advice that I would leave for any young man that is to come after me is to keep his hand in the hand of the one who sustains life in and of itself. The great Tupac Amaru Shakur often posed the question, "Who do you believe in..." (Shakur, 2002). I believe the creator of the universe and my belief in my respective family is what has brought me to this point in the academy, which is a Black male doctoral candidate in counseling psychology. To my beautiful Black brothers, I have unwavering faith you will prosper and do the work on the shoulders of giants before us had the hope that we would do: each one reach one.

REFERENCES

Duckworth, A. L., Peterson, C., Matthews, M. D., & Kelly, D. R. (2007). Grit: Perseverance and passion for long-term goals. *Journal of Personality and Social Psychology, 92*(6), 1087–1101. doi:10.1037/0022-3514.92.6.1087

Rampersad, A. (1994). Mother to son. In A. Rampersad & D. Roessel (Eds.), *The collected poems of Langston Hughes* (p. 30). New York, NY: Vintage Books.

Shakur, T. A. (2002). Who Do U Believe In. On *Better Dayz* [CD]. New York, NY: Interscope Records.

CHAPTER 16

THINGS FALL APART TO FALL IN PLACE

Jajuan S. Johnson

Upon deciding to write this chapter, I pondered on the focus of my story. There are many facets of the human life and varied experiences of Black gay males in the American south. Do I discuss educational disparities experienced... Talk about processes of reconciling my spirituality and sexuality... Tackle the challenges of navigating social constructs of Black masculinity... All of these issues overlap, so where do I start... And more importantly, where do I end... So, I thought I would just tell a bit of my story, which encompasses the broad themes of struggle and resilience.

I grew up during difficult times in a small rural town called Hayti, located in the Missouri Bootheel. The population of the city has never exceeded 3,500 and the poverty rate soars higher than the national average. Life was often unpleasant for a boy who walked with a twist and greased his lips with Vaseline. I would often ask myself, "How in the hell did we end up here..." Although I was born and raised in this spot—on Highway 55, I never quite felt it was home— and I was reminded daily I didn't belong there. So, I spent most of my childhood dreaming about a place where I could be my best self.

I grew up in Cleveland Apartments, located between the railroad tracks and a bean field. We were the "first family" of the housing projects. Partly, because we were the first to move there in 1977, the year before I was born. I was told it was quite a step up from the shotgun house where my mom grew up in Hayti Heights where indoor plumbing was a novelty—and roads unpaved until the late 1980s. The railroad tracks near the projects were a grim reminder of the Jim Crow South—and maintained its purpose of separating the races even in the 1980s and 1990s. My grandmother often referred to the east side of tracks as "the White folks part of the town" and encouraged us not to go over there.

My parents were teenage lovers during the time of my conception. It was not socially acceptable for a teenage girl to be pregnant. Some even offered to adopt me. My mother was often told by older women who couldn't bear children, "You're such a pretty girl, give me that baby and live your life. Everyone is entitled to a first mistake." But she sternly responded, "No, this is my baby." It was not uncommon for children of teenage mothers to be given to an older relative or be raised by the grandparents as their own. This is probably why I always called my mother by her nickname "San," short for Sandra. I called my grandmother Dester Johnson, "mama." I can imagine this probably caused my young mother to be ashamed and resentful. She bore the labor pains but I called someone else "mama." She earned the title because it was her body that nurtured my fetal soul.

Life in Hayti consisted of the best and worst of times. It seemed as if the deck was consistently stacked against me. I am quite sure other Black boys felt this way as well. My secret and sometimes evident desire for boys further pushed me to the margins of the community, but this ostracism provided an opportunity for me to construct my own sense of masculinity. Being on the fringes of society had certain advantages; you definitely learn to think independently. Gazing in the bathroom mirror was my escape from the harsh realities of my existence. I would stare deep into my brown eyes with tears flowing down my face and tell myself I would someday do something great. I was quickly brought back to reality as my mom banged on the door yelling, "Jajuan! Get out that bathroom, I got to get ready for work." I didn't know where this strength or resilience originated but I found pleasure in rebelling against incessant insults and grim predictions about my future by others. I can remember making comforting proclamations to myself as early as age eight.

Attending school was a horrid experience in this town I called "home." Oftentimes, to cope with the mental, verbal, and physical abuse I would simply daydream, staring out of the window while at school—believing and hoping one day a change would come. These mental drifts and strategizing how to navigate teasing and bullying on the school playground often clouded focus on class assignments. Eventually such survival mechanisms would prompt failing grades and placement within learning disabilities classes in the seventh grade—an environment I knew I didn't belong and only increased shame. It was one thing to be called a faggot, but to be labeled as a dumb sissy was an entirely different fight.

At age 12, my mother began courting a man from Arkansas whom I initially liked, but upon discovering he wanted to marry her and relocate us from the only place I knew as home quickly changed my attitude towards him. My disposition toward him abruptly switched from fondness to hate. The thought of a life in a home with another male was jarring. My father was often present but I grew up in a house and neighborhood of Black women who set the rules and standards for living—but the world I knew was about to change and I had no opinion in the matter. My mom married and off we went to Osceola, Arkansas to live with a man I didn't quite like but the change I dreamt had come; just not the way I imagined. The blending of two families consisted of positives and negatives. My mom was promoted to manager of the housing projects in Hayti where we grew up, which warranted a daily commute, and my stepfather was a fireman. We became the quintessential Black middle-class family, which was a psychosocial adjustment.

Life took a major turn the day my stepfather drove me to Osceola Junior High School to transfer and enroll me in classes during the Summer of 1993. The school counselor, Mr. Robert Naylor, was probably my saving grace. He looked at my school records from Hayti Junior High School (which clearly indicated I was a low performing student enrolled in learning disability classes) and then gazed at me. I vividly recall him saying, "You look like a smart kid... I want to place you in the regular classroom for one semester to see how it goes." I am thankful for his grace and good judgment. It was definitely the first time I remember being called smart. I surely knew how it felt to be called dumb, even by my mama. On the first day of school, everyone was fascinated by this neatly dressed new kid wearing K-Swiss sneakers, a striped evergreen and white hooded shirt and Levi jeans— and for some reason, they all thought I looked smart. I was clever enough to think, "Well, if they think I'm smart, maybe I should pretend I am." I didn't know how long this special attention from students and teachers would last but I took it as an opportunity to reinvent myself. For the first time in my life, I felt people viewed me as a human being. Yes, I was sometimes teased for being a "feminine boy" but their genuine intrigue of my slightly Midwestern accent tampered any excessive taunting. It was a new school and a town where no one knew me, so I felt I could create a new identity even if I felt it was a lie. But it wasn't a lie, I literally began experiencing the life I daydreamt about, now it was time to set goals, create a strategy, and do the work. I recall coming home from school and writing short-term goals on a set of index cards. By the end of the semester, I accomplished each goal. I was an honor student, elected to the student government association, and had a great rapport with my teachers and fellow students. During that moment, I truly believed I could beat the odds through education, integrity, and service—and these have been the guiding principles of my life. It was amazing that the change I was most resistant to, changed my life for the better—and each year I've practiced the principle of setting higher goals and standards for my life.

After graduating from Osceola High School as vice-president of the class, I continued my dream of pursuing higher education. I earned a bachelor's degree in communications at Arkansas State University and completed a Master of Divinity at Oral Roberts University in Tulsa, Oklahoma. Upon returning to Arkansas, I have worked in the public and private sectors and also had the wonderful opportunity of doing humanitarian work in Eastern Europe visiting prisons, safe homes, and doing outreach to encourage marginalized men and boys. Most recently, I earned a Master of Arts degree while currently completing a doctoral degree in Heritage Studies at Arkansas State University. I have been fortunate to serve on numerous boards and advise leaders on social justice matters.

I am a firm believer we are a self-fulfilling prophecy. With tears streaming down my eyes as a boy child in Hayti, Missouri, I dared to dream that I could make a positive difference in the world. I think my life thus far is truly reflective of the statement that things fall apart to fall in place.

I often encourage the young men to read, think, and create. Reading not only calms the mind and soul but also stimulates the imagination, which broadens one's perspective of the world. Think. Because we live in a culture hostile towards the humanity and divinity of men of color, it is imperative we practice critical consciousness which is a process of analyzing oppressive systems and taking action against elements threatening our existence. Create. We must use our gifts, talents, and unique abilities to produce something positive that will not only change our lives but also forge clearer pathways for those who will precede us.

CHAPTER 17

THE MENACE OF IMMIGRANTS

Reflections of Growing Up in Organisms Against My Development

Oscar Espinoza-Parra

I want to attest to the positive and significant impact immigrants provide to the growth progress of the United States. However, I am not able to dismiss the constant assault against immigrants in different types of living organisms (e.g., schools, legal, political, media). There are individuals and multiple organizations who do feel immigrants are criminals, rapists, social welfare loaders, and tax burdens. These labels prescribe an array of negative stereotypes. In rare instances, these perceptions may be true in small cases, but the fact is that this constant messaging against immigrants is unwarranted and damages the very foundation and structure of how this country came to be. The central focus of this writing is the high incidence of negative messaging directed toward immigrants. In many ways, the degree of exposure of these adverse messages accumulates through time and has a detrimental effect on individuals' cognitive system.

I am a person who migrated to the United States. I did not know I was an immigrant until I entered third grade at a Las Vegas elementary school. I learned at a young age that my various social identities compounded together intersected to represent a menace to individuals and organizations in society. The constant toxicity of the messages of my external environment expressed the inferior mentality associated with immigrants. Not only was I an immigrant that did not speak the English language, but I was also a liability because I was perceived to be automatically less capable than native English speakers due to not knowing how to read, write, communicate, and think in the English language. Even as a child, I felt the internal and cognitive harm caused by the perception that I was a hazard to society. I could not understand why being an immigrant threatened the very U.S. systems in which I wanted to participate. The culprits of these messages were sometimes teachers and administrators who label students intellectually less capable because of not having mastery of the English language. During these school years, I was programmed to believe that my capabilities were inadequate.

Immigrants from across the world were part of my English as second language courses. We were innocent immigrants who came to this country without any knowledge of this country, its inhabitants, customs, culture, language, and systems. In my case, not a single English word existed in my brain. In this sense, my knowledge of the English language and American culture was a blank slate. My disadvantage stemmed that I was a transplant unfamiliar with the new environment. As such, I did not possess the capabilities to speak, think, and write in the English language. Even though I was 8 years old when I entered formal U.S. education, I started to learn the skill of acquiring the English language at a level of a novice. My third grade teacher served as my initial instructor who taught me the fundamentals of the English language and developed my first lessons of culture, customs, and values of American democracy. Since this stage, I studied the English language and immersed myself in practicing and improving this skill.

During my formative years, I learned that I had three strikes against me. I was (a) undocumented, (b) Mexican, and (c) an immigrant. Not only were there cultural and xenophobic fears against immigrants, but there is a stronger feeling of discontent towards Mexicans. The currency of being a Mexican male student was also not very valued within my learning environments. The habitants of my environment revealed their prejudices, actions, attitudes, and perceptions towards Mexicans.

I also did not succumb to lessen my cultural, ethnic, and national identities just because being Mexican was heavily misrepresented. I lived in a household where I was loved and reared to be proud of my Mexican background. I was fortunate my home was a sanctuary place where I was be free of those toxic messages. Even at a young age, I discerned how my formal school environment would not teach me about my cultural heritage and how my ancestors contributed to the development and success of this country. I had to take on these lessons independently and acquire a cognitive perspective taught by my parents. I worked hard, studied, participated, and learned. I made the best out of my life based on the knowledge and resources presented to me during my journey. My parents inoculated me to not listen to those external threats.

Growing up, I continued to receive negative words toward my character that expressed continuous venomous messages about immigrants who did not come the "legal" way. It is a reality and an experience that immigrants live with every day. The media, school, legal, and political systems multiply these overt and hidden aggressions. Being undocumented also presented challenges. For example, I was discouraged during my ninth grade year of high school. I was selected to attend a Nevada Test Site event that required submission of my social security number. However, I did not submit my paperwork to my instructors because I did not have any legal standing. We were at the final stages of being approved by the U.S. government for my permanent residency. I did not have the courage to inform my teachers.

In my 11th grade year, I received the news that the federal government approved our residency. Five years later, I became a U.S. citizen. I am now an example of an individual who leads a civic and professional life that contributes to the foundation of U.S. democracy. I am a manifestation of a dream that came true. I am an example of an immigrant who continues to capitalize on every opportunity. As I reflect on the current stage of my life, I can affirm the success I have achieved since my arrival into Las Vegas, Nevada. I have obtained a Doctor of Philosophy in Higher Education. As part of my dissertation, I completed over 250 pages of original research (not a bad accomplishment considering I once could not speak a word of the English language). I presented research at the top tier of higher educational national conferences and published in various outlets (e.g., book chapters). Every time I write, I think of my 8 year old self. I revisit him and this stage of my development. I celebrate this young boy who took the courage to learn and master the English language.

I also know that I speak, write, and communicate English (my second language) better than most native speakers and it did not come at the cost of losing my Spanish language. I stand in affirmation of the research conducted by Claude Steele about stereotype threat. His research gave me the power to name my existence and what I have witnessed since third grade and all the way to my terminal degree. In reflection, microaggressions and negative experiences strengthened my character. All the words and actions toward me did not change my life direction. I confess that these past declarations of my academic and intellectual activities scarred me but did not altered my sense of power and talent.

My identities continue to be influenced by my immigrant origins and by my Mexican upbringing. I am a threat to those who continue to promote an agenda of radicalism and who do not give much thought and application of science and data to inform them of the lived experiences and contributions of immigrants. I represent a promise because I now have four college degrees and have the scholarship and knowledge to support my thinking and actions. My identity will always remain that of an immigrant; the difference now is that I am a documented successful Mexican immigrant who is proud of my beginnings and my journey.

We have a responsibility to reframe the conversation of immigrants. We have to begin to discuss the toxicity and hurtful words that these structures and individuals perpetuate to those most invisible and with the least power. We need to dialogue about the cognitive and internal damage caused to children and adolescents in lessening their progression and personal development. Notably, how damaging it is especially when individuals are still learning and developing and have not reached their optimal potential.

It is time to honor the lives of immigrants. Immigrants shape and strengthen our local communities. Immigrants pay taxes, regardless if they are documented or not, and contribute to local, state, and national economy. Immigrants own vehicles, homes, and businesses, and contribute to the creative and scientific advancement of this country. To the contrary, immigrants do learn the English language (at different levels), hold full-time positions, participate in political parties, vote, go to church, and engage in various civic activities. The majority are law-abiding individuals who aspire for their children to go to college and be successful in American society. Immigrants may start at the bottom with the least amount of resources. But I can assure you, most immigrants, by the end of their lives, they have moved their lot from where they first started. The majority of immigrants I know have achieved significant successes and deserved to be recognized for their contributions.

In closing, I offer readers the wisdom of my hardworking parents:

1. *Believe in yourself and work toward developing your talents and skills.* Be the master of your domain and apply a positive mentality to your experience and development. The amount of dedication you foster within yourself will strengthen your capacities.
2. *Build a sanctuary where you can be free of negative messages.* This can be your home where you can cultivate positive images, promote your well-being, be free of stress and toxicity, and escape from the outside world.
3. *You are capable of achievement and deserve success.* Celebrate being a pioneer in your own life story and honor the wins that you achieve along the way.

4. *Work hard.* Preparation and persistence are ingredients that contribute to skill and talent development. The amount of time you dedicate to your success will reap you significant benefits.
5. *Love all your social identities.* Celebrate your uniqueness even those that are not understood; these accentuate and provide the distinctiveness of your individuality.

CHAPTER 18

BE YOURSELF AND THE WORLD WILL ADJUST

Tyrone C. Hamler

MASCULINITY, BLACK IDENTITY, SOCIALIZATION, ACADEMIA

The path I have taken to doctoral education has been unique and complicated, but there is no part of the journey that I would change. I was born and raised in the inner city of Cincinnati, Ohio and attended Walnut Hills High School, a college preparatory high school that prepared me to further my education. My mother was a civil service worker for the City of Cincinnati and my father worked as a maintenance worker for Cincinnati Metropolitan Housing Authority up until his death. My mother was instrumental in preparing me for the challenges that I would experience pursuing my education and instilling within me a drive to succeed no matter what the circumstances were. Being one of 11 children, my mother did not have the support that she needed to pursue education. My mother's family was centered around the idea of "18 and out" and my grandfather heavily encouraged independence but did not value education in the same way. As an only child, I was still a part of a large family that grew up in public housing in Cincinnati. My parents lived together and I grew up with my father in my home. My father was an alcoholic who abused drugs throughout my childhood. Despite his substance abuse, he was able to maintain full-time employment. My parents divorced when I was 16 years old, and within seven years my father died of hypertensive heart failure in his home. Years of binge drinking and substance abuse took a huge toll on my father's health. Many factors contributed to his death, but now I understand that he harbored a resistance to seeking medical care that was derived from his early life experiences and a feeling of disconnection from general society. His mother had five children by five different men, and none of them were involved in the children's lives. My father's dad was married and had a family who did not accept my father or my grandmother as a part of their lives. He had the intellect to pursue higher education, but he never had the support to pursue his interests. He was a smart man, and he had the capacity to see the world in different ways that transcended narrow conceptualizations of what Blackness has come to mean but was broken down by his family circumstances.

From my earliest recollections of school, I was always considered different. During elementary school my classmates would call me "Black Genius," and that moniker started to keep me separated in some ways from the other Black kids at school. I was consistently either the only or one of the only Black students on the annual honor roll field trips. I was singled out for reading often and "talking proper" at school and within my family. My mother was steadfast in her support of my education and took me to the library regularly and provided me with the support to pursue my interests. In junior high and high school, I began to become even more isolated. It was clear that I did not quite have a place in any of the established social groups. I was able to interact with my peers who looked like me and those who did not, but I had no place that I belonged. For some, I acted "too White" or had a diversity of interests that isolated me from Black social groups; while in other groups I still felt like I did not belong because there were many cultural experiences that we did not share. I recall overhearing my peers make comments about how I dressed, the music I listened to, how I talked, and I recall the sting of being misunderstood because I did not fit into the narrow parameters of what constituted Black masculinity as a teenager. I continued to walk my own path and not allow others to define my Blackness or limit me within the confines of what others believed was appropriate behavior. This was a painful and alienating experience, and I felt that I had two options. The first option was to assimilate and try to blend in so that I could stop being ridiculed by my peers, and my second option was embrace who I was and continue to discover and define my own Blackness.

What I ended up doing at first was a combination of both of those options. To identify with my peers, I began to smoke marijuana and use other drugs. I created an alternate persona where I was free to live, experience, and be judgment free. This version of myself had the courage to move between social groups and used drugs and alcohol as the commonality that bonded me to the groups that I encountered. Drugs and alcohol helped medicate my social anxiety and depression while making me feel comfortable enough to explore my identity within social spaces. Looking back, I realize that I wanted to "dumb down" in order to fit in. Navigating that balance is critical to being able to express your complete self as an adolescent. This period was one of the first times that I truly began to feel accepted across social groups. As a teenager I felt that I needed this type of acceptance from my peers, and as my drug use escalated I received more positive reinforcement as my social connections grew. I believed that I had found an identity. At home, this was going over poorly with my mother, and by this time my father had essentially dropped out of my life. As I struggled through finding my identity before drugs and alcohol, I believe that my father was unable to relate to me and wanted me to be more "normal." For my father "normal" fell within the narrow confines of what masculinity came to mean for him having learned amongst other men who grew up without fathers. This tension became a theme in our relationship as I grew into an adult who consistently tried to reach out to a father who was unable to reach back or lend a helping hand. I remember always thinking that I never wanted to be like my father. I never wanted to make drugs and alcohol centerpieces of my life. However, in a struggle to be accepted I ended up doing the exact thing that I swore that I never would. I began to let drugs and alcohol unravel my life. As a child I was ridiculed by my peers for getting good grades, but as a teenager I let my grades spiral until I was faced with limited options for my college education. Once I entered college, I was still deeply involved in substance abuse and what I now recognize as a search for my identity.

I went to the University of Cincinnati and was placed on academic probation after the first semester; then, subsequently suspended due to continued poor grades. During this time, I was unsure about receiving my college education. I spent the following year away from college working in food service. This year away from school was a formative period of time where I learned the value of education. I also learned how to cope with depression and anxiety without the aid of drugs and alcohol. Working at these jobs taught me valuable lessons about the importance of navigating work environments and difficult supervision situations. I have built on these lessons as I have continued my education and had to navigate through the political environment of a PhD program. Here is where I began to discover my own motivations that fueled my desire to return to school. At this time, I conceptualized going back to school as atoning for past mistakes; the mistakes I had made during my first year of college and later years of high school. After a year out of school, I enrolled at Cincinnati State Technical and Community College as a full-time student while working two jobs. Cincinnati

State Community College is where I rediscovered my self-confidence, motivation, and drive to be a scholar. After 2 successful years, I received a Community College transfer scholarship and transferred to the University of Cincinnati where I enrolled in the social work program.

During my senior year as a BSW student, I was an intern at a local hospice agency and experienced the sudden death of my father in the midst of my first internship experience. This experience indelibly changed my perspective on social work and my approach to learning. With support from the faculty, students, and the agency I finished my internship and elected to complete the Advanced Standing MSW Program with a specialization in health and gerontology. After working for 6 years, I applied to several universities to pursue doctoral education and chose Case Western Reserve University. No PhD program is perfect, but learning to navigate as a person of color in a primarily White institution provides major challenges that can make surviving and thriving in the program quite difficult. You will encounter both implicit and explicit racism in the university setting. Learning how to advocate for yourself and when to seek out counsel from those who have been there before are both key. The most valuable advice that I have learned during my long journey from failing out of college to completing the PhD program is that you have to be yourself. Time and time again I have benefited from bringing my authentic self to the table. I haven't tried to hide or obscure who I am, and where I come from. I have learned to understand that my past is a valuable asset and I accept everything that my journey has given me—both good and bad. Trying to be someone else is a waste of the person that you are and the uniqueness that you bring to academia and the world. You are valued, your contributions are valuable, and your perspective is necessary and needed. Be yourself and the world will adjust.

CHAPTER 19

MEMOIR OF A FORMER IMPOSTOR

C. Emmanuel Little

My entire life has been an extensive search for belonging. Growing up as an extremely shy pastor's son in Macon, Georgia meant growing up with various privileges but also never quite being able to fully participate in the "in" crowd, out of fear of judgment, shame, punishment, and so on. In some ways, the classroom was where I felt most at home and in control of how people perceived me and perhaps, how I perceived myself. In other ways, it has also been the place where I've felt the most like an impostor. This narrative describes how I navigated through such challenges.

MY UNDERGRADUATE EXPERIENCE

I started college in Fall 2003 after graduating in the top 10 of my high school senior class. As a gifted student since the second grade, I was fortunate enough to gain a near-full academic scholarship at a prominent institution in Georgia. As part of the first living-learning community for the honors program, I lived on the same floor in a residence hall with other

Gumbo for the Soul, pages 93–97
Copyright © 2019 by Information Age Publishing
All rights of reproduction in any form reserved.

members of my cohort. As one might guess, there was a considerable lack of racial diversity. Many of my peers were from more affluent suburban enclaves elsewhere and thus, attended schools that were better-resourced. It didn't take long for me to start questioning my own abilities. Throughout my life up to that point, I'd usually been among the smartest in my class. Now... I was literally one in the number. On one hand, this is perhaps typical of any college experience—when you reach the next level, your peers are others who have had similar academic prowess as your own. However, when you are one of just two Black students (both males) in the program, both of whom come from the same city with a comparably disadvantaged K–12 education, it's easy to feel as if you don't belong. Take my attire for instance; my cornrowed hair, du-rag and Dickies shirts (standard attire for younger Black men in my hometown in the early 2000s) stood in stark contrast to the preppy polo shirts and Birkenstocks sandals that proliferated the campus.

These feelings crystallized early during my freshman year. I vividly remember a final project (perhaps ironically, in an interdisciplinary course about Utopian societies) in which we were required to form groups midway into the semester. I, already withdrawn and unlikely to initiate interaction, was among the last without a group. That left myself and two other unclaimed individuals to form a group. Realizing the unfortunate circumstances that brought us together, we used our project to make light of our situation and designed the concept of a utopian community meant for apparent outcasts like ourselves. While the project and presentation was well-received and ended with us being chosen to present at a conference, such an experience was nonetheless emblematic of the isolation I felt. I felt like an impostor. I was completely unlike the others and felt hyper-aware of this observation at every possible juncture.

This impostor status, of course, did not stop me from being featured in a program brochure in an effort to showcase the little racial "diversity" the program did have. In the brochure, I'm pictured sitting in a chair in the background, sunken and staring into space as the guest lecturer is talking. I'd offer that this is not the kind of picture to include in a brochure if you want to showcase how engaged your students are, but I suppose it was the "best" picture available. (*Author's note:* Well over a decade later, I still keep a copy in my office as a reminder.)

Fortunately, I was able to find community. Given the lack of racial diversity, I was easily identified by five other Black male freshmen who shared my feelings of isolation. One of these gentlemen was the only other Black male in my honors program. We began hanging out and unwittingly formed a de facto peer-mentoring group. We even came up with a name for ourselves: *The Coalition* (or in shorthand, as we'd call out to each other across campus: "C-O!"). The Coalition brotherhood played a crucial role in boosting my confidence and I quickly moved from feeling like an impostor to maintaining the confidence from knowing that I belonged. We hung out together, played ball together, and even hosted some of the most popular radio shows on campus! I eventually became program director of the student radio station due largely to The Coalition pushing me to the microphone in the first place. I flourished not only in such extracurriculars but also academically, with my brothers serving as accountability partners. In 2007, I graduated cum laude with a degree in mass communications (a shy introvert like myself...imagine that!). Five out of six of us graduated within 6 years, constituting a direct counter narrative to the often-bemoaned low graduation rates of Black males across the nation.

WHEN ACADEMIA THREATENS YOUR SANITY

A few years later, I ended up working as a diversity coordinator after a 3-year stint as an admissions recruiter. I came full circle, using my experiences to help younger Black men in college and drawing upon my success stories with the Coalition as guidance. I enjoyed the work and felt I was truly making an impact with those who were identifying similar challenges that I faced as a freshman. That enjoyment soon waned as I experienced many microaggressions that come with being a Black face in a White space. At one point, my White male supervisor, upon reading a grant I'd written needing his approval, remarked over the phone "this is one of the most well-written grants I've ever read. Who helped you..." *Who. Helped. You...* The words echoed through my mind for a few seconds and I stuttered, telling him that I wrote it myself. *Imagine that.* Stunned into angered silence and unable to continue the conversation, I muttered a "thank you" and quickly got off the phone. Despite the fact that I'd attained a master's degree by then, he assumed that there was no way I could've written this myself. I was an impostor, again.

I quickly turned to trusted colleagues and mentors about my experience (this was simply one of several during this time period). They coached me on how to deal with a supervisor who clearly saw me as incompetent, despite the plethora of evidence suggesting otherwise. They spoke life into me and assuaged the quickly growing anger into a much more productive sense of motivation. A quick study, I learned how to strategically navigate that space and soon ended up in a different office, performing the same role but away from his supervision.

Several years later, I began a PhD program at one of the most prestigious programs for higher education administration in the country. And of course, the old demons revealed themselves again: *These students are on a higher level than you. You're not ready for this. Was I simply an affirmative action admit... There must have been an error when I received my acceptance letter.* Or, when someone heard that I was continuing to work full-time while taking doctoral coursework at an institution 90 minutes away, "That's...not smart at all." Only this time, I had the tools necessary to cope. *I am smart and I contain multitudes that you cannot even imagine. Watch me work.* Today I am finished with my coursework and in the beginning stages of my dissertation process, preparing to take my comprehensive exams as I write this essay. I'm also a father of a 2-year-old, a husband, and *still* a full-time employee. I am a walking counter narrative to those who insist that I'm not smart enough, or that I cannot possibly do what I do, daily. In other words, I *know* I belong here.

ADVICE

Peers and Mentors

I cannot stress enough the importance of reaching out to peers and colleagues who identify with your journey. In both of my previous anecdotes, I'm positive that I would not have successfully navigated those situations without their guidance and willingness to hold me accountable. I had mentors also who opened doors for me where others wouldn't have even bothered. My biggest professional mentor is the person who helped recruit me to enroll at my alma mater. At the time, he was a vice president and now is a president of an HBCU. Throughout my journey as both a student and professional since the day I stepped foot on a college campus, guidance from individuals like him have helped order my steps. As a result, I've navigated around many pitfalls that could have otherwise derailed my career. If you are a person of color and working in academia, it is crucial to find spaces where you can not only network with others that share your experiences, but also vent and receive wise counsel without fear of judgment or retribution.

WWWMD...(What Would a White Male Do...)

There is no greater proof of the indomitable, if irrational confidence and temerity allowed White men than our current president. Unfettered with the weight of societal discrimination regarding race or gender, they behave as if the world is their oyster. There is none of the second-guessing, the "maybe I'm not good enoughs," and general hesitation that those in marginalized populations feel. And of course, this is to be expected when you're buoyed by centuries of White male supremacy in your favor. We who are not White men have good reason to be cautious in how we navigate the world. However, I've learned that the concomitant reluctance that the rest of us feel—to ask for raises, to request larger budgets, to apply for that aspirational position, to ask for what we deserve in general—can cause considerable difficulties in the future. While we know of the multiple ways in which inequalities manifest themselves in academia, as the old adage goes: closed mouths don't get fed. You can't win the game if you never at least shoot your shot. You are enough. Don't let impostor syndrome block your blessings, beloved.

SECTION III

RACIAL DISCRIMINATION

A century ago, W. E. B. DuBois (1903) noted that the "problem of the twentieth century is the problem of the color line." Building on DuBois' assertion a century later, critical race scholars (Ladson-Billings & Tate, 1995; Lynn & Dixson, 2013; Milner, 2010) argue that race and racism are endemic to American society. That is to say, race and racism are foundational to America's social, political, economic, and educational institutions. As such and because race still and always will matter (West, 1993), people of color, particularly men of color, become victims of many acts of racialized violence including discrimination. Racial discrimination explains the inherent dangers of shopping while Black and Brown, walking while Black and Brown, and driving while Black and Brown—to mention a few.

Media and the popular press have documented instances of men of color who faced racial discrimination. Take, for example, Colin Kaepernick, a Black male football player, who was racially discriminated against and banned from the National Football League (NFL) for "taking a knee" to protest racial injustices in Black and Brown communities (Watson, Hagopian, & Au, 2018). Kaepernick followed the trend of many Black and Brown athletes including Muhammed Ali (a professional boxer) who used their professional sport platform to speak up and out against racism and racial discrimination.

In Section III, contributing authors do not take a colorblind approach (Milner, 2010)—the idea of ignoring issues of race and racism—as they reflect on their personal and collective experiences. They understand the salience of race and racism and how these constructs have and continue to inform their lives and everyday lived experiences as men of color. While these men share individual stories of racial discrimination, they call attention to the systemic ways racial discrimination operates in American society.

REFERENCES

DuBois, W. E. B. (1903). *The souls of black folk: Essays and sketches.* New York, NY: Johnson Reprint Corp.

Ladson-Billings, G., & Tate, W. (1995). Towards a critical race theory in education. *Teachers College Record, 97*(1), 47–68.

Lynn, M., & Dixson, A.D. (Eds.). (2013). *Handbook of critical race theory in education.* New York, NY: Routledge.

Milner, H. R. (2010). *Start where you are but don't stay there: Understanding diversity, opportunity gaps, and teaching in today's classroom.* Cambridge, MA. Harvard Education Press.

West, C. (1993). *Race matters.* Boston, MA: Beacon Press.

Watson, D., Hagopian, J., & Au, W. (2018). *Teaching for Black lives.* Seattle, WA: Rethinking Schools.

CHAPTER 20

WHAT WAS INTENDED FOR MY HARM, GOD INTENDED FOR MY GOOD

A Black Male Overcoming the Odds

Lucian Yates III

I hated school!! No, I really hated school! I hated the teachers. I hated the impersonal nature of schools. I hated my choices. I hated it all! Had someone told me, these many years later, I would be working in schools, I would have called them many multisyllabic "cuss" words! All I wanted to do was GET OUT! My parents wouldn't have it any other way.

But, as the Biblical character, Joseph said, "You intended to harm me, but God intended it for good to accomplish what is now being done, the saving of many lives" (Genesis 50:20, New International Version). So, to encourage others who may have had some difficult times in school, had bad memories of teachers and the process, I decided that I must write an autoethnography of my racialized schooling so that others can learn from my experiences, change their trajectory, and "save many lives."

By far, this is the most difficult piece that I have ever tried to write. Although autoethnography has its origins in sociology and social anthropology (Tedlock, 2005), it has become a staple in the education literature. Autoethnography requires the writer to do two things—look inward (autobiography) and look outward (ethnography; Tedlock, 2005). Bochner and Ellis (2002) went further to explain that autoethnography requires the writer to do three things: Look at self (auto), examine culture (ethno), and engage in research (graphy). Tedlock (2005) defined autoethnography as both a theory and a practice which "straddles the domains of lived experience and recollected memory... and with time spent alone in reflection, interpretation, and analysis..." (p. 160). Therefore, to maintain integrity, reflexivity, and accuracy, the author must exhibit great care in explaining the lived cultural experiences; and with diligence extract the embedded learnings.

Methodologically, I will narrate four episodes in my K–12 schooling experiences, step away from the events, and attempt to extract meaning for myself and for the reader. Although I experienced these racialized episodes, I have not given much thought to their meanings and how others can benefit. Hopefully, this will give voice to countless other students as they navigate schooling and give educators pause to reflect on actions, intended or otherwise, that adversely impact students of color.

I grew up in an idyllic, quaint, little antebellum town in central Kentucky. It was the oldest permanent settlement west of the Allegheny Mountains, started by Daniel Boone and James Harrod. I was the fourth of six children (three girls and three boys) who lived in this poor community. In fact, I discovered I was poor in a graduate sociology class many years later.

In my little community, there were clear lines of demarcation—Blacks lived in one space, Whites lived in another; and poor Whites in yet another. Everyone knew his place and one dared not to cross those imaginary, yet real racial and economic lines. Our schools were segregated, our churches were segregated, and for the most part, our worlds were separate and unequal.

EPISODE 1: FIRST DAY OF SCHOOL

Education was important in my home. My mother was the salutatorian in her high school graduation class but could not go to college because her mother could not afford it (prior to Pell grants and government loans). My father had attended college to become a medical doctor but had to quit to help support his mother and siblings after his father died. They knew the importance of education and they emphasized that it was something "they," meaning White folks, could not take from you.

I remember my first day of school like it was yesterday. I could hardly sleep the night before in anticipation of going to school. It was almost like the nervousness and restlessness that children experience on Christmas Eve as they wait for Santa Claus. My three older sisters had sufficiently prepared me for school. I asked questions about reading and they taught me to read simple stories. I had a rudimentary grasp of math and could perform simple mathematical tasks. They also taught me about the sociology and rules of school—how one is to behave while there!

That first morning, first day of first grade, was my first day of school! I did not have the luxury of kindergarten—no school-based kindergarten, no Head Start, just private provided kindergarten. We (my classmates and I) did not or could not afford private preschool, so our first day of school was the first day of first grade!

I put on my new "school clothes." As I entered the room, my teacher was the bespeckled lady who I had seen at church many times before and I saw sitting on the porch when my sisters and I went sidewalk roller skating. She did not have a degree. The rationale at the time was: "You don't need a degree to teach Negro children." She went to Kentucky State University for in-service training each summer. She taught Grades 1–3 in one classroom, without a teacher assistant. Now, I think we call it *non-graded primary*.

She printed each student's name on the board in the manner that only elementary teachers can do. We were instructed to go stand under our name, which was to see if we could recognize our names and to establish our readiness level to begin the learning process. All of the students began to stand under their names, except me. I saw a name on the board that was similar to my name, but it was not my name. The teacher asked, "What about the one right here, honey..."

I responded, "That's not how you spell my name!" The teacher had misspelled my name!

EPISODE 2: SCHOOL INTEGRATION

For the first 4 years of my schooling, I attended a three-room segregated school with only three teachers. Ms. Jeanette Taylor taught Grades 1–3, Ms. Mary Helen Pittman taught Grades 4–6, and Mr. Robert Jackson taught Grades 7 and 8 and served as the de facto principal. His major job was to prepare us for "the White high school."

In our school, we did not have physical education, music, art, or for that matter, a library. When the White school received new books, the "hand-me-down" books from the White schools were delivered to us. Many were outdated, littered with racial epitaphs, and other gross notes to us. In fact, we were studying that there were 48 states, when, in fact, there were 50. During that time in the late 1950s, we could not get a library card at the local library! So, for many of my classmates, the world of books was closed to us.

While in fourth grade, it was announced that it would be the last year for West Side Elementary. We were all going to "the White high school!" Emotions were all over the place: from excited to apprehensive to scared! Some looked at this as a time to expand horizons, to meet new friends, and begin to chart our destinies. For me, I guess my emotions were mostly complex: I was scared and anxious, and I often wondered, "Would I be good enough..."

In late summer, it was announced that my teacher would be Ms. Perry, the wife of the United Methodist Church minister. In my elementary understanding of Christianity, I knew that she might be fair to us for she was a believer! And was I right. Ms. Perry encouraged us, taught us to believe in ourselves, and co-signed what many parents had taught their children, "You can be anything you choose to become as long as you are willing to work hard at it!"

I saw some guys with whom I had played Little League baseball and lo and behold, they were in my class. We talked about things that fifth grade boys talked about—baseball, football, basketball, and all things sports. We were not quite yet interested in girls, but they had their giggly spells about us. When I would try to engage them, they called me a nigger! I was devastated. I finally understood what it meant to be considered "less than."

Ms. Perry in her own way tried to mediate the situation. She talked to both sides about name calling and verbal put downs. She quoted the little riddle, "Sticks and stones may break my bones, but words can never hurt me," but she had not experienced racism! The sting never left. All of the apologies in the world would not relieve the diminished view of self and the "fracturedness" that racial epitaphs can cause. I took this microaggression throughout the rest of my K–12 schooling. It was not until I started to read the writings of civil rights leaders and other revolutionary writings of that era that I began to understand who and whose I was and the very weight and responsibility that that carried with it.

EPISODE 3: FLUTOPHONE STORY

Ms. Perry was a wonderful teacher, but Ms. Sallee, the music teacher, was another story. The music teacher rolled the piano into our classroom every Monday at 2:00 p.m. for our 45-minute music lesson. She was a cold, distant person who treated us with disrespect and disdain. I remember to this day the smell of her cheap perfume and the blob of red rouge on each cheek. Just as bad as her treatment of us was the repertoire of music she had us singing. She said, "Sing this song with conviction and enthusiasm...I wish

I was in the land of cotton, old times there are not forgotten. . . ." Then she made us sing, "The boll weevil is a little black bug come from Mexico they say . . . ." Plus, we sang each of the songs from the military academies. Such brainwashing!

She also "taught" us to play the flutophone. It was a little plastic instrument that closely resembled the recorder. Remember at West Side, we didn't have music, so we knew nothing about the flutophone! Hell, we didn't even know which end to put in our mouths. Talking about disdain, this was the ultimate! She would roll her eyes at us, make snide remarks, and from my fifth-grade estimation, she was just a poor excuse for a teacher.

I made a vow: "When I get back in the sixth grade, I'm going to know how to play this damn thing!" First, I started taking piano lessons from the organist at church. My lessons were 75 cents per week and when my parents discovered that I was taking piano lessons, I owed the teacher $17.25. Each week, I would make up a lie: "Momma didn't have any change today; Momma wasn't home when I left; Momma will send it next week; Momma didn't have any more checks; or on some weeks, I would save money from running errands and pay for my own lesson. I did all of this just to conceal that I was taking piano lessons (remember, in the early 1960s, it wasn't cool for boys to take piano lessons).

Second, we did not have a piano! I drew the keyboard on the cardboard from my dad's laundered shirts and practiced on it. When the sexton rang the bell for Sunday school, I would run down the street with my piano book under my arm, just to practice on a real piano before the next week's lesson. Unbelievably, that summer I learned to read music. I read in the flutophone book, "If you cover all holes, that's middle C; raise the pinky on the right hand, that's D . . ." I taught myself how to play the flutophone that summer!

When we returned in the fall, Ms. Sallee asked, "Who wants to take the lead on this song . . ." I raised my hand. She tried to ignore me, but I wouldn't let her. I said, "Ooh, ooh, ooh, I want to do it!" She looked at me as if to say, "Nigger, you know you can't play it!" She finally said, "Okay!"

She counted it off: one, two, ready, play. I played that thing flawlessly! She said, "Very good, when did you learn to do that . . ." I knew God would give me my opportunity and did I ever take advantage of it! I responded to her question, "Don't you worry about it, you didn't teach me!"

Once I proved to her that I was capable of learning, I wanted to stop taking piano lessons. My mother said, "No! You started it and you're going to finish it! Keep taking piano lessons!" So now, when I'm upset, disappointed, or frustrated, I go to my baby grand and play Rachmaninov, Beethoven, Bach, Liszt, Chopin, gospel, or the blues! What she meant for my bad, God turned it around for my good!

SPEECH AND BAND

There were always two activities that I wanted to participate in—band and speech. Band, because of my new-found love for music. I wanted to major in music in college and participating in the marching band would be a plus. Speech, because I was now developing a passion for social justice and law school was definitely a possibility. However, because of racism, both of these options were closed to me.

The high school marching band was an award-winning aggregation with intricate formations, marching sequences, and beautiful music. I wanted to be a part of it! The band director flat out said, "I don't want any niggers in my band." And *no one* challenged him! A public school and gross discrimination was practiced with no advocates for Black children. It was probably 6 or 7 years later that a Black student was permitted to participate in marching band.

Speech was a similar story. The forensics/debate team at my high school was an award-winning program and one of the best in the nation. Students participated in forensics/debate meets across Kentucky and the nation—and usually they won! Their conquests were publicized in our weekly newspaper! I knew that a good grounding in speech and debate would be a plus for law school. I went to the counselor—they never came to us, unless there was a problem! So, I went to her and said, "For my career goal (going to law school), I'd like to register for speech and debate next year. To my chagrin, she said, "I don't think that will be possible."

"Why not..." I asked.

"Ms. Bess [as in Bess Williams] teaches speech in her home across the street," was her response.

"So..." I continued to question.

"She said 'Before I'll teach a nigger in my home, I'll stop teaching altogether,'" was the counselor's quote of Ms. Bess.

Devastated, I could not understand why the world of speech, just like marching band, was closed to me simply because I was a Black. Again, there were no advocates for Black children. They allowed Ms. Bess to continue teaching speech and debate without ever teaching a Black student!

DISCUSSION

These events were real, they were not exaggerated or embellished! The devastating effects were also real! Many students believed the hype and never aspired to anything beyond those general-track classes. However, some of us said, "You think I can't, watch me!" We went on to great things—lawyers, teachers, doctors, ministers, and yes, even a provost and vice president for academic affairs. These episodes, although they were meant to demean and keep us in "shackles," God had a different plan. He knew because I was armed with these experiences, I was the ideal person to help make a change for future generations. He knew that:

1. Poor and non-White students and schools are more likely to be staffed with ineffective, inexperienced, and poorly trained teachers.
2. Poor and non-White students are often excluded from rigorous curriculum.
3. Culturally competent teachers are a must for students of color achievement.
4. Every child needs a champion or an advocate.

And for the past 41 years, in five different states, from P–12 through graduate school, I have been that vessel God has used to bring about His will and for that I am thankful.

I remember saying at a faculty meeting, "These are my children. I am their parent, and I am their advocate. Don't mistreat them, for you'd be safer kissing a piranha."

So, my friends, believe me when I tell you, regardless of your experience in the educational system, your destiny is not tied to what other people believe or think about you, it's tied to what you believe and think about yourself! As my parents said, "Get the education for no one can take that from you." Ms. Perry also said, "You can be anything you want to be, if you're willing to work hard enough for it!"

These episodes, though extremely painful and emotional, awakened a sleeping giant and have emboldened me to stand and advocate for the locked out, pushed out, and the forgotten. Just like Joseph, "You intended to harm me, but God intended it for good to accomplish what is now being done, the saving of many lives." (Genesis 50:20 New International Version). Peace.

REFERENCES

Bochner, A.P., & Ellis, C. (2002). *Ethnographically Speaking: Autoethnography, literature, and aesthetics.* Walnut Creek, CA: AltaMira Press.

Tedlock, B. (2005). The observation of participation and the emergence of public ethnography. In N. K. Denzin & Y. S. Lincoln (Eds.), *The SAGE handbook of qualitative research* (3rd ed., pp. 467–481). Thousand Oaks, CA: SAGE.

CHAPTER 21

COMING HOME

The Social and Educational Consequences of Being a Formerly Incarcerated Chicano Convict Criminologist

Oscar Fabian Soto

THE FORMATION OF A "CRIMINAL"

As a Chicano from the San Diego region, my sociological imagination has been informed by my childhood in La Calle,[1] a predominantly White community in North San Diego County fraught with racial inequality. Institutional racism, police repression, and a thriving school-to-prison pipeline (Yosso, 2006) shape the experience of people of color in La Calle.

Growing up, I did not feel connected to my peers, teachers, or the school district. At La Calle Middle School, the only place I felt connected, I was successfully thriving in many academic subjects. This made me an honor roll student. Once I reached La Calle High School, I was pushed to remedial classes that were filled with people of color. The instructor for these courses was Ms. Smith, a short blond-haired woman. Every block period, instead of teaching her students, the class was subjected to watching Disney movies. The other days we would read Dr. Seuss's collection of books and practice our cursive writing, a typical third grade U.S. class. Instead of engaging with the students, she often threw tantrums if students were talking during the movie, reading, or writing time. In her class, she had strict zero tolerance policies that often sent the "troubled" students to the principal's office. I was one of these students. Ms. Smith sent me to the principal's office so often that I was labeled a bad student and started my association with La Quinta Continuation School. This school was labeled the troubled school and is where I met most of the *homies* (friends). After school, our hangouts consisted of house jumping. This meant that we would go from one friend's house to another, setting up boxing matches, doing drugs, and drinking alcohol. Once put in this path, I was pretty much expected to join the neighborhood gang, end up in prison, and perhaps even face death. I became a pushout. I witnessed, firsthand, how structural inequalities in educational institutions limit not only people's educational access and success, but also shape their life course.

As a young adult, I served time in the San Diego County jail. In addition to my sentence, I was assigned mandatory probation until restitution was paid in full, which was finally paid off on June 9, 2017. Prior to this sentence, I was facing a conviction for two felonies and six misdemeanors. Since I refused to snitch,[2] I was convicted and ordered to pay restitution.

My story illustrates how social institutions heighten what Rios (2012) calls the youth control complex. The youth control complex is a system of social institutions, such as police, community centers, and schools, who treat youth's everyday behaviors as criminal activity. These social institutions hyper criminalize and hyper surveil youth of color for their unique behaviors. Pushed out youth are then marginalized in this caste system we call the *modern-day slavery*, meaning mass incarceration.

One year after I was released from the San Diego County jail, I walked into a classroom at California State University, San Marcos, to start my Introduction to Justice Studies class. Classroom 1204, the placard read in the Social and Behavioral Sciences building. As I entered the classroom, sitting in the center seat of a plethora of desks facing two large white boards, a full sleeve tattooed Chicano. As I made my way to the back of the classroom, students began to funnel through the door, 5 minutes before the class began. The clock hit five, and still no professor. Five minutes passed, when the tattooed Chicano wearing a black *Guayabera*[3] shirt and a black Fedora hat with a small grey feather on the left side, approached the white boards. His name Dr. Xuan Santos. Unlike the typical professionalization of faculty across campus, Santos embodied a stereotypical *pelon* (bald) Chicano *cholo*,[4] and lectured with a passion that demanded social change. I had found my mentor!

Prior to me taking Dr. Santos Introduction to Justice Studies, I navigated California State University, San Marcos through a discrete lens. The lens that narrates and governs the experiences of many formerly incarcerated people: The less interaction with your peers the less people know about your "troubled" past. I was afraid of the stigmatization that would threaten my credibility as a student (Goffman, 1963). Once stigmatized, people label you as inadequate to pursue an educational degree. Michelle Alexander (2010) describes how people of color and formerly incarcerated have become second-class citizens. She calls this a racial caste system. The racial caste system is a system that creates stigmas and discrimination. This system prevents formerly incarcerated people from achieving a successful reintegration into "civil" society, with 77% of people returning to prison within 5 years. Through my experience, I was afraid of experiencing backlash from people knowing of my criminal record. I had enough backlash and discrimination from employment institutions; one, because of my criminal record and two because I was a person of color. This experience is true for many formerly incarcerated people, according to Pager (2007). My educational experience is critical in describing the multidimensional criminality formerly incarcerated and persons of color receive via invisible punishments (Travis, 2002).

Thanks to a mentor like Dr. Santos, I was able to embrace my life experience as a motivation factor to continue my educational career. Instead of shaming, Dr. Santos provided a platform to empower, not only myself, but those in the community. Dr. Santos became a role model, a mentor, and a friend because of the similar experience growing up in Boyle Heights, Los Angeles. One day I was walking towards Dr. Santos' office, an office located on the fourth floor of the Social and Behavioral Science building, and saw what looked like a line of students leading towards a door covered with social justice memorabilia. I walked into Dr. Santos' office, cutting in front of all the students. As I walked into his office, I felt comfort and at peace. Dr. Santos' office is covered with social justice posters, sugar skulls representing different aspects of his life, and Mexican relics from Aztec sculptures to *zarapes*.[5] He asked me to sit down, and to my surprise Dr. Santos further asked me if I wanted take part in a panel of scholar activists that would speak in Lewiston, Idaho. I gladly accepted his offer. Throughout this trip, the panelists gave their testimony to middle, high, and Native American reservation schools. The trip also consisted of speaking to law enforcement officers about community organizing and gang intervention programs. This trip gave me the platform to speak freely about my incarceration history, as well as, the struggle of overcoming this stigma. Suddenly, being incarcerated was a tool to continue on the path towards a doctorate degree in sociology. No longer was I ashamed to state that I have been in the *pinta* (jail/prison), even though I was strongly encouraged to hide my past from going public.

CONCLUSION

Social institutions can have tremendous negative power over the lives of individuals—the power to outcast them from academia, the power to label them as deviant, the power to transform a person's life in a negative way—but may also have positive power: the power to educate marginalized groups, and the power to transform an individual's life in a positive way. In my experience, this power came from my mentor and true OG (he defines this as, not an original gangster, but Opportunity Giver), Dr. Xuan Santos. Mentors, like Dr. Santos, stand with the oppressed to combat the oppressor. This is a mentor who mentors those formerly incarcerated, immigrants, people of color, and any other individual that stands against the status quo. They help guide people through social institutions like the educational ivory tower and the hierarchal prison system, which are one in the same.

In this essay, I have shared a brief autoethnography of my past and personal struggles through several institutions: the streets, academia, and post-incarceration. I know I run the risk of tainting my credibility as a scholar, but with 2.3 million incarcerated and 7 million under the criminal [in]justice system, there will be a continued avalanche of underrepresented and underprivileged communities coming to academia. To them I say, find a mentor that fights for social justice, social change, and is supportive, not only through your education, but throughout your life. In addition, maintain the family support system which helped me get through the difficult times.

NOTES

1. I will use pseudonyms throughout the paper to protect the identities of persons and places.
2. The act of snitching is sharing information with law enforcement incriminating other individuals. Snitching is a violation of what Anderson (2000) calls the code of the streets, which are informal and formal rules that govern the lives of people in the neighborhood. Snitching can bring repercussions to you and/or your family.
3. A lightweight open-necked Cuban or Mexican shirt with two breast pockets. In addition, it has two pockets over the hips, and typically has short sleeves.
4. Someone who is stereotypically labeled to have adopted elements of a Mexican gang member dress, language, or culture.
5. A poncho-like colorful blanket, typical of Mexican culture.

REFERENCES

Alexander, M. (2010). *The new Jim Crow: Mass incarceration in the age of colorblindness.* New York, NY: The New Press.
Anderson, E. (2000). *Code of the street: Decency, violence, and the moral life of the inner-city.* New York, NY: Norton.
Goffman, I. (1963). *Stigma: Notes on the management of spoiled identity.* New York, NY: Touchstone.
Pager, D. (2007). *Marked: Race, crime, and finding work in an era of mass incarceration.* Chicago, IL: The University of Chicago Press.
Rios, V. M. (2012). *Punished: Policing the lives of Black and Latino boys.* New York, NY: The New York University Press.
Travis, J. (2002). Invisible punishment: An instrument of social exclusion. In M. Mauer & M. Chesney-Lind (Eds.), *Invisible punishment: The collateral consequences of mass imprisonment* (pp. 15–36). New York, NY: The New Press.
Yosso, T. J. (2006). *Critical race counterstories along the Chicana/Chicano educational pipeline.* New York, NY: Taylor & Francis.

CHAPTER 22

WHEN I WOKE UP TO BEING BLACK

Christopher J. P. Sewell

The house that I grew up in was exactly four blocks away from two different elementary schools. If you went in one direction, the majority of the students in the school were Black and if you went in the other direction, the student population was predominantly White. My mother made the decision to place me in the school, PS 203, that happened to be majority White, for a host of reasons. Going to the White school was very different as most of my peers went to school in the other direction. While I was too young to note any distinct impact or difference, going to the White school proved to be of significance as I think about my schooling beyond Grades K–5.

Before diving into my experiences at PS 203, it is important to know a bit about my family background. I grew up with my mother's family (I have never met my father), who immigrated from Jamaica in the 1960s and 1970s. If you were to look at my maternal grandmother or great-grandmother, you might think that they were White women. They could name their Irish and Syrian Jewish ancestors who came to Jamaica in the 1800s. All of my grandmother's sisters, who could potentially pass as White women, married men who were darker skinned. As a result, my family members range in all colors of brown and beige. For me, then, skin color was not a predictor of anything. My family made it a point to stress Jamaica's motto of "Out of many, one people" to speak to the diversity of people we had in our family. So, when it was time to go to school in 1987, I did not think anything of the diversity of students that would become my peers.

Looking at my pre-kindergarten class picture, I am one of two people of color (the other student was an Asian girl). Despite being the only "chip in the cookie," I began what would be life-long friendships with several of my White peers. My friends came to my birthday parties and their families took me to see different parts of the city, exposing me to various activities that were unfamiliar to, or of no interest to, my family. I went to my friends' houses after school and I became, to some extent, the stereotypical "Black-White boy" due to my school affiliation and nerdiness.

As a schoolboy, it did not bother me. I worked to construct a persona of a smart Black guy (and I am sure I was also pegged as queer) as it worked to my advantage in building relationships with my peers and my teachers. Even as more Black students joined our classes as the years progressed, I was able to secure a reputation as a reliable and smart kid who was well-liked amongst his peers. I was able to not fall into being labeled as a problem or at-risk, even as my family's financial circumstances changed when my mother went back to school when I was in the third grade. In reflection, teachers viewed this "me" as non-masculine. I was seemingly not a threat to the Whiteness around me nor was I actively working to be "pro-Black." I felt comfortable, accepted, and wanted by everyone. On some levels, I felt invincible as I never got into any trouble despite a growing ego as one of the few Black boys in a gifted space; that was until the fifth grade.

Fifth grade started off shaky; I should have known it was going to be a challenging year when the school was delayed for asbestos removal. The inevitable move to middle school loomed over me and my peers as we studied to take placement exams for the gifted and talented middle schools in our district. While we were very collaborative in nature in years prior, this process seemed to bring out the worst in some of my peers. One student in particular, Kaitlyn*, whose mother happened to be a teacher in the school, worked to harass and bully all of the Black students in the class. Whether it was stealing their glue, hitting them on the head with a Woody the Woodpecker pencil, or other sorts of shenanigans, Kaitlyn seemed to have every person's mother come to the school for something that they did in retaliation for her misdeeds. She never got called into the office and her mother never attended these meetings with the other parents. It seemed that she simply had it out for any of the people of color in our class.

Looking back on the situation, I thought that I was immune to Kaitlyn's conniving ways. I never sat near her in class, we were not in the same friend circle, and we shared no mutual interests. As much as I knew I was Black, I never thought to make that the reason that would cause strife between me and any of my classmates, Kaitlyn specifically. I just chalked it up to her not being a nice person. That was until she lied on me.

We were both monitors for first grade classes during our lunch period. This meant we were to walk our respective classes to lunch, help them get situated, eat with them and bring them back to their classes to wait for their teachers' return. One day, I was asked to substitute in the class that she worked in because someone was absent. Kaitlyn lied and said that I did something wrong to a student, which led to us having a verbal altercation. I thought it was all over until I got back up to class after lunch and was told that my mother had to come to school. I was flabbergasted. I had never been in trouble. What was my mother going to say... Why was this happening to me... All of my Black classmates who had their trials with Kaitlyn came to me as I sobbed uncontrollably in the stairs. I felt like they wanted to tell me a big "I told you so." Instead, they told me that they had my back and would make sure that some of our other peers, with a propensity for fighting would be alerted.

I went home and told my mother. While upset, she immediately told me not to worry as she had been in communication with some of the other mothers who had similar experiences. A few days later, she went to the school where she made it very clear that she saw this issue as being around race. While I had grown up thinking my schoolmates were simply friends, some of whom happened to be the same complexion as my grandmother, I was now viscerally aware of the differences that existed. I listened to my mother put the school officials in their place and let them know she would not tolerate this treatment of me and any other student of color in the class by the institution. She used choice words to let them know that she would not respond to anything more from them in regards to Kaitlyn as she knew they were biased, especially since her mother was a teacher in the school. At the end of the meeting, while I was not suspended, a mediation was scheduled for Kaitlyn and I to work out our difference.

In the middle of graduation practice, Kaitlyn and I were pulled to discuss our differences by the very same assistant principal who called my mother to the school. Feeling as if I were going to be berated, I did not have high hopes for the session. As I relayed my story, Kaitlyn rolled her eyes, huffed, and made noises. Halfway through my statement, the assistant principal said, "I can see how this behavior you have, Kaitlyn, is causing issues if this is how you are behaving in this session." It was my moment of vindication. He had no choice but to recognize that I, the Black boy, did nothing; I was simply a victim of her White privilege and positionality in the school. He sent me on my way to continue with practice while he sat speaking to her about demeanor and behavior.

The whole experience made me become more aware of not only my surroundings but also who I was. It taught me, that even though I was built up to be different or better, that I was going to always be viewed as a Black boy from Brooklyn. No matter what class I was in, my peers and I would always be looked upon differently and seen as a potential threat to the egos of our peers. From that point forward, I made sure to always be aware of my positionality and the ways in which my Blackness would be perceived as a threat. I could no longer see myself in isolation; rather, building alliances and friendships based in our shared experiences as Black kids in a White space became critical to our survival in gifted programs.

As I reflect on this experience now, I believe that I would push young Black men in similar situations to do three things: (a) *Always let your work speak for itself*—be humble and work hard so that the reputation, that exists alongside the narratives that others want to make of you, is stronger; (b) *Do not forget where you came from*—while I was never standoffish to my friends at home, I did not think about how to fully merge those two beings and became lost in my whiter surroundings. It became critical to remember the lessons I not only learned at home, but also from my peers on my block, in order to think about the ways in which I may have been shielded from reality and remain humble; (c) *Never be afraid to speak up*—as much as I saw what Kaitlyn was doing to my peers, I sat by since it was not happening to me. Never be afraid to call out when you see racism at hand. While it may feel awkward, it is the right thing to do as you and your peers deserve to always be in a safe and welcoming space.

CHAPTER 23

THE POWER OF FORGIVENESS

Joseph Matthews

The police officer pulled me out of the car in handcuffs and walked me down the long dark hallway to my jail cell where I would stay my first night. Many people in my life had said this is where I would end up, starting back when I began to act out due to the pain and anger I was holding inside. I believe it started when they said I had a learning disability, then placed me in special education. Being treated like I was not as smart as the other kids in my class, like something was wrong with me, made me hate my teachers. Being racially profiled as if I had committed a crime when I was just trying to walk down the street made me hate the police. Growing up in poverty without the things kids need to live made me hate life. So, there I was, 17 years old, a high school dropout, and in jail—exactly in the place where they said I would be. The first night was the worst as I began to realize that this small, cold, and quiet room with no windows, where I couldn't look outside and daydream and see the sun, was my new home. Like many other young people in lockup, I had fallen for the trap. Some of my cellmates looked at being locked up as a badge of honor. We have all seen the Hollywood images of people in jail. They show the inmates walking around acting hard. They made it look really cool. What they don't show on the videos or movies are the sounds of men crying from broken heartedness and loneliness. They don't show them talking to themselves because there is no one else to talk to, or the screaming out for help as horrible things are being done to them.

It wasn't until I saw the look in my mom's eyes on her first visit that I began to understand how wrong I was about the lifestyle I was living. She was already stressed from raising us with no money, struggling to feed us, not knowing if she would get the call that I had been killed. Now she had to deal with me being in jail. I remember her telling me she loved me before she left. I didn't have the heart to tell her that I loved her too because I knew that regardless of what I said, my actions were saying the opposite. My actions were saying, "I wish to hurt you." All this time I was looking at the decisions I made through very selfish eyes only thinking about how they affected me. I didn't think about the impact it would have on the people who cared about me, especially my mother. I had never felt so heartbroken as when I thought about how much I was breaking her heart. Not only did I begin to resent the unloving space that I was physically in, I also began to resent the unloving mental space I was in. There was no doubt that I had been mistreated by others throughout my life. But I started understanding that in order to be free mentally and stay free physically I would have to forgive everyone who had hurt me in the past. Most importantly, I would have to forgive myself. I needed to do this so I could let go of the pain that I kept revisiting over and over again.

Shortly after being released from jail, the new person I was becoming was tested when I decided to return to school. I needed to see if I could finish and maybe have a chance at going to college to play football. From the first day I walked back in the school many of the teachers looked at me like I was the ghost of a person who had returned from the dead. A few even asked me why I was trespassing. They couldn't believe that I was a student again. That year I endured teachers watching and waiting for me to do or say something out of line so they could jam me up. I even got approached by a police officer who worked at our school. He told me a few teachers made a bet that I would not graduate. This just made me focus even more. They thought I was the same Joseph they had come to know a few years earlier, but I wasn't. I had been through many life-altering events and had committed to pulling myself, my mom, and my family out of poverty. I was focused like a fighter and no matter what was said or done to me, I always took a step back to think about it before I responded.

One week before graduation, my forgiveness was tested. I was invited to a party. When I arrived, the dude who had snitched me out and got me sent to jail was in the building. It was all I could do to contain myself as he smirked at me, as if saying, "I'm not afraid of you." I was trying to ignore him and just have fun but my friends had other plans. They wanted me to beat him up, or give them the green light to do so. I had made a commitment to changing, and forgiving people from my past, so I told them to let it go. After catching an ear full from them for not wanting to get even with him, a fight broke out. During the chaos the homie said, "Joseph, let's get him! Now is our chance." And for one split second, I thought about knocking him out, but something deep inside of me said, "Let it go," so I turned around and left. Before I could take two steps I heard gunshots. When I turned around I saw someone standing across the room with a gun pointed in the air. It was the dude who had gotten me sent to jail. That is why he had the smirk on his face when he saw me. He was not afraid because he was packing heat and waiting for me to approach him so he would have an excuse to kill me. I was so relieved that I didn't cave in to the pressure to seek revenge. Because I had truly forgiven this dude, I was able to make a decision that saved my life and the lives of my friends.

Exactly one week later I walked across the stage as a high school graduate in front of an auditorium full of people who didn't believe in me, had bet against me, and talked about me like I was dead. It seems like people would have cheered really hard for me when they called my name considering everything that I had been through to graduate. Instead, the room was dead silent. The truth is, it didn't matter because I had learned that I didn't need the approval or applause of others to understand I had accomplished something big.

That summer I loaded up my bags and headed off to college to fulfill my lifelong dream of becoming a college football player. A few years later I walked across a stage again, this time as the first college graduate in my family. I went on to become a special education teacher. I worked with kids who had been labeled and mistreated like me, teaching them to never give up on life because the dreams they have can be accomplished. I taught them that they are not who society has told them they are. They are so much more. Shortly after becoming a teacher, I wrote my first book about my life, titled *The Dropout* (Matthews, 2008), and began sharing my story around the county. Today, I have written five books and I am working on my sixth. I have also earned two master's degrees in education and I am working on finishing my doctorate from a prestigious Ivy League university in New York City.

I have taken every negative thing that people tried to do and say to me and turned it into something positive, but what if I hadn't learned to forgive... What if I had not learned how to let things from the past go so I could grab a hold of the future... What if I started a fight with the man who got me arrested... One of the things I have learned on my journey is that you cannot hold on to pain from the past and your dreams for the future at the same time. One will eventually destroy the other. In this world, those who develop the ability to let the anger go and turn pain into positivity are the ones who succeed.

If I could leave you with a few words for the journey, I would ask you to:

- *Look at school and life as if they were the streets.* Just like you would not allow someone to walk up to you on the streets and punch you in your face without fighting back, don't allow life or school to punch you in the face without fighting back. Just like you would not allow someone to walk up and steal the shoes off your feet, never allow them to walk up and steal the dreams out of your heart.
- *Forgiving others who have wronged you doesn't mean they've won or that you're weak.* It means that you are the stronger person and that you are now focused on winning. Practicing forgiveness is one of the best gifts you can give to yourself. Letting go of past pain gives you space to embrace better days.

As I reflect on my troubled childhood. I think of all of the fallen homies that never made it to adulthood with me. As I dedicate my books and talks to them, I also use their stories as lessons for the next generation. This is what those reading this book must do, survive and succeed so you can help the next generation make it. Know that your life is valuable and that which you need to succeed, already exists inside of you.

REFERENCE

Mathew, J. (2008). *The dropout: How a lost kid found his dream.* CreateSpace Independent Publishing Platform.

CHAPTER 24

STONY THE ROAD WE TROD

Black Males Share Lived Experiences With Police Brutality

Antonio Ellis and Eddie Vanderhorst

As natives of Charleston, South Carolina, we often frequent the city of North Charleston, which is approximately five miles from downtown Charleston where we were born and raised. On April 4, 2015, the unjust shooting of Walter Scott, a 50 year old Black male, brought North Charleston into the national spotlight. Michael Slager, a 33-year old White male officer, shot Scott eight times in his back as Scott was running away from him. Slager claimed that Scott attempted to take away his taser prior to the shooting. However, cellphone video which circulated on social media and in the popular press, contradicted Slager's assertions. Feidin Santana, a local barber who was on his way to work, captured the interaction between Scott and Slager via his cell phone video camera.

This incident and others have caused many local North Charleston citizens to constantly worry that their lives will be unjustly taken by police officers. We are no different. We have similar fears as professional Black men who are striving to make the world a socially just place. The first author

(Antonio) is a Black male college professor whose scholarship focuses on social justice issues in Black communities. The second author Eddie, a doctoral student in criminal justice, is developing a research agenda on effective policing practices in Black and Brown communities.

We both believe, like many North Charleston residents, that local police officers use Black, poor, and other vulnerable people to prosper economically. For example, it is widely believed that North Charleston police officers target Black males at night and plant illegal drugs on them. It is also believed that the same police officers give local citizens speeding tickets illegally in order to make their quarterly quota. In addition, we have overheard fellow community members mention that local police officers handcuff Black males, while taking their money for personal use during the search and seizure process. In many of these cases, they do not make any arrests. Given these examples of police misconduct, police support appears to be strong among mainly White citizens who live in the suburbs of North Charleston. Citizens who reside in urban centers lack trust due to their lived experiences and negative interactions with officers. Instead of these citizens viewing police officers as professionals who will protect them, they are viewed as people who sabotage and physically harm Black bodies with no remorse. To this extent, in selected cases, police officers in North Charleston have been known to mentally abuse and publicly shame citizens.

In this chapter, our aim is to shed light on our lived experiences with police brutality and racial profiling by North Charleston police officers. We hope our collective stories elucidate the stories of other Black males who have been subjected to police brutality. While police brutality is often associated with physical abuse, we challenge readers to also think about police brutality in terms of mental abuse, which includes public shaming and humiliation. Although our recent experiences with police brutality did not end in physical death as was the case for so many other Black males including Walter Scott, they ended in what P. J. Williams (1991) and Bettina Love (2013) call "spirit murder." That is, our experiences of racial profiling and police brutality in North Charleston, South Carolina, denied us our full humanity. Instead, we were faced with "personal, psychological, and spiritual injuries...through fixed, yet fluid and moldable, structures of racism, privilege, and power" (Love, 2013, p. 302). Such injuries denied "inclusion, protection, safety and acceptance" (p. 302) and demonstrated how "stoney [yet] the road we trod" (Johnson & Johnson, 2010). Despite all of this, we still strive to overcome. We start this chapter off by sharing our stories. As such, we use a storytelling methodology, which is prevalent in many critical theories, for example critical race theory, which challenges issues of race, racism, and social injustice. We conclude with what we believe are recommendations to dismantle police brutality in predominantly Black communities.

ANTONIO ELLIS' NARRATIVE

During the fall of 2014, I was driving home after a long day of teaching and grading papers at the College of Charleston, when I was abruptly pulled over by a North Charleston police officer. While driving under the speed limit, I vividly recall seeing a Crown Victoria police car following me for approximately three miles. As I changed lanes, the officer changed lanes, while continuing to get closer to the tail end of my car. Upon coming to the conclusion that I was being followed, my heart started racing with anxiety. I immediately thought about the many African American males, including Donte Hamilton (Milwaukee), Eric Garner (New York), John Crawford III (Ohio), Michael Brown Jr. (Missouri), Ezell Ford (California), Dante Parker (California), Akai Gurley (New York), Tamir Rice (Cleveland), Rumain Brisbon (Phoenix), Jerame Reid (New Jersey), Tony Robinson (Wisconsin), Phillip White (New Jersey), Eric Harris (Oklahoma), Walter Scott (South Carolina), Freddie Gray (Maryland), and others who are not listed, who were unjustly killed by the state due to police brutality. While nervously driving, I eventually saw the officer turn on his blue lights, as I pulled over into the margins of the road. I stopped in a lighted area to lessen the chances of my being physically harmed by the officer.

As I sat waiting on the officer to approach my car, I kept both hands on the steering wheel, while trying to think of additional ways to make the police officer not feel threatened by me. Black male bodies are often identified as threats without being a threat. As an African American male who is speech impaired, I was afraid and extremely uncomfortable. At least three minutes passed before the officer finally approached my car and asked for my driver's license and registration. While the officer was taking my credentials back to his car, I heard police siren sounds approaching from afar off. However, the sounds continued to get closer by the minute. Eventually I realized the officer who pulled me over had called for backup. In that moment, my heart started racing and eyes became filled with tears. Seconds later, two backup officers aggressively commanded that I step out of my car, place both hands on the hood of my car, and spread my legs. Both officers patted me down and emptied my pockets, while the third officer shined his bright flashlight on me.

Thereafter, they searched my car. While searching my car, they saw my college faculty identification card under the armrest. One officer asked, "Is this a fake faculty identification card ... " I responded by saying, "Yes sir, it is a real faculty identification card." In order to further prove the validity of the identification card, I added, "You can look me up on the college website." At that point, all the officers walked a few feet away and got into a huddle, leaving me with my hand still on the hood and legs spread apart. After approximately five minutes of being in a huddle, the officers walked back over to me saying, "You may get back in your car. We looked on the college website to make sure that your faculty identification card was legitimate." When I asked why I was pulled over, one officer said, "We thought you were someone else, and you'd better get going." In order to avoid further conflicts, I left the scene with anger in my heart. I felt as if I was initially stereotyped and profiled as a Black male who was driving through the city of North Charleston. However, at the same moment, I felt somewhat privileged once the officers realized my professional status as a faculty member at a popular local predominantly White college. If I did not have my faculty identification card, I wonder about the outcome of this situation. Could I have been the next #SayHisName hashtag on social media...?

EDDIE VANDERHORST'S NARRATIVE

It was a cold wintery night in 2006, I was driving through North Charleston, South Carolina with my 2-year-old daughter in the back seat of my car. As I was traveling through the city, I was alarmed as I saw blue lights come on behind me. Not only was I alarmed, but my 2-year-old daughter was even more alarmed. She began to cry and scream hysterically. In the moment, I tried to calm her down, while concurrently trying to figure out why I was being pulled over by the police. When the White officer approached my car, he shone his flashlight into my daughter's face and demanded that I do something to "shut the baby up." At that point, I became furious internally with the police for using such language while referencing my daughter. My first thought was, "Who in the hell is he talking to..." However, I did not allow my anger and inner rage to cause me to act out of character in front of my daughter.

Thereafter, the officer asked me for my license and registration. When he went back to his car with my credentials, I used that time to calm my daughter's emotions to the best of my ability. Nevertheless, she was physically shaking and breathing heavily at an abnormally fast pace. While I feared for my safety, my primary concern was the comfort of my daughter. In the midst of comforting my daughter, similar to the first author's story, more police cars arrived on the scene. I was told to step out of my car, while leaving my daughter in the car alone. When my daughter noticed that I was exiting the car, she became even more emotional than she initially was.

As I carefully exited the car, two White officers abruptly pushed me against my car and proceeded to handcuff me. Although I was being physically abused by the police officers, I still was focused on the well-being of my daughter. As the officers used excessive force, I asked, "May I call a family member to come and get my daughter..." One officer called the number I provided, while the other informed me that I was being detained due to my suspended driver's license. While driving with a suspended license does warrant an arrest, it does not justify the fact that I was physically abused by the officers. I neither resisted arrest, nor posed a threat to them. In addition, my 2-year-old daughter should not have been traumatized by professionals who are hired to protect citizens. I often wonder if I would have been treated differently if I was a professor at a prestigious local college, like my co-author.

RECOMMENDATIONS TO THE AFRICAN AMERICAN COMMUNITY

As fear continues to penetrate the hearts and minds of local citizens, it is imperative that community organizers hold local elected officials accountable for challenging unethical behaviors of law enforcement. Over the last 3 years, local civil rights leaders in North Charleston have hosted marches and rallies to draw attention to police brutality, in light of the murder of Walter Scott. While marches and rallies are somewhat useful, marching and rallying alone does not create ethical change. Instead, we contend that change is more likely to occur when local officials are provoked to make public policy decisions regarding law enforcement, which would in turn hold police officers accountable. To this extent, we believe that a local civilian review board (CRB) should be formed in the city of North Charleston. The primary purpose of a CRB is to ensure that police are complying with local and federal laws, in addition to facing the necessary consequences when they fail to comply with the law.

RECOMMENDATIONS TO MALES OF COLOR

While African Americans and other minority groups have experienced social, economic, and political progressions in America, the treatment of people of color by law enforcement remains a national dilemma in the city of North Charleston and throughout the United States. While every assault on communities of color may not be publicized nationally like the Walter Scott case, males of color can do the following to help eradicate police brutality:

1. Formulate police brutality prevention groups in highly targeted communities, such as North Charleston.
2. Partner with local K–12 schools and higher education institutions to continue raising police brutality awareness, including educating students on ways to appropriately communicate when approached by law enforcement officials.

3. Become active in local neighborhood councils to ensure that police officers are being held accountable for behaviors that are contrary to protecting citizens.

If law enforcement officers continue to invoke fear into our communities, while physically and mentally harming citizens, we doubt that trust will be built under these treacherous conditions. While we continue to fight for justice in the murder of Walter Scott, among others, we must remain vigilant, by striving to ensure that all citizens in the North Charleston community are safe. As an African American male who is a professor of education and another who is an aspiring professor of criminology, we are constantly thinking about ways to ensure that Black lives will one day matter to law enforcement throughout the United States of America. While we centered our discussion on police brutality in North Charleston, South Carolina, we advocate for equity and fairness broadly.

REFERENCES

Johnson, J. R., & Johnson, J. W. (2010). *Lift Ev'ry Voice and Sing*. Decca.

Love, B. L. (2013). "I see Trayvon Martin": What teachers can learn from the tragic death of a young Black male. *The Urban Review, 46*(2), 292–306.

Williams, P. J. (1991). *The alchemy of race and rights: Diary of a law professor*. Cambridge, MA: Harvard University Press.

CHAPTER 25

THE RACE

Dwight Gordon II

America so often wants to paint a picture of a country that is a melting pot of harmony. From Woody Guthrie (1944) singing "This land is your land this land is my land, from California to the New York Island, from the Redwood Forest to the Gulf Stream waters, this land was made for you and me"; to the Statue of Liberty's heartfelt inscription, "Give me your tired, your poor, your huddled masses yearning to breathe free, the wretched refuse of your teeming shore. Send these, the homeless, tempest-tost to me, I lift my lamp beside the golden door!"

I, however, learned in the harshest of ways, that this land is not made for you and me, nor am I a part of the tired, poor, huddled masses yearning to breathe free, that this country readily and willingly wanted to accept. No, I was the citizen covered under Americas 13th Amendment, Section 1 "Neither slavery nor involuntary servitude, except as a punishment for crime whereof the party shall have been duly convicted, shall exist within the United States, or any place subject to their jurisdiction." This is the American citizen I had engraved in my mind at 5 years old growing up in Nashville, TN. The country music capital, the city where today everyone so readily flocks to, the city that currently sees growth of 100 new residents per day.

Imagine your family moving into a new home. You are living without a care in the world, a young innocent child who knows no color, no Black or White—just people. Now imagine having your innocence shattered over the course of a night.

One peaceful night after living in a community for about a week, my father was finalizing our move at our apartment, and everyone in the house was sound asleep. After falling asleep, I was awakened by the piercing sound of glass shattering and a brash banging. Frightened and not knowing what was happening, I pulled the covers over my head praying whatever it was would just go away. Maybe I was dreaming, maybe this was just a nightmare...As I was hiding under my covers, my mother rushed to the room and snatched me and my sister into her arms and hurried us into her bedroom.

While cowered in the corner of my mother's room, curious while still very fearful, I glanced out the window to see what I believed was a ghost. I was confused, "Could it be a ghost..." What I saw resembled the imaginary ghosts from cartoons, covered in white sheets, running in the dark, but mommy told me ghosts aren't real. "What is happening..." I asked myself. I vividly remember my mother beating on the wall with a hammer yelling, "Leave us alone!" Repeatedly, "Leave us alone!" Who were these people... What did they want...And why were we the target of their anger...After what seemed like hours the ghosts went away, leaving me, my sister, and my mom in a frantic state. My father arrived a short time later and we quickly packed our car to leave this place where we were no longer welcomed. As we drove from the house in the middle of the pitch dark night, I stared at the cross in our front yard burning bright as the sun; the image was permanently scorched into my brain. For it was not a cross of redemption, or an episode of Roots, or a documentary on slavery in the 1800s. This was no civil rights era movie in the 1960s, this was 1985 in Nashville, TN. In the midst of this perceived nightmare, was my first face-to-face encounter of racial discrimination, a hate crime. I would later learn that the perceived ghosts on that scary night were our next door neighbors dressed in white sheets or Ku Klux Klan (KKK) attire. They behaved this way in order to frighten and make known to my family, that us colored folk where not wanted nor worthy to live beside them.

The journey towards the pursuit of my doctoral degree is a constant reminder of that moment in time, of not being wanted or accepted based on the color of my skin. Fittingly, as much as time has changed, things consistently have remained the same while being Black in America. If one looks around with an open mind, it is evident that racism is still an active part of our society. Philando Castile, Tamir Rice, Trayvon Martin, and Sandra Bland were reminded at different ages and stages in their lives that they weren't wanted in America and that this land was not their land. They were young gifted lives snuffed out before they were able to fulfill their highest gift to society.

As an African American male, it is not the hate I experienced as a child in Nashville or these taken souls that made me pursue a PhD. Instead, the pursuit comes from a drive, a fire, a desire to run a race, and reach a goal that was placed in me from birth. The pursuit of a doctoral degree brings so much adversity, so much anguish, and so much mental tussle. The adversity I have experienced while being Black in America has most definitely prepared me for the trials and tribulations associated with obtaining the highest educational degree. There's assertiveness, being humble, being prepared, knowing how to eloquently express your thoughts with just enough assertiveness, yet without appearing threatening towards authority. All of these things I learned while dealing with racial discrimination in America, and yet they so easily can be translated to the pursuit of challenging tasks we may encounter in life.

Dealing with racial discrimination has been the plight of African Americans since being brought to this country. As I personally reached milestone after milestone at 10, 18, 21, 25, 30, and 36 years of age, I'm reminded of every person who looked like me but was never allowed the opportunity to attend high school or college due to being imprisoned or worse, killed because their melanin was a few shades too dark. Over the course of my life I have learned that in a White-washed world I will constantly be reminded that I am not good enough, my education is not good enough, and perhaps I did not earn nor do I deserve a postgraduate degree. I have also realized that, "I must strive to run the race just a stride faster and harder as to leave no doubt of my qualifications."

One may ask where my strength, my drive, my motivation come from… Honestly, my strength, drive, and motivation starts with my faith. My faith in God, my family, and a close circle of peers within my doctoral program has continually helped me to bear the cross which is the pursuit of this degree. Research shows that less than 3% of the world's population has a doctoral degree. This, in itself amounts to a monumental amount of pressure to complete a doctoral program. It is not only the pressures associated with school that challenge me, it is also work, family, and life in general that keep me reluctant about my ability to persevere. The journey has not been easy by any means, in fact it has been the polar opposite with a constant questioning: "Why am I pursuing this degree… Am I cut out for this…" These have been consistent questions for my colleagues and I as we endure through this program. Without our faith, prayer, and dependence on one another for support and encouragement to fight the good fight and continue the journey, we would most likely respond to these questions of doubt with a resounding, "No!"

Beating the odds of racial discrimination, overcoming the obstacles of society's labels of not good enough, not the right color, and personally pursuing a graduate degree until almost 10 years after I finished college has been nothing short of a miracle. My immediate family has no college graduates prior to myself. I graduated from high school with a C average, even though I scored a 27 (out of 36) on the ACT as a freshman. I was often told by those who knew me best that I wouldn't graduate from college, because I was the proverbial "wild child." In hindsight, these things never deterred me from college or pursuing my doctoral degree; in fact they pushed me towards it.

Having a strong support system is absolutely paramount in pursuing a postgraduate degree. Personally, I am in a committed relationship with an engineering professor who holds a PhD, and I have many friends who have PhDs in various fields of study. The encouragement I receive by having instant access to those with similar struggles as I endure is never taken lightly. Whether their PhDs are in engineering, education, kinesiology, nursing, or psychology, there is no shortage of those who offer me a plethora of advice and support. This becomes paramount because the task at times becomes so hard that it appears unattainable or insurmountable. A simple, "Hang in there, doc" or "You can make it," goes a long way.

Ultimately peer support, faith, like-minded individuals, and self-motivation will start you on your journey of carrying this cross and it will also carry you the long days and nights when you want to quit. Finding the strength to turn your adversity into triumph requires a plan and a road map few have managed to mesh together. The 8th president of my esteemed school, Tennessee State University, the late Dr. James A. Hefner, always reminded us, "Every morning in Africa, a gazelle wakes up, it knows it must outrun the fastest lion or it will be killed. Every morning in Africa, a lion wakes up. It knows it must run faster than the slowest gazelle, or it will starve. It doesn't matter whether you're the lion or a gazelle—when the sun comes up, you'd better be running."

REFERENCE

Guthrie, W., & The U.S. Coast Guard Band. (1944). *This land is your land*. MENC. [Audio]. Retrieved from the Library of Congress: https://www.loc.gov/item/ihas.100010446/

CHAPTER 26

A BLACK MAN'S STORY OF EMPOWERMENT

Why I Stopped Begging Whites to Accept My Blackness

Raymond Adams

On August 28, 2016, Chance the Rapper, an African American hip-hop artist, tweeted the hashtag entitled #*Blackboyjoy* in where he essentially authorized the need to celebrate the personhood of every Black boy and man of color in White America[1] at the 2016 MTV Music Video Awards. Sadly, this seemingly innocuous proclamation to inspire and affirm Black men and boys' right for happiness wasn't openly embraced by those in the majority. As I reflected on the venomous rhetoric espoused by both White and Black men toward the #*Blackboyjoy* on my Facebook feed, it forced me to recognize how race and racism has intersected not only in White America but also within my own life. For this reason, my utilization of critical race theory (CRT) seeks to critically analyze how White racist systems of education have imposed psychosocial barriers upon my overall identity as a scholar of color as well as a man of color in White America.

This unapologetic re-storying gives #*zerofucks* about how those outside the African diaspora will choose to interpret my critique of how Whiteness intersects with race and racism. However, it should not dissuade the reader regardless of their race or gender from absorbing how my narrative is representative of this country's historic race problem. I argue Whiteness' woeful ignorance to how race and racism intersects within education perpetuates the racialized experiences of Black boys and men of color. Too often I have read scholarly articles that temper the real experiences of racism for White comfortability as it relates to the dominant narrative about Black males in schools. Let me assure the reader(s) my African spirit doesn't entertain nor allow such White minimization on my storytelling as I don't need nor seek White validation for my happiness.

WHAT THE HELL IS CRITICAL RACE THEORY AND WHY DOES IT HATE WHITE PEOPLE

Critical race theory (CRT) arose during the early '70s to address the inadequacies of the critical legal studies in answering the byproducts of race and racism within the U.S. judicial system (DeCuir & Dixson 2004). Over time, this theoretical framework has been used in an interdisciplinary manner to explore the phenomenon of race, racism, and power (Carbado & Roithmayr, 2014; Malagon, Huber, & Velez, 2009). Research has shown that CRT posits the following five basic tenets:

> (1) Acknowledging that racism is an invisible norm and White culture and (privilege) is the standard by which other races are measured; (2) Committing to understanding that racism is socially constructed and expanded and an inclusive worldview is required for true social justice; (3) Acknowledging the unique perspective and voice of people of color as victims of oppression in racial matters and valuing their storytelling as a legitimate way to convey knowledge; (4) Engaging interdisciplinary dialogue and discourse to analyze race relationships (Mcdowell and Jeris, 2004); (5) An understanding that racism is systemic, and that many current policies and laws are: (a) neither ahistorical nor apolitical; and (b) are situated to privilege Whites and marginalized minoritized groups. (Muhammad, Dunbar, & Douglas, 2013, p. 491)

I AM A MULTILINGUAL MAN OF AFRICAN DESCENT PUT SOME RESPECT ON MY NAME

In continuing the conversation as to why I choose CRT to critique Whiteness and how it intersects with race and racism, I will utilize the CRT tenet of "counter storytelling" (Solorzano & Yosso, 2001a; 2001b) to recount my first racist experience with a White middle school teacher in White America's educational system. This tenet of CRT, as described by Solorzano and Yosso (2002), is "a tool for exposing, analyzing, and challenging the majoritarian stories of racial privilege" (p. 32). As such, in a recent journal newsletter of Division for Culturally and Linguistically Diverse Exceptional Learners, Adams (2017) speaks to how "This incident began because of the teacher's perception of my 'phonological difficulties' (Oetting & Garrity, 2006) during an English in-class exercise" (p. 13). In this class exercise, we were required to annunciate the vowels, consonants, and even identity the certain verbs and adjectives in the body of sentence. It's important to note that I was the only bilingual person (Louisiana French and English) in the classroom of peers and my linguistic aptitude to White English was not on par with my cohorts as of yet. Nonetheless, when I went to the board I struggled with completing the task asked of me by the instructor on record. Instead of acknowledging my difficulties with positive affirmations I was forever scarred with the following phrase: "Were you raised in a barn, you lazy barnyard nigger..." To this very day, I still remember the teacher's name, his face, even the anger in his words; unfortunately, his actions would not be the last time I encountered Whiteness during my educational journey.

MY HILLMAN COLLEGE EXPERIENCE

Before I go any further I want to educate the reader(s) born after the early 90s on the significance of the subheading. There was a sitcom entitled *A Different World*[2] (1987–1993) where a fictitious college, Hillman College, modeled after renowned Historically Black Colleges and Universities (HBCUs), educated a large majority student body of African descended folk with a few sprinkles of Whites here and there. With that said, it serves as a perfect backdrop into why I am forever grateful to my current institution, Jackson State University, in rewiring my overall sense of duty to Black and Brown bodies suffering under White Supremacy. Prior to becoming a doctoral student at The Jackson State University, I attended a predominately White institution with an R-1 status (top tier research institution) in Midwest White America for my doctoral education. It was because of this poor advising; I experienced 3 years of race-based stress and feelings of being an imposter (Cokley, McClain, Enciso, & Martinez, 2013). For instance, one of my former advisors (White cisgendered male) questioned my research agenda even my ability to conduct research at the doctoral level. Equally important, their critique of my scholastic aptitude, laid the foundation for justification by White administrators to recommend my dismissal from the program with no attempts at remediation to address my shortcomings, which signifies how Whiteness intersects with race and racism.

LIKE LIL BOOSIE SAID "WE GOING TO SHOW DA WORLD"

Lil Boosie after Tupac Shakur is one of my all time favorite rap artists. His recent song entitled, *We Going to Show Da World,* which is a track from his album *Touchdown 2 Cause Hell,* edifies my resilience within education; in addition, it informs my three simple recommendations to other males of color:

1. You must remain encouraged no matter how difficult the situation(s) and push through to earn what is rightfully yours (e.g., high school diploma, bachelor's, master's, PhD).
2. You must remain cognizant of the how racism intersects within the various systems of education.
3. You must always know how powerful your story is; no matter, your prior or current circumstance(s) you can overcome them in order to re-story them for others suffering in education in silence.

NOTES

1. The author's usage of White America throughout the chapter serves as a means of resistance to the erroneous "colorblind" ideological notion that all Americans are treated equally regardless of race, class, gender, sexual orientation, or religion refer to Twitter hashtags of #Kajuan-Raye, #KwadirFelton, #NabraHassanen, #SandraBland, #ChynaGibson
2. For more in-depth understanding of this cultural gem, please refer to the following hyperlink: https://en.wikipedia.org/wiki/A_Different_World/

REFERENCES

Adams, R. D., (2017). The lived experience of a Francophone speaking Louisiana Creole of color in Northeast Louisiana in an English speaking school system. *Multiple Voices for Ethnically Diverse Exceptional Learners, 7*(1), 13–14.

Carbado, D. W., & Roithmayr, D. (2014). Critical race theory meets social science. *Annual Review of Law and Social Science, 10,* 149–167.

Cokley, K., McClain, S., Enciso, A., & Martinez, M. (2013). An examination of the impact of minority status stress and impostor feelings on the mental health of diverse ethnic minority college students. *Journal of Multicultural Counseling and Development, 41*(2), 82–95.

DeCuir, J. T., & Dixson, A. D. (2004). "So when it comes out, they aren't that surprised that it is there": Using critical race theory as a tool of analysis of race and racism in education. *Educational Researcher, 33*(5), 26–31.

Delgado, R., & Stefancic, J. (2012). Critical race theory: An introduction. New York, NY: New York University Press.

Malagon, M. C., Huber, L. P., & Velez, V. N. (2009). Our experiences, our methods: Using grounded theory to inform a critical race theory methodology. *Seattle Journal for Social Justice, 8*(1), 10.

Muhammad K., Dunbar, C., & Douglas, T., (2013). "Derrick Bell, CRT, and educational leadership 1995–present," *Race Ethnicity and Education, 16* (4), 489–513. doi:10.1080/13613324.2013.817770

Solórzano, D. G., & Yosso, T. J. (2001a). Critical race and LatCrit theory and method: Counter- storytelling. *International Journal of Qualitative Studies in Education, 14*(4), 471–495.

Solórzano, D. G., & Yosso, T. J. (2001b). From racial stereotyping and deficit discourse toward a critical race theory in teacher education. *Multicultural Education, 9*(1), 2–8.

Solórzano, D. G., & Yosso, T. J. (2002). Critical race methodology: Counter-storytelling as an analytical framework for education research. *Qualitative inquiry, 8*(1), 23–44.

CHAPTER 27

THE EMANUEL CHURCH MASSACRE AND THE SCHOOL ACROSS THE STREET

A Black Man's Narrative of Two Racialized Conflicts

Nathaniel Bryan

Like the feelings many Black people convey during assaults on Black communities (Johnson & Bryan, 2016), the Emanuel Church Massacre[1] angered, traumatized, and confused me. On June 17, 2015, a 21-year-old armed White male, Dylann Roof, entered a predominantly Black historic church in the heart of downtown Charleston, South Carolina. Although I live in a different part of the state, Charleston is my home. Dylann worshipped with 12 church members including children who were attending a typical Wednesday night Bible study. After sitting through an entire hour-long worship service, he shot and killed nine of the 12 parishioners who had previously welcomed him that night with open arms.

Included among the victims were Rev. Clementa Pinckney, Mr. Tywanza Sanders, Mrs. Cynthia Hurd, Rev. Sharonda Coleman-Singleton, Mrs. Myra Thompson, Mrs. Ethel Lance, Rev. Daniel Simmons, Rev. DePayne Middleton-Doctor, and Mrs. Susie Jackson. The ages of the victims ranged from 26 to 87 years old. Similar to the works of Baker-Bell, Butler, and Johnson (2017) as they honored victims of anti-Black violence, I list these names to memorialize these victimized individuals. Two surviving members (Polly Sheppard and Felicia Sanders) of this horrific tragedy hid from Dylann and/or pretended to be dead. Polly Sheppard stated that Roof told her he would spare her so she could tell others about the tragedy.

As the tragedy unfolded, I could not avoid thinking about my experiences as a Black male assistant principal who worked in "the school across the street" from Emanuel African Methodist Episcopal Church between 2007–2009. Brunson Academy (pseudonym) is a predominantly White magnet school. My experiences were replete with racialized issues that produced what Baszile (2011) calls a "riot in my soul" or the "critical rant on race, rage, and ignorance" (p. 150). Now, I must carry the burden of both Emanuel church and Brunson Academy—two racialized narratives at the center of a place I call home. The purpose of this chapter is to not only to share my racialized experiences in "the school across the street," but also my reaction to the night I heard about the Emanuel church shooting to demonstrate the confluence of White racial violence against Black bodies, from the schoolhouse to the church house. To that end, what follows next are my stories written in my way.

THE NIGHT I HEARD ABOUT THE EMANUEL CHURCH MASSACRE

It was approximately 10:05 p.m. I simultaneously was sitting on my bed, looking at television, and perusing Facebook. Five minutes later, a news caption shot across the television scene that caught my attention like never before. "Mass shooting in downtown Charleston, South Carolina at Emanuel AME Church and mass shooter still on the loose." I was confused and became dumbfounded at the moment. I was trying to locate Emanuel AME Church in my mind. I had heard the name of the church so many times before but could not locate it at that juncture. It took me awhile to figure it out. All of a sudden, it came to me that it was the church across the street from Brunson Academy. I scrambled to dial numbers of family members in the area to alert them about what had just happened. Every number I dialed, there seemingly was no response. I called my mother. No response! Then, I called my sister. No response. I texted my brother because I knew he would not answer his phone. "Hey, I hope you are home...there is a mass shooter on the loose in the area." Three minutes later, he replied, "Yea, I know... I just saw the news and I am home." This came as a great relief because he often enjoys Charleston's downtown nightlife. I replied, "Ok, I am glad you are home."

The moment I concluded text messaging my brother, news updates flashed once again across the television screen. "Mass shooting in downtown Charleston... mass shooter on the loose... police are looking for a White male approximately 21 years old wearing a grey hoodie and Timberland boots." I thought to myself, "White male... what the heck is a White male doing at Emanuel this time of night..." I began to think about the recent gentrification of Charleston and considered that Emanuel may have diversified its church population.

Facebook posts from friends who were requesting prayers for loved ones who were suspected to be in the church interrupted my personal thoughts. Post after post contained biblical scriptures and encouraging words from those who sought to uplift worried individuals. My attention returned to the television. Local news media began to provide more information about what happened. "It is suspected that eight people have been shot!" I was becoming more worried. I thought, "Shot... My God... are there any survivors..." It was as if the news reporter read my mind. She responded, "The coroner is now on the scene and one person is being rushed to the hospital." I saw images of policemen and firefighters rushing to the aid of one victim while also trying to console family members who waited outside of the church to learn more about the status of their loved ones. A moving image of a young Black man (who is a friend of my family) with tears streaming down his face alerted me to the severity of what had happened.

I was glued to the television but could not stop hearing the Facebook chimes from my Samsung Galaxy III phone that alerted me of new posts. People began to post... "Eight people are dead, you all please pray!" My heart dropped. I could not believe what I was reading. Shortly thereafter, I read the tragic news from the television screen. The Facebook posts were confirmed. One news reporter said, "Eight people are confirmed dead... one is in critical condition at a local hospital." I could not believe what had happened in my hometown. I thought, "This couldn't be... we just got over the Walter Scott shooting... how much more can we bear..." Walter Scott, a 50-year old Black male, was shot in the back by a White male North Charleston police officer, Michael Slager.

Moments later, news reporters relayed that family members and other community members were being redirected to the Embassy Suites hotel that is in close proximity to the church. The same reporter indicated that bomb threats were being made which forced family members and others out of the hotel. At that same juncture, news arose that they had captured the accused shooter. I was finally relieved.

A few seconds later, I learned that they accosted the wrong guy. More information about the accused guy was being disseminated via news media. "A White male...wearing a grey hoodie, jeans, and Timberland boots is still on the loose. If you have any information, please dial your local police office."

Perplexed, I attempted once again to call family members who lived in close proximity. My phone rang several times....No response! I laid down and apparently fell asleep only to awake to morning news indicating nine people had died in the Emanuel shooting. I was debilitated. I was worried about the names that would soon be listed as victims. I grabbed my cellphone to check Facebook, which is a normal morning routine. Some Facebook friends started to post names and images of family members who had died in the tragedy. "Sleep well Senator and Rev. Pinckney!"..."RIP Auntie Susie!"..."Damn Wanza (Tywanza), we just spoke the other day!" I could not believe what I was seeing. I was in complete shock.

In the meantime, my mind kept going back and forth between the images of the church and the school I so fondly remembered. I re-envisioned being in my office at Brunson Academy where I tended to look out the window towards the church. This was a customary practice that brought solace to me when things were not going so well in the school across the street. I could always depend on those picturesque images of Emanuel AME Church and its stained-glass windows that lifted my downtrodden spirit. Those images were surely divine. Although I never had the opportunity to enter its doors, I knew it was a sacred place. I knew it was a place where Black people went because they needed peace from an unjust world. I became disheartened because it was that peace that was violated the night evil entered Emanuel church's doors.

Old wounds reopened and the concomitant pain brought back to mind the racialized agony I felt while working at Brunson Academy. My mind could not stop going back and forth between the church and the school. I started thinking about how I was going to write about these tragedies. I will never forget...

THE DAY I WAS CALLED A N-WORD:

It was a day within my fourth month on the job. It was a beautiful morning; the sun was shining, and the smell of a hot Southern breakfast consisting of grits, bacon, eggs, and biscuits emanated the cafeteria area where students congregated to eat before the bell rang to start classes. I stood in the cafeteria's doorway, monitoring to ensure the safety and well-being of the children, which were the expectations for teachers and administrators who were "on duty." This did not preclude me from enjoying breakfast myself.

During my assigned duty, it was customary for me to allow the children to intermingle as they moved from table to table interacting with their friends. I allowed them to engage as such because this was one of the only times that they were able to enjoy an unstructured moment as the school schedule was inundated with structured academic responsibilities with minimal time integrated for recess. It was a magnet school for gifted and talented students.

Amid their childhood exchanges, the noise level rose significantly among them, particularly among a group of Black children (the few who had attended the school). I was comfortable with the noise level; however, one of my White female colleagues, Mrs. Boxx, was not so happy about it at all. She was about 5'6" with long blond hair and pale White skin. She rudely approached me to discuss her concerns. With one hand placed on her hip and the other pointing directly towards the group of Black children in the corner, she exclaimed, "Dr. Bryan, don't you think the children are too loud...I have asked the group in the corner to settle down several times but they refused to listen to me. I think you need to say something to them!" I replied, "Mrs. Boxx, I think they are just fine. I think they are all just enjoying a little time together." Apparently frustrated, she uttered in a low voice, "I am tired of these niggers! I need you to do your job!" I immediately reported her to Sara, the school principal who was concerned. This was another racialized incident that I had to add to a list that I had already collected from my experiences "at the school across the street."

CONNECTING THE CHURCH AND THE SCHOOLHOUSE

The more I began to think about the racialized violence surrounding the Emanuel church massacre and the racial microaggressions I faced at the schoolhouse, the more I began to realize how much they were all interconnected. My critical race discernment or my spiritual third-eye helped me to not only see the undoing of Black bodies and spirits, but the emboldening of White supremacy that is pervasive in our schools and society at large. Woodson (1933/1990) contend that Black children learn to despise themselves in schools because of culturally unresponsive curricula which constructs Blackness from deficit perspectives. However, through the same curricula, White children, like Dylann Roof, come to despise Black people and as a result, carry out a lynching agenda, which starts in the school house. As a conclusion, recommendations are provided to support Black male administrators who work in predominantly White (magnet) schools.

RECOMMENDATIONS FOR CURRENT AND FUTURE BLACK MALE ADMINISTRATORS

1. Don't be afraid to stand up against racial injustice in predominantly White schools.
2. Find opportunities to engage in self-care to combat racial battle fatigue or the psychological duress associated with fighting against racial injustice.

NOTES

1. I do not refer to the attack as the tragedy of the Charleston 9 as most people suggest. I avoid using such expression because it seems to sanitize an unsanitary/unsanitized act of racial violence that is grounded in historical White terrorism against Black communities.

REFERENCES

Baker-Bell, A., Butler, T., Johnson, L. (2017). The pain and the wounds: A call for critical race English education in the wake of racial violence. *English Education, 49*(2), 116–129.

Baszile, D. T. (2011) Riot in my soul: A critical rant on race, rage, and the limits of formal education on these matters. In E. Malewski & N. Jaramillo (Eds.), Epistemologies of ignorance in education. Charlotte, NC: Information Age.

Johnson, L., & Bryan, N. (2017). Using our voices, losing our bodies: Michael Brown, Trayvon Martin, and the spirit murder of Black male professors in the academy. *Race Ethnicity, and Education, 20*(2), 163–177.

Woodson, C. G. (1990). *The mis-education of the negro.* Trenton, NJ: Africa World Press. (Originally published 1933)

CHAPTER 28

FROM HOPELESSNESS TO THE HALLWAYS OF HIGHER EDUCATION

Lawrence Scott

"Why am I still here..." This is the proverbial question that I continuously have to answer daily. Having grown up in a home in which drugs were used and sold, placed in handcuffs more than once, shot at, and having lost several of my friends due to senseless violence, I realize that I need daily confirmation of the existential meaning of my life. The purpose of this chapter is to illustrate how locating your purpose, developing an action plan, and remaining resilient, will solidify your desired success no matter the impediments.

While in elementary school, I lived a stable life. I was an A honor roll student, a part of a local church, Pop Warner football player, and a cub scout. When I was 9 years old, my parents divorced, and my life would change forever. Every year, I would rotate schools between my mother's home in Charlotte, North Carolina to my father's home in San Antonio, Texas. This situation would take an abrupt halt during my eighth grade year, when several students were shot during a gang shootout at my feeder high school.

My mom decided that she wanted me to attend a school called Victory Christian Center in Charlotte, North Carolina. that focused on discipline, leadership, spirituality, and academics. This decision would be a lifesaver as my father sold drugs out of the home and eventually became addicted to crack cocaine. This school helped me understand my purpose in life, which was far beyond the current lifestyle of drinking 40-ounce bottles and selling drugs. Even back then I knew my purpose was to provide equitable opportunities of success for those who grew up like me.

When I arrived in Charlotte to live, now 14 years old, my only plan was to survive. As a single mother, rearing two Black male teenagers, my mom did the best she could. Even though we had meager accommodations, I never felt underprivileged. My mom always instilled thankfulness (to God) in all things, and to always serve others. We didn't have furniture, so we ate, watched TV, and slept on the floor for about 8 months. I never stayed at home because my mother and older brother were always working as my older brother helped provide for the family. Once I came home, I would do my homework, then "go outside and play."

It took me no time to start walking the streets and playing basketball with the neighborhood drug dealers. The major difference was that I was going to a predominately African American church school that taught leadership through spirituality. While there was a sparse amount of Black male mentors in San Antonio, at this school, half the staff were strong, family-oriented, mission-minded, Godly Black men whose goal was to reach young men like me. This exposure provided a counterbalance to ubiquitous archetypes of disreputable Black men I would see in my neighborhoods in both San Antonio and Charlotte.

The paradigmatic shift occurred at 15 years old, when I met my English teacher and basketball coach, who would serve as one of the most influential persons in my life. Since my mom worked two jobs and she couldn't pick me up from school, Mr. Bego would take me home from basketball practice. He would talk to me about life, and how to envision and plan out strategies of success. This was the first time I personally encountered a family man that looked like me, had several degrees, was published, and with a love for God and a mission to serve students. During his classes, he would make us complete 2-year, 5-year, and 10-year goal sheets. He would guide us through introspective exercises that would anticipate obstacles. He knew that even the best plans will be tried by the fire of the process. Having Mr. Bego in my life gave me a roadmap to success, but didn't necessarily insulate me from extrinsic negative forces that would plague my latter high school and early college years.

At 17 years old, the summer before my first year of college, I dealt heavily with racial profiling. I was fired from a job that I had for over 3 years because some waitresses said I was stealing their tips. Unfortunately, at the time, I didn't have the linguistic tools or social capital to address the disproportionate institutionalized marginalization and disempowerment that certain enforcement officers practiced. During this summer, some friends and I were hanging out at an apartment complex after playing a few games of basketball. After about 20 minutes, around seven cop cars and 10 cops came around the corner and ordered us on the ground. At the time, I was not worried since we didn't do anything wrong. We were then handcuffed and placed on our knees as they searched us. After about 12 minutes of questioning and intermittent derogatory statements about the way we were dressed, we were released. When I asked them why they did this to us, one of the officers replied, "You fit the description of people who have been breaking into several apartments this week." I was devastated that this could happen in the land of the *free*. This systemic oppression began to crush my confidence and I started doubting my life's contribution. As I became older, I began to read about Martin Luther King, Malcolm X, and others who were on a path of resistance and their resilience recalibrated their mission. Most notable, my faith in God helped me persist beyond the resistance.

Now at 18 years old, my freshman year in college, I thought I was able to escape the malaise that plagued my teenage years. I was one of few Black males that lived on campus. One night as my friends and I were walking towards campus, one of the campus officers pulled us over. He checked our IDs and mentioned that we were stopped because we were jaywalking. After we proceeded to tell him we were students at the university, he ended this interaction with, "I got my eyes on you." Again, I was completely flabbergasted that even on a college campus this type of profiling existed. A month later, I decided to hang out with one of my friends, Mike from my old neighborhood. While arriving on campus, the police stopped us for failure to use the turn signal. We were ordered to get out of the car. This time, I knew I was going to jail because there were drugs, alcohol, and weapons in the car. They searched the car and found the contraband they were looking for the whole time. Being the man he was, Mike said:

> Larry, you are in college and doing something with your life. I will tell them that everything is mine and you were not aware of anything when you stepped in the car.

His sacrifice changed the course of both of our lives. When he was released, he enlisted and did a successful 8-year stint in the U.S. Marine Corps. He then started a lucrative job in the oil fields in Texas and is doing well with his new family. Since that day, we have intermittently kept in touch, as I thank him profusely for his sacrifice. We both knew that what he did that night ushered in a passion and purpose that was bigger than the both of us. Every time I give a speech, I talk about Mike and how his desire to make sure I pursued my dreams was another impetus to keep pushing for other young Black boys that are facing their giants.

Despite the fact that I was homeless at a time after this occurrence (lived with my pastor, Pastor Keith Graham), faced several deaths of others close friends and family members including my grandparents who helped rear me, I always knew that there was a greater purpose for living and I wanted to live out the legacy of those who sacrificed for me. Living by the *purpose, plan,* and *process* principles helped me give back in ways unimaginable. Now as an assistant professor in educational leadership at a 4-year university, and an executive director over a nonprofit which has given over half a million dollars in scholarships since its inception, I can now be a role model and conduit to others who grew up like me. To start your journey of finding your purpose, you must ask this basic, but complex question: "Why are you here..." God created you for a reason! Once you have established your "Why," create a plan that is measurable, dated, specific, and feasible. For instance, a statement in my plan said, "By Fall of 2001, I will secure a job as a teacher in San Antonio ISD and begin my master's degree in counseling."

Lastly, you have to understand that achieving your goals is a process. You will experience many hardships but take solace in knowing that this is all a part of the process. Build momentum by celebrating the small victories with those who helped you succeed. A series of small victories lead to a victorious life. Also, find mentors who have achieved your desired goals, and make them a significant part of your social network and cadre of counselors. Mentors will help you stay cognizant that trials are temporal and will only improve your story of resilience. Furthermore, to win in life, put yourself in uncomfortable situations that will force you to grow (disequilibrium). For me, that was vying for leadership positions throughout high school and college.

Finally, and most importantly, to win in this life, *never give up*! I vividly recall asking my girlfriend to marry me on the Eiffel Tower in Paris, and she said "no." She said "yes" 7 months later and we have been married for over 14 years. Plans may change, but your purpose will remain the same, despite incessant rejection. Never giving up, my dad has assumed his role as my father and he is an amazing grandfather to our children. Living with these principles of finding my purpose, creating a plan of action, and going through the process helped me transition from being hopeless in the *hood*, to navigating the hallways of higher learning and allowing me to give back in ways I could have never imagined.

DEDICATION

This chapter is dedicated to the memory of Damontre Pamilton, Shomari Lewis, Joshua Vargas, and Willie Ruth, and Johnny Scott.

CHAPTER 29

TO LEAVE OR NOT TO LEAVE

That Was My Contemplation

Jamel Miller

I am currently a PhD candidate at Midwestern University or MU (a pseudonym), a predominantly White institution of higher education (PWI). I am a Black man who is the father of a daughter and two sons. I entered MU when I was 29 years old, making me a nontraditional student with major responsibilities. MU is the third PWI that I have attended in my postsecondary career. The first two colleges I attended were in the South where the local and college demographics were more diverse compared to MU. I highlight this distinction because it is important to contextualize my experiences in relation to these institutions. Based on my experiences from all three schools, I have realized how racism manifests itself as well as the ways racism impacts me as a Black man. Therefore, I have a story to tell. Sharing my counter narratives about my own school experiences is inspired by critical race theory's (CRT) imperative to expose racism and challenge dominant ideology (Solórzano & Yosso, 2002), particularly as it relates to Black males, so that my stories may empower them to succeed. In this chapter, I do not pretend to be neutral or colorblind. I want other Black males to know that encounters with racism are inevitable. I believe that informing them of my past experiences can prepare them with distinctive insight, skills, and strategies to navigate racism. Though I cannot predict the manner in which racism will occur for other Black men, I do believe that sharing stories regarding race and racism offer nuggets of information useful for defeating racism.

Research has documented the experiences of Black students at PWIs, particularly, revealing their daily experiences with racism (Von Robertson & Chaney, 2017). Harper's (2009) article entitled Niggers No More: A Critical Race Counternarrative on Black Male Student Achievement at Predominantly White Colleges and Universities highlighted how Black students, particularly Black males at PWIs constantly endure a process of dehumanization. Further, it is important to know, discuss, and address these negative school experiences because they are detrimental to personal well-being and academic success (Von Robertson & Chaney, 2017). Though it appears to be no panacea for curing racism, I am writing this chapter to offer my recommendations which could help Black males navigate hostile and racist environments. Therefore, in the ensuing sections, I tell my story through a series of racial vignettes that detail my experiences being a victim of race and racism on a predominantly White college campus. In conclusion, I offer recommendations for Black males who may be victims of race and racism and find themselves in similar contexts and situations.

OVERT RACISM IS NOT A THING OF THE PAST: PURSUING EDUCATION WHILE BLACK

I did not encounter much overt racism in my undergraduate and first graduate school experiences. The graduate school experiences that I will be speaking on in this chapter include only my experiences at MU. I argue that the higher number of Black and Brown students enrolled at my undergraduate and first graduate institution played a role in minimizing overt acts of racism from peers and staff. Reflecting back, I feel that the perpetrators (college peers and faculty) of racism were less inclined to commit overt acts of racism because there was a higher presence of Black and Brown bodies. I say this because in general when a group of people are not marginalized, they have the numbers and power to resist.

Additionally, my non-collegiate priorities barred me from hanging around on campus as much as traditional students. My priorities included working jobs so that I could earn money not only to pay for costs associated with school but also to take care of my children sufficiently. Hence, I was a full-time father and student. Despite my nontraditional status, I was not immune to racism. I frequently experienced racial microaggressions from school peers, faculty, and staff. Through the various microaggressions, I found out that many of my White peers and faculty held a deficit view of Black men. However, they spoke positively of Black males who played sports or were affiliated with an organization.

I GUESS ALL BLACK MEN LOVE BASKETBALL

My first time being racially profiled in an institutional setting and called nigger was on MU's campus. One incident involved a campus police officer. In this incident, a male friend (who is Black) and I left the gym. We got into my car to drive back to our apartments. My friend and I saw a police officer before we got into my car and noticed him watching us the whole time. I knew that my license, registration, and tag were valid, so I really did not think I had anything to worry about. However, I was wrong. I fastened my seat belt and proceeded to drive following the speed limit. As I drove off the officer followed us for about one mile. Finally, he turned his lights on and pulled us over. He walked up and asked for my driver's license. I asked him, "Why was I pulled over..." He replied that I did not have my seat belt fastened. That was a lie. I had seen him watching us before I got into my car, so I made sure to follow the laws. Consequently, my seat belt was fastened. I asked him if was he suggesting that my seat belt was off... He said, "No. I see that you have it on now." I asked him why he needed to see my license considering that he acknowledged that my seat belt was fastened... He replied that he had the right to ask me anything he wanted, especially knowing that locals frequent the gym to play basketball. He assumed that we were not students but males who frequented campus just to play basketball. My friend in the passenger seat recorded the entire stop on his cell phone. I mentioned to the officer that my friend had recorded the stop with the cop's acknowledgment of the unlawful stop after I had confirmed that my seat belt was fastened. Further, I told him that he never asked if we were students but that he had no problems implying/stereotyping that we might have been Black locals shooting basketball. Even if we were, locals are permitted to utilize the gym with a pass. Therefore, his assumption confirmed that we were racially profiled, and I told him that I would not give him my identification. Once he found out that we had the stop recorded, he tried to walk back his statements. He mentioned that he did not mean to profile us, so he let us leave. That was problematic because we were not only racially profiled, but his comment "he did not mean it like that" is indicative of more troubling, deeply ingrained, racist, and stereotypical beliefs about Black men.

HIGHER EDUCATION DOES NOT MAKE BLACKS IMMUNE TO BEING CALLED A NIGGER

One day after class I got into my car leaving to go home. On my way home, I stopped for a red light. While waiting for the light to turn green, two White males pulled up in a small pickup truck. I was in the right lane and they were in the left lane. While stopped I noticed the two laughing, looking around and giggling, and demonstrating immature behaviors. Suddenly, the guy on the passenger side signaled for me to roll down my window. I did because I thought he was going to tell me something about my tire. As soon as I rolled my window down, the light turned green, and they both yelled "stupid nigger" and sped off. I was fuming, mad, and frustrated. However, there was nothing I could do about it. So, I proceeded home.

THE LONELY JOURNEY

My experiences have exposed me and taught me how to identify, circumvent, and navigate racism. However, I am not necessarily prepared for the next overt or subtle act of racism. I have experienced overt and subtle racism in academic classrooms and social atmospheres. I have experienced and witnessed racial microaggressions daily. Racial microaggressions are "unconscious and subtle forms of racism that often go unnoticed when juxtaposed with more visceral, overt expressions of racial animus" (Von Robertson & Chaney, 2017, p. 261). For example, in many of my past classes I was the only Black male. I was often seen as the radical one and a representative of the Black community and its issues. In my classes, I appeared to be the only one interested in Black literature, overlooked for group work, or the last to be asked for my input. For Black males, being marginalized on a predominantly White college campus is not anything new, akin to not having many Black professors. In my experiences, this has been consistent—I have not had any Black professors in my graduate school experiences. What is more disheartening is that in my graduate school experiences at MU, when I thought I had found Black professors who would (or could) serve as mentors, offer insight on navigating racism, dedicate the time, patience, and leadership to help me develop into a quality researcher and educator, this turned out not to be the case. Although I am matriculating towards graduation, I have not enjoyed my college career—not because I doubted my intellectual ability; rather, I felt that the environment was unsafe, unwelcoming, and not inclusive. The title of this chapter, *To Leave or Not to Leave: That Was My Contemplation*, characterizes my personal battle of constantly negotiating whether I wanted to complete my higher education degree at

MU due to my experiences. The next section discusses recommendations for Black males to matriculate successfully to graduation.

TAKE HEED TO THE RECOMMENDATIONS OF INSIDERS

The following is my list of recommendations (though not exhaustive) for navigating a hostile and racist college environment. One of the first things I believe is essential to Black perseverance is for Black males to change and control the narrative about them. I believe that this entails that Black males establish a strong sense of self, healthy respect, and love for themselves and other men of color. In addition, I encourage Black males to learn as much as possible about the college they will attend so that they will have a better understanding of the campus climate. Because we live in a society that constantly diminishes the worth, positive images, and aspirations of Black men, we must not compromise who we are as strong people who have survived extreme racial oppression. We are living proof of what can happen when we love ourselves and aspire. Knowing who we are and where we have come from is a testament of our fortitude. Therefore, we must continue to share our counter stories that disrupt deficit narratives about us. For Black people, the use of counter stories has always served as conduits for revolutionary liberation (Baszile, 2014). Through our stories, we can accomplish self and community love. We must continue our work to eradicate racism as well as highlight Black contributions to society.

REFERENCES

Baszile, D. T. (2015). Rhetorical revolution: Critical race counter storytelling and the abolition of White democracy. *Qualitative Inquiry, 21*(3), 239–249.

Harper, S. R. (2009). Niggers no more: A critical race counternarrative on Black male student achievement at predominantly White colleges and universities. *International Journal of Qualitative Studies in Education, 22*(6), 697–712.

Solórzano, D. G., & Yosso, T. J. (2002). Critical race methodology: Counter-storytelling as an analytical framework for education research. *Qualitative Inquiry, 8*(1), 23–44.

Von Robertson, R., & Chaney, C. (2017). "I know it [racism] still exists here:" African American males at a predominantly White institution. *Humboldt Journal of Social Relations, 39*, 260–282.

SECTION IV

OVERCOMING NARRATIVES OF FAILURE

Men of color have inherited a society designed so that they would fail. In other words, institutional inequities have attempted to hinder the plight of many men of color. As mentioned in the introduction of this book, men of color are what Upchurch (1997) referred to as being "convicted in the womb." In other words, chances for upward mobility have been stymied by an educational system that was not designed to meet their academic and social needs (Warren, 2017), an economic system built on efforts to keep them "at the bottom of the well" or in the lowest socioeconomic brackets in society, and a justice system designed to create a pipeline of men of color who become trapped in both school-to-prison and prison pipelines (Alexander, 2010; Curry, 2017). Curry (2017) acknowledges that system of failure are intentional in a society where men of color, Black men in particular, are constructed as threats to White people's existence.

However, despite these institutional inequities, many men of color have overcome systems designed to entrap them and narratives of failures. In Section IV, we highlight the narratives of men of color who were courageous in naming systems of inequities that were designed to ensure their failure. What was most powerful about these narratives, stories, and counter narratives were their personal and collective will to fight and pushback against these systems to demonstrate their will to overcome. In most cases, these Men developed personal strategies and sought out macro and micro-level support systems to ensure they did not become victims but instead victors despite their circumstances. It is prudent to suggest that while some men of color have overcome inequitable systems, this idea does not suggest that all men of color have overcome. We have not overcome until all men of color overcome. There is still much work to do to tear down systems of failure that continue to plague the lives and livelihood of men of color in the United States.

REFERENCES

Alexander, M. (2010). *The new Jim Crow: Mass incarceration in the age of colorblindness.* New York, NY: The New Press.

Curry, W. (2017). *Man-not: Race, class, genre, and the dilemmas of Black manhood.* Philadelphia, PA. Temple University Press.

Upchurch, C. (1997). *Convicted in the womb: One man's journey from prisoner to peacemaker.* New York, NY: Bantam Books.

Warren, C. (2017). *Urban Preparation: Young Black men moving from Chicago's Southside to success in higher education.* Cambridge, MA: Harvard Education Press.

CHAPTER 30

BECOMING THE VICTOR

Victor L. Powell

At 4:14 p.m. on Tuesday, April 6, 1982 the temperature was about 37°F when my mother and father welcomed me into this world. Being born at Methodist Evangelical Hospital in Louisville, Kentucky forever connected me to the roots of my Bluegrass State. The first few hours of my life, were some of the scariest moments for my parents because I was not breathing and had complications that quickly needed attention from the hospital staff. As a result of my challenging beginning, my Vietnam War Veteran father chose to name me Victor; an overcomer of life's early obstacles. Leon was given from my Birmingham-native mother. From day one, I've proudly adorned Victor Leon Powell like a tailored-made suit.

Growing up straddling the Mason-Dixon line of the Ohio River, race and discrimination lingered throughout my childhood. These evils of old showed themselves in the redlining of neighborhoods in Southern Indiana and the Louisville Metro area, and in the ever-present Confederate flags prominently displayed on the bumpers of cars, on the front lawns, and proudly worn on the shirts of local citizens in the mall.

My home base was a small suburb called Jeffersonville, Indiana, nestled closely to the Ohio River's edge. The small town outside of Louisville was home to only 21,000 people, a population that has more than doubled since that time. In 1982, the city of Louisville, my backyard across the river, was home to about 690,000 people, most of whom I was related to by blood or other personal or professional affiliation. Growing up in a large family, I regularly encountered people who knew my brothers, parents, or our extended network of family and friends. The youngest of three boys, I often was called "Lil' Powell" or "William and Linda Powell's boy." This wasn't a major issue to me; but it did spur me to make a name for myself and blaze my own trail.

BECOMING A VICTOR: THE ELEMENTARY YEARS

Riverside Elementary School is where my early childhood education took place and where many lasting memories were created. A product of the standardized testing era, I came to know Indiana's version, the Indiana Statewide Testing for Educational Progress (ISTEP), all too well. In all my attempts, I never earned a passing score on the reading or writing sections of the assessment. This triggered insecurities about my abilities in these areas throughout my educational experience. Perhaps the most significant event of my elementary experience was being retained in second grade due to my poor reading and comprehension skills. On the other hand, it highlighted my positive performance in mathematics, art, and physical education. While other students were earning praise for reading through our Book It program, which encouraged reading by rewarding with Pizza Hut® coupons, I was receiving positive affirmation from physical education and art teachers, memories I still cherish today. As detailed by author of *The Five Love Languages: How to Express Heartfelt Commitment to Your Mate*, Gary Chapman, (2009) there is power in words of affirmation. Recognizing that this has been my primary love language since elementary school, I have realized the importance of knowing how to target my areas of growth and remain aware of how I receive and relay information.

My anxiety related to standardized testing and education, in general, continued throughout junior high and high school. But my strategy for combating tests and the metaphorical brick walls in my life was to never stop trying. As a child of the 1980s, I learned from the popular movie, *The Goonies*, that "Goonies never say die" (Bernhard & Donner, 1985). As a result, I was the student who studied Chemistry for hours and was excited to earn a D– because failing was not an option. To some, such a grade would have been unacceptable and met with criticism. But my parents valued how hard I worked on a challenging subject and this shaped my character. It developed the character of a man who has been an educator for more than 12 years.

> *If there is no struggle, there is no progress.*
> —Frederick Douglass

BECOMING A VICTOR: THE HIGH SCHOOL YEARS

High school taught me the value of social capital and the importance of treating everyone with dignity and respect. As an athlete, I realized that my actions on the basketball court, conversations with teachers, and interactions with underclassmen were being watched by people I knew and those I did not. On the court, my head coach taught me how my ability to control my rage and emotions under pressure was valuable to me, our team, and our school at large. Recognizing my connectedness to the larger group helped me to channel my energy and develop coping strategies on the public stage of the basketball court.

Like basketball, the classroom became a competitive stage. Given academics weren't always my strength; my actions were often calculated and purposeful. When I spoke, I tended to quote my peers and teachers rather than the voices in the text. Why... I learned more when there was quality classroom dialogue instead of student silencing lectures. I also believe I learned to offer others the gift of affirmation when using their thoughts to highlight an important point within the context of an exciting classroom discussion. Not realizing it then, but my auditory learning style caused me to remember information in the long-term, which was critical to my incline towards academic achievement.

The importance of how I treated others wasn't crystallized until my collegiate years. Through the mode of the day, AOL Instant Messenger, out of the blue, a young man who was a freshman when I was a senior in high school contacted me. He said, "I don't know if you remember me, but when we were in school I looked up to you. I watched how you treated me and the girls in our school. I noticed all those things and wanted to pattern myself after you." As I read his words, it humbled me and caused me to be thankful for attempting to treat others around me how I wanted to be treated. Further, we never know who is watching us and what they are taking from our walk in this life. I could have easily led this young man down the wrong path, but because of my relationship with Christ and the Holy Spirit, who directs me, this young man didn't see me, but God operating in me.

BECOMING A VICTOR: THE COLLEGE YEARS

Anderson University (AU) was the training facility for sharpening my blades of grit and perseverance. Because my parents allowed me to go on all of my basketball recruiting visits alone, I was able to see coaches' and universities' true motivations and what they really thought of the time I would spend on their respective campuses. I made the decision to commit to AU, in large part because of the words of my head coach:

> Victor, I know other schools have promised you this and that. I am not going to do that. You have to earn your playing time here. What I can promise is that we will give you the support to graduate and that we will help you grow as a young man.

In choosing AU, a private Christian college in Anderson, Indiana, I turned down full scholarships to multiple Division II, Junior College, and National Association of Intercollegiate Athletics (NAIA) universities, but I gained so much more.

One of my first lessons in grit was on the hardwood of O. C. Lewis gymnasium. As a freshman, this was my chance to show my new teammates my tenacity and determination of character, my basketball skill set, and my work ethic. My goal was to have my teammates and coaches make statements about me similar to how Elgin Baylor spoke of my favorite player, Kevin Garnett:

> When I first saw him, he had the best athletic skills for his size of anyone I had ever seen at that stage. He's really thin, but it doesn't matter. With his agility and coordination, he can give people trouble at the power forward, small forward and center positions.

For each drill, I wanted to be first. I had to win every line sprint, and no one was going to play harder at defense than me. In all the small things, I made it my mission to shine. Although it wasn't easy my hard work paid off. By the time my first fall practice began, I had proven to my teammates that I was the premier defender, even as a freshman. It offered me a spot in starting lineup from time to time; gained me more playing time; and respect from the team, all of which built my confidence as a young man.

Academically, AU trained me to never stop pushing for my goals and dreams. My *training day* metaphor, was brought to life when my grade point average did not allow me to remain a Mathematics major; when I sought to transfer because I didn't see others who looked like me; or when I made it to my final semester and received an email from the administration explaining I was one credit short of graduating with less than 8 weeks left in school. These circumstances brought that young boy from Louisville to choose who I was going to be in the face of hardship. The meaningful relationship I had built with my mathematics advisor, who suggested I continue on within education, and the personal bond that developed with the university registrar, who vouched for me when my credit proposal was sent to the university advisory committee, gave me what I needed to continue on. Their support allowed me to maintain a focused attitude when things were hopeless and gave me the strength to face the storms that came my way.

A Victor was who I was predestined to be. A Victor is who I am becoming.

4 RECOMMENDATIONS ON BECOMING THE VICTOR

1. Understanding the setting in which you came to be
2. Developing resilience
3. Embracing social capital and discourse and respect
4. Remaining focused through the storms of life

REFERENCES

Bernhard, H. (Producer), & Donner, R. (Director/Producer). (1985). *The Goonies* [Motion Picture]. United States: Warner Brothers.

Chapman, G. (2009). *The five love languages: How to express heartfelt commitment to your mate.* Chicgo, IL: Moody.

CHAPTER 31

OVERCOMING THE OBSTACLES AND BREAKING THE BARRIERS

Jeremiah N. Taylor

I was born and raised as an only child to my mother in Galveston, Texas. I had many struggles academically as I progressed through school. My mother a well-educated professional woman, was constantly looking for ways to improve my reading comprehension and mathematical skills, but her efforts were met with little improvement and results. Teachers requested to retain me, because I showed a lack of improvement in regards to state standardized testing. My mother would refuse to retain me, because she felt that I was not motivated and just refused to apply myself. Therefore, summer school and my mother's summer workbooks were endless. I was repeatedly chastised for simply confusing the letter "P" and the number "9," the letters "b" and "d," even confusing nickels and dimes.

By the time I made it to high school and began to score low on ACT/SAT testing, my mother realized that I desired to do well, but there were barriers that would not allow me to be successful. It took me three times to pass college entrance exams, but ultimately I was able to take college

(Dual) credit courses my senior year along with emergency medical technician (EMT) courses. I excelled in all social studies and EMT coursework. This really confused my mother, because I was so strong in so many areas, but very weak in others.

I quickly realized that I needed to resolve my academic issues if I planned on going to college. With no other choice, my mom went to a psychologist and had me tested for learning disabilities. The results revealed that I had dyslexia, mild dyscalculia and attention deficit disorder (ADD). The psychologist explained that in order to be successful, I would require accommodations both in the classroom and during any type of testing. By the time I was diagnosed with learning disabilities, I was preparing for my first year in a community college. As soon as I enrolled as a nursing major, I went to the student services department and immediately turned in my files for accommodations. I was allowed accommodations such as, extended time on tests/assignments, calculator for math related classes, and audio recorders for lectures. During my first year of college, I realized that I must be my own advocate, if I expected to receive accommodations and assistance as a college student and young adult.

Once a student has made the college aware of their disabilities, it is illegal for a college to deny accommodations. Through the civil rights statues of the Rehabilitation Act of 1973 and the Americans with Disabilities Act (ADA) of 1990, federal law prevents college institutions from exposing students with disabilities to discriminatory acts. The purpose of Section 504 in the Rehabilitation Act of 1973, is to protect individuals with disabilities from discrimination for reasons related to their disabilities. The ADA broadened the agencies and businesses that must comply with the nondiscrimination and accessibility provisions of the law (U.S. Department of Education, 2017).

The task of getting accommodations in college may seem simple, but it is very challenging. As a transitioning student from secondary school, I was told to just turn in my files once in college and all would go smoothly, but I was met with questions from faculty as to why I required special privileges. At times, I noticed that Caucasian students were treated with more responsiveness, but as an African American male I was treated as if I was looking for an easy way out of working as hard as my peers. It is unfortunate that many postsecondary faculty members have little to no experience teaching students with disabilities (Yuen & Shaughnessy, 2001). Faculty and staff tend to be willing to make accommodations for students with physical or sensory disabilities but are not as willing to provide accommodations for students with disabilities that are not visible, such as emotionally disturbed (ED) or learning disabilities (LD) (Aksamit, Morris, & Leuenberger, 1987; Vogel, Leyser, Wyland, & Brulle, 1999).

I quickly graduated with a 3.1 GPA and an Associate of Arts degree. Finally, it was time for me to apply to nursing school. I chose to apply to the College of Nursing at an HBCU (Historically Black Colleges and Universities). While waiting to be accepted, I submitted my disability/accommodation files. Days later I received a call from the director of student services at the university who was African American, but apparently not orientated to ADA laws. She stated that she reviewed my files and saw that I have met the minimum requirements for the college of nursing, but there was no way I could be successful in the program given my long list of disabilities. The director went even further to say that if I'm interested in the medical field, I should consider a vocational option; such as "medical records." Not realizing that the director of student services had basically broken the law, I felt so angry, inferior, and discouraged.

From that point on I decided to never submit my files requesting for accommodations ever again. I decided that I was going to be successful and make it my mission to obtain a bachelor's degree and I started to advocate for students who struggle academically. I decided that if I was going to do this with no accommodations, I needed to have a strong relationship with God and be around encouraging people. Therefore, my mother recommended her alma mater where she received her master's degree, LeTourneau University in Longview, Texas. LeTourneau is a private Christian university that required biblical based classes. This was just what I needed in order to stay encouraged while in school. My mother and I went to the admissions office and submitted an application to the school of interdisciplinary studies (education). Within a week I was accepted and given a schedule. Five days later my mother passed unexpectedly and Hurricane Ike hit Galveston on the day that was supposed to be her funeral. Galveston was declared a national disaster site. I was forced to have my mother's funeral and burial while being banned from Galveston. The next week after finally having my mother's funeral, I was scheduled to start my first day of class at LeTourneau University. Initially I was going to just not go and eventually drop out, but I thought about how proud my mother was when she enrolled me, and I knew that I was not going to let that be in vain. The first day of school I stepped off the elevator, turned right and saw my mother's class picture displayed on the wall. At the bottom of the picture there was a scripture; "'For I know the plans I have for you,' declares the Lord, 'plans to prosper you and not to harm you, plans to give you hope and a future'" (Jeremiah 29:11, NIV). After that first day, it was routine for me to walk off the elevator, turn right, look at my mother's class picture, and read that scripture before class. I continued to do that for 2 years until my graduation. Looking back, the 2 years at LeTourneau went by very fast which solidified that being an education major was not going to be a career but a calling from God. As a student with dyslexia, dyscalculia, and ADD; I graduated Magna Cum Laude. I went on to pass two teacher certification tests to teach all subjects fourth through eighth grades. Yes, as a teacher with dyscalculia, I'm certified to teach mathematics.

Following my graduation, one of the greatest moments in my life happened when I submitted a letter to the student services director and the president of the HBCU regarding the student services director's discouraging words. Along with the letter I submitted my degree and a graduation picture. I went on to become, Teacher of the Year (for best practices), Galveston Academic Booster Club Honoree for 3 years, "Slice Above" Teacher of the Year by Galveston Chamber of Commerce for 2 years, and 2016 African American Image Award for Education. After teaching a little over 2 years, I realized that there were many African American children who had been misdiagnosed with disabilities. Additionally, I noticed the unfair and incompetent management of children with disabilities.

Therefore, I decided to attend Houston Baptist University to obtain a Master of Education specializing as an educational diagnostician. With this degree I'm able to test and diagnose children with disabilities and make recommendations for student success in the classroom.

In order to overcome, I had to put my faith in God and not in accommodations in regards to success. My rough start in academics has become the foundation of my career and calling as an educator. Having a learning disability does not mean that you are inferior or will always be illiterate. A person with a learning disability just learns differently compared to their peers. Once a person with disabilities has discovered how or what allows them to learn, the sky's the limit. In order to be successful, I did the following:

1. Gained knowledge about my learning barriers/disabilities and proven research-based recommendations for success. It's important to know how learning disabilities affect your learning in a class or during homework, studying, in class assignments, and exams.
2. Had a vision and goal to obtain.
3. I became my own advocate. I did this by knowing myself well enough to know what I needed in order to be successful.
4. Got an accountability partner or mentor. By having a partner or mentor, I had someone to keep me focused, and learned how to socialize with others through collaboration.
5. Most importantly, I stayed spiritually grounded, and listened to my calling by allowing God to direct me.

Today I am a doctoral candidate who continues to advocate for children in and outside the classroom. My personal mission statement is, "I will be an exceptional husband, father, mentor, and servant. I will invest in my future at all times by inspiring and enhancing all children holistically beyond the classroom." This mission statement is in my classroom and my home office. My mission statement serves as a vision and goal that we all should forever strive to achieve as professional Christians in this challenging world.

REFERENCES

Aksamit, K., Morris, M., & Leuenberger, J. (1987). Preparation of student service professionals and faculty for serving learning disabled college students. *Journal of College Student Personnel, 28,* 53–59.

U.S. Department of Education. (2017). *Protecting Students With Disabilities.* Retrieved from https://www2.ed.gov/about/offices/list/ocr/504faq.html

Vogel, S., Leyser, Y., Wyland, S., & Brulle, A. (1999). Students with learning disabilities in higher education: Faculty attitude and practices. *Learning Disabilities Research & Practice, 13*(3), 173–186.

Yuen, J., & Shaughnessy, B. (2001). Cultural empowerment: Tools to engage and retain postsecondary students with disabilities. *Journal of Vocational Rehabilitation, 16*(3, 4), 199–207.

CHAPTER 32

MAN ENOUGH TO ASK FOR HELP

Overcoming a Learning Disability and Family Issues

David C. Hughes

It all started in Beaumont Texas—the least educated major U.S. city according to the 2014 Wallet Hub study (Wermund, 2014). Albeit Beaumont's lack of education, I was born while my parents where in college. At 6 years old, burying my father was the beginning of my plight. Growing up in a single parent household, navigating school with severe dyslexia, and dodging society's target on my back as an African American male were a few struggles I had to overcome. This is my story of how I overcame by asking for help.

Thirteen months after my grandmother's passing, my father passed away due to an asthma attack while supervising his Boy Scouts in the California Mountains. And soon after my father's passing, the last member of my paternal family—my father's uncle—passed as well. Witnessing so much death by age 7 triggered depression, suicidal thoughts, and anger on the inside. I felt so alone, and it was only my mother who recognized these new

Gumbo for the Soul, pages 169–172
Copyright © 2019 by Information Age Publishing
All rights of reproduction in any form reserved.

emotions I felt. Without realizing it, my mother instilled the "culture of asking for help" in me by placing me in counseling at our home church. Without my mother asking for help, I dare say I would never have been able to sort through my issues.

From first grade to fifth grade, I attended four different elementary schools in two different cities. Despite changing schools frequently, my mother's teaching background made her a stickler for making sure I kept up with my schoolwork. Going into the sixth grade two things happened that would forever impact my life—my mother's second marriage and my dyslexia diagnosis. Despite my mother being a stickler, I constantly struggled with schoolwork due to a learning disability. Shortly after my mother's marriage began, her new husband became abusive. Looking to escape the abusive environment, we moved in and out of women's shelters over a 2-year period.

Ironically, these shelters symbolized both pain and passion in my life. The shelter is where I found my passion for sports. This passion—of which I had no idea at the time—would help me find my purpose in life. During private counseling sessions, it was suggested I use football as an outlet for my anger. Like my late father, my outlet became football. This was the perfect sport for me as it taught me discipline, teamwork, and allowed me to physically release my frustrations without getting into trouble. In retrospect, football was the best thing for my career as a former Sport Management University Lecturer and a Corporate Development Associate in the NFL.

My counseling sessions birthed my interest in sports. I ended up working for an NFL team after I graduated from college. Interestingly, the thought of playing football and my passion for it would have never crossed my mind unless my mother asked for help and insisted on counseling. Her advocacy on my behalf helped me find my passion.

Though my mother was my biggest advocate growing up, at times I felt she sided against me. She sided against me in one specific circumstance—my stepfather. My stepfather and I never got along and at a young age I would stand up to him when he tried to disrespect my mother. My mother, however, would often side with him after I stood up for her. The final straw in my stepfather's and my relationship was when two of his family members jumped my mother. To this day (over 15 years) he has never apologized to me nor spoken to me about it. The disconnect my mother and I had because of my stepfather reignited the very anger she advocated for me to receive help for.

My home life dysfunction caused my middle school years to be filled with anger. I willingly fought anyone—friend or foe—who even thought about disrespecting me. For example, from 6th–8th grade, I got into four fights just on campus. My anger in school occurred because I felt so helpless in my abusive home trying to defend my mother from my stepfather and his family.

Due to my dyslexia, I had to spend more time studying than all my peers. I had to re-read my assignments multiple times in order to get a good understanding. Interestingly, the elongated study time kept my mind off of my home situation and kept me out of trouble. Because I had to spend much longer studying I ended up with a better understanding of coursework than my peers and outperformed them academically. As a result, I was able to get accepted into Morehouse College.

The 2 months prior to beginning my matriculation at Morehouse College, my parent's house was foreclosed during the subprime mortgage crisis. As a result, I went to college homeless and had lost every possession I ever owned—including my late father's possessions. Starting over for me was difficult, but necessary, because I had nothing else but my mother.

Even though my mother was legally married, she was my only source of support. As most married couples do, my mother filed joint taxes with her husband. However, my mother did not work at the time I went off to college and her husband made too much money for me to qualify for Federal Student Aid. Yet, he would not cosign a loan or help pay for my college education. Going into my junior year, my student loan would not cover all of my tuition and my mother lost her job due to cutbacks in the school district. Shortly after midterms, I was purged from all my classes and kicked out of my dormitory due to lack of money.

Being homeless for the second time in less than 3 years, while not being enrolled in school for the rest of that semester, did not stop me from achieving my goal of becoming a college graduate. I asked my teachers to allow me to continue attending class on an audit basis. They said yes. Through this obstacle, I was able to develop both independence and a work ethic to persevere.

While auditing classes, I moved in with my college best friend until I was able to get an apartment. Then it was time to straighten out my financial aid issues. The assistant director of financial aid told me that my estimated family contribution (EFC) was too high for her to help me and the scholarship money went to students who really needed it. After 2 weeks of not being enrolled, I went to see her again to let her know that my EFC was not my reality. Torn between believing me and not believing me due to the paperwork of my parent's income, she called my stepfather. On speakerphone she said, "Hello, Mr. X this is the assistant director of the financial aid department at Morehouse College. Do you know your son David Hughes has been dropped from his classes and removed from his dormitory due to lack of payment..." He said, "Yes, I know, but that's between him and his mother. I don't care what happens to him; it's not my business." With a look of shock and disgust on her face, she just said, "Okay" and hung up the phone. After the phone call, she apologized to me for not believing me earlier. Once I asked for help from that moment on, I was put on academic scholarship and never had to pay for Morehouse College again.

Despite my delayed graduation, I made the best of the situation. Since I was not officially in school that semester, I used my time to gain work experience interning in the Marketing Department at Georgia State University and on 790 Sports Radio with the "Two Live Stews." I was also able to intern for ESPN, The Orange Bowl Committee, and the University of Miami athletic department all before I graduated. Each of these experiences allowed my first job out of college to be with the Houston Texans in the ticket sales department. In addition to working in the NFL, I started my master's degree studies at Prairie View A&M University. One year and nine months after graduating with my bachelor's degree, I was able to start teaching at the collegiate level. Currently, I am in my last year of my PhD program and doing a predoctoral fellowship at an Ivy League intuition. I was able to do these things because I asked for help. I found mentors that chose to help me succeed and I was willing to put in the work and make sacrifices.

In retrospect, one of my biggest mistakes in high school and undergrad was being afraid to ask for help. My logic at the time was I would not ask any teachers for help because I did not want to seem stupid due to my learning disability. Unfortunately, this approach hurt me more than it helped me. As you see from my journey, once I was able to get over my fear of seeming dumb and asked for help, I overcame anger issues, performed much better academically, and professionally. After asking for help I was able to continue school with no money, internships, and scholarship money. Based on my experiences I encourage you to do the followings things: Find out as early as possible, what you would like to do as a career. Ask someone who is successful in that profession to mentor you. Understand that when you do ask for help, it is a sign of strength not weakness. Also, be aware that not everyone will go out of his or her way to help you. However, you do not need everyone to help you, only the right one, so do not get discouraged if you ask and get told, "No." Lastly, if you need help finding a mentor, look into Big Brother Big Sister of America, 100 Black Men, any fraternity or sorority (graduate chapter) in your city, local church, or a teacher at your school.

REFERENCE

Wemund, B. (2014, September 16). Beaumont is least educated major U.S. city, study says. *The Houston Chronicle*. Retrieved online from https://www.houstonchronicle.com/local/education/campus-chronicles/article/Beaumont-is-least-educated-major-U-S-city-study-5758815.php

CHAPTER 33

FOR SPECIAL EDUCATORS WHO HAVE CONSIDERED GIVING UP WHEN THE RAINBOW IS ENOUGH

A Retrospective and Prospective Essay on Being a Black Male in Specialized Education

Brandon C. S. Wallace

BACK THEN

When I was growing up, I didn't speak; I didn't talk; I couldn't put sound to words. Although, I was never formally evaluated or diagnosed, I concluded (because special educators often do this kind of conjecturing) that I was suffering from selective or progressive mutism (maybe traumatic, but I can't think of just one, single instance that would have led me down that road)—anxiety disorders that result in a child not being able to speak. So when my teachers would question my work, give me unjustifiable grades, or even mistreat me, I could not get the words out to protest or resist, even though I knew what I wanted to say; I had an inability to verbalize my words.

In my early years, I would process it all (feelings, conversations, etc.) in my head, but I didn't know how to transform those thoughts into speech—a nightmarish disposition wherein the wheels attempting to revolve in your mind are in a state of stasis. This inability to advocate for myself, especially considering my mother worked nearly three jobs at any given time in my childhood and early adolescence and no other adult was around to help me navigate a predominately all-White school system, left me in despair and depression; I was voiceless, helpless, and (seemingly) hopeless. Sometimes, I think that the only way I escaped the too often disproportionate clutches of specialized education was because I was so well-mannered in class (and by well-mannered I just mean extremely quiet).

Around the age of 12, my family and I moved from Connecticut to Prince George's County, Maryland in the mid-'90s, and that God-destined, down-south move saved my life. Teachers were much more used to African American students of a wide-spectrum of cognitive levels, as opposed to the all-White schools that I had been bussed to in elementary years. I was exposed to teachers who encouraged me, made me feel safe and smart, and teachers who went out of their way to recognize a light in me, especially in high school. Finally, I had Black male English teachers, like Mr. Beidleman and Dr. Williams, who introduced me to Black male writers, like Haki Madhubuti and Langston Hughes. I could finally see myself as an educator, as an intellectual. And the ability to see myself apart from so many myopic metanarratives that just didn't fit the person, the man I was inside. Seeing Black male educators in my formative middle and high school years made me feel like it was possible and attainable to have more opportunities for my future.

Sometimes on this tedious educational journey, both as a beneficiary and as a benefactor, I have been met with a lot of tension and disdain. Many have used my age, race, and even gender to discount me—calling me unqualified and many other deleterious names to where I feel uneasy even placing them in this piece. The hurt, so bad and stinging at times, made me want to run away, give up, or worse, retaliate with schemes and venomous words, too. Can I tell you how I stayed above the fray and refused to engage in the toxicity of those moments... The secret is in a two-letter word. This single word—so powerful that it has perpetuated hope in me when I thought all hope was lost; it has made my life's work of ensuring disproportionality for students with disabilities is addressed and, as best as I can, mitigated and solved. It quiets the rumble and butterflies in my stomach when I'm in a room of thousands and speak about evidence-based practices and national assessments and prisons-to-pipelines. I say this word to myself. God says it to me; I repeat it—daily. I say it in my mind. I whisper it to myself; I remind myself of it. It's an imperative, a command that has been moving me from one landing to another, one platform to another, one city to the next; it's one simple word—*Go*.

RIGHT NOW

When I get discouraged by the insurmountable obstacles that are in front of me, strategically placed there by systems that have been masterfully designed to hinder my process and progress, thwart my attempts, and destroy my very life—I still go. I go with tears in my eyes. I go with a broken heart; I go with a lack of strength; I go with gray hairs popping up from the crown of my head; I go. I go whether or not I have allies; I go when I know there are adversaries waiting for me; I go because I know that the strength that I have in me and the cause that I am fighting for is greater than any crass word, harsh remark, tactless stare, or ridiculous, snide quip that is gossiped behind my strong, Black, professional back.

I go and provide training and technical assistance around standards-based individualized education programs (IEPs) because they should not be edicts for a life sentence of imprisonment—composed to simply strengthen a pipeline that is funneling our young boys and men into prisons and street corners—displacing them, making them strangers and misfits in their own communities. I go to challenge the homogeneity and hegemony that happens in urban education, especially in specialized education (Skiba et al., 2006).

I go—knowing that I may have to walk away unpopular and unwanted. I go and write curricula that is taught at the Johns Hopkins University, one of the top graduate schools of education in the country, because I know that the specialized education curricula that I write will influence and impact the new generation of urban teachers throughout this country. That same curricula will provide support for so many students that I have come so vicariously enamored with because they are me and, in so many cases, I am them. I just go.

THE FUTURE

To all of you future, and novice, and new, and ready, and hungry, and waiting, and soon-to-be, and already are, and even seasoned educators of color—I need you all to stay encouraged and remember these four ideas:

1. When you're the only young, gifted, and Black brother in the room, the same room, mind you, that critical decisions are made concerning many students of color, and they are trying to "other" (Powell, 2015) you while you are trying to fiercely dodge all those microag-

gressions that, strangely enough, keep on getting thrown in your face—Go. Go right in the room, sit down at the table, especially because He has already prepared it for you in the midst of your enemies, and speak and share, and let them know you came to fight for students who can't fight for themselves.
2. When you're the only melanin-enhanced, cool, Obama-esque brother on stage in a room filled with folks who already see you as less than, not enough, or whatever other nonsensical conclusions they have come to because they are, themselves, inferior to your amazing gifts and talents, Go. Walk right up to that podium and let your voice ring, sing so loudly that they will have to hear you, even though they may not want to.
3. When you are one of the only beautifully intelligent, brown and sandalwood imbued, almond-rounded headed young man in an entire school building filled with academic faculty that look nothing like you but are teaching kids that could certainly be your family members, go and speak and educate those amazingly awesome students of yours. Go and show (not tell) them how amazingly smart they and you are. Go and tell them how brilliantly capable they are, and you are. Go and tell them that you will never give up on them because you, yourself, have never been given up on, which has, undoubtedly, left you teaching your learned craft in front of them.
4. When everyone wants to throw the kids that look like you into special education, not because they need specially designed instruction, but rather because they simply just don't want to *deal* with them anymore, go into those IEP meetings, whether they receive you well or not, and speak up when the constant treachery of disproportionality is being ignored and folks are pretending like Daquan has a developmental delay—knowing good and damn well that a 5-year old boy isn't supposed to sit still for 90 minutes anyway. Mentor as many as you can but learn to take as much time as you need for your self-care along the way. Go, and remember Trayvon, Tamir, Freddie, Stephon, and all the rest of those young boys whose blood cries out from the ground beneath us. Give them a culturally relevant experience that they can use and engage and excite them throughout your lessons (Gay, 2002).

Go and demystify the inappropriate fascination of misrepresentations and stereotypes about Black boys. Go and be you. Go and get knowledge. Go and teach somebody. Just go.

REFERENCES

Gay, G. (2002). Preparing for culturally responsive teaching. *Journal of Teacher Education, 53*(2), 106–116. doi:10.1177/0022487102053002003

Powell, J. A. (2015, May 30). Keynote: The mechanisms of othering. Retrieved from https://www.youtube.com/watch...v=Cs3mtCqC8S4

Skiba, R. J., Simmons, A., Rittet, S., Kohler, K., Henderson, M., & Wu, T. (2006a). The context of minority disproportionality: Practitioner perspectives on special education referral. *Teachers College Record, 108*(7), 1424–1459.

CHAPTER 34

SPECIAL EDUCATION TO HIGHER EDUCATION

Speech Impediment to a Degree in Speech Communications

Burgess Mitchell

Growing up in a large family played a significant role in my life. I was the ninth of 10 children raised in Franklin, Louisiana. I grew up on Mitchell Street, which is also my surname. My mother, the late Bessie Bray Mitchell, completed high school. However, my father, the late Ulysses Mitchell Sr., had to quit school at an early age because in the 1940s, like most boys in rural southern Louisiana, he had to go to work in the sugarcane fields. Years later, my father became a roofer; he had to do metrics and measurements that required numerous calculations. Dad was very good at fixing things with his hands. Mother, a housewife, was excellent at solving problems relative to the souls of her ten children, as well as over 30 grandchildren and 30 great grandchildren. Whereas my parents were not afforded the opportunity to get formal schooling, they instilled in us that education was significant. However, my educational plight did not come without its share of struggles and challenges.

ELEMENTARY SCHOOL

Memories of my early elementary school days were riddled with demeaning labels and low self-esteem. I had to repeat the second grade for not making satisfactory progress. In short, I failed. I did not like school because so many of my experiences were frightful and harmful.

During second grade, I was labeled as retarded. Merriam-Webster's Dictionary (n.d.) defines the word retarded as "slow or limited in intellectual or emotional development." Today's terminology would have identified me as learning disabled. I was placed in special education, a form of learning for students with exceptional needs, such as learning disabilities or mental challenges.

My primary learning disability was a speech or language impairment, defined as a communication disorder such as stuttering that has an adverse effect on one's educational performance. In so many words, I stuttered. Like Moses in the Bible, "I was slow in tongue."

Children teased and belittled me because of the way I talked. Their looks and comments were embarrassing so I dealt with it by speaking publicly as little as possible. Also, I answered in short sentences to make my faltering of words less noticeable. My speech disorder led to other issues such as low self-efficacy and social anxiety.

PARENTAL INVOLVEMENT

Mother helped me rise above my speech impediment, educational, and personal barriers. She and my father blatantly refused to accept my inability to learn holistically. They believed that with hard work, determination, and nurturing educators, I would perform well. Consequently, my parents rejected the Louisiana Social Security Supplemental Income (SSI) offered on my behalf.

AN ATHLETE IS BORN

My high school days were filled with peaks and valleys. I was introduced to the triple jump by my brother Sidney in the ninth grade. He became the coach for a day. His theory was: "Today, I'll teach you everything I know about the triple jump; tomorrow you'll have to practice on your own. Study techniques and practice will allow you to be one of the best triple jumpers in the country, if you want it bad enough." The triple jump became a welcomed challenge for me because I could be on a team and compete while combining timing, speed, power, and agility. As a triple jumper, I gained a quiet confidence and became a fierce competitor while maintaining a humble spirit. While in ninth grade, I placed first or second in all track and field meets.

My sophomore year was supposed to be the year I would dominate in the triple jump but I failed a course at midterm that left me ineligible to compete. I was distraught because even though the triple jump is an individual event, I let my teammates down. My stellar performances in the triple jump would have earned our team valuable points. Unfortunately, I could not even practice with the team. Again, I felt the effects of my special education and learning disability. After speaking with my coach and teammates, I was committed to growing academically and athletically. I developed a strategic plan and I dedicated myself to working at least 3 to 4 hours a day on academic and athletic preparation for a year.

Junior year started off with a bang! I was academically eligible to compete and I broke my brother Sidney's triple jump record during the first track meet. I was still not a stellar student, but I worked hard academically. The entire year I was one of the top three finalists, jumping distances over 44 feet, until the district meet. There, I jumped over 46 feet for the first time ever. This qualified me for the regional meet, where I jumped over 46 feet again. Three days before the 1986 Louisiana State Track and Field Meet, I wrote, "48' 0" on the track locker room chalkboard during my time of reflection and strategic preparation. If you believe it, you can achieve it.

During my senior year, I became one of the top five triple jumpers in the nation, earning invitations to the Golden West Track and Field Meet in Sacramento, California, Yale University, and Chicago Invitational, all while still attending little Franklin Senior High School in Franklin, Louisiana. I jumped over 50 feet and earned many accolades. Due to my athletic success, I was asked to speak to inmates at the local jail. I was terrified because remember, I stuttered. After some coercing from my brother Sidney, I agreed to speak. As fate would have it, I talked for 45 minutes without a stammer. On that day, I was delivered from stuttering.

MY COLLEGE YEARS

Graduation from high school was a major milestone. I was recruited by many colleges and universities to participate as a track and field athlete. I chose to attend Blinn Community College which became one of the most dominate track and field programs in the country during the 1980s and 1990s. My arrival at Blinn College was scary. It was my first time leaving home for an extended period, and the athletic dormitory was right next to a cemetery. I cried every day for 3 weeks after my parents dropped me off at college. However, things improved once I learned Brenham was the home of Blue Bell ice cream!

The campus climate was a learning experience because we had an international team of athletes from Canada, Jamaica, Mexico, South Africa, Sweden, Zambia, and the United States. This team was a perfect picture of diversity, which was reflected in its nationalities, race, religions, beliefs, and customs. It made for a rich cultural experience. Overall, I grew spiritually, socially, academically, and athletically. I was an all-American athlete and earned an associate's degree from Blinn College.

My success at Blinn College earned me a track and field scholarship to the University of Texas at Austin to compete as a triple jumper. I was a successful athlete and ultimately earned my bachelor's degree in speech communications. Once I completed my eligibility to triple jump, I interned with the athletic department's academic counselor. In this position, I assisted the academic counselor with monitoring athletes' academic progress. I coordinated tutoring and mentoring programs, and I aided with academic advising. Little did I know that 25 years later, I would be doing the same type of work as assistant dean for student services in the School of Engineering at Vanderbilt University.

COMING FULL CIRCLE

As an assistant dean, I can identify with the many difficulties that life presents to a student because I have endured my struggles. In 2009, while working as assistant dean, I earned a master's degree in education administration. Currently, I am pursuing a doctoral degree in educational leadership. I persisted from special education to higher education.

I grew up in Franklin, Louisiana, but I now reside in Franklin, Tennessee. I have come to know that Franklin, Louisiana was named after Franklin, Tennessee. So, I guess fate would have it that my journey would take me many miles only to end up in another Franklin. Whereas I once stuttered, I now spend a great deal of my time enunciating and presenting in many forums.

Years later, when I graduated from the University of Texas at Austin with a degree in speech communications, my mother said to me, "Burgess, the state of Louisiana offered your daddy and me an SSI check stating that you were retarded." She went on to say, "I know my son. He can learn like any other child, so the State of Louisiana or no one else can offer us enough money to make him think that he can't learn." She went on to say that if I had a learning disability and just could not learn, they would have taken the money. It wasn't that my parents could not have used the money, but in my mother's mind, it would have been to my detriment.

Thank you, momma and daddy, for helping me take my most successful triple jump from special education to higher education; from speech impediment to a speech communications degree; and now from an elementary education system who said, "We think your son is slow" to having an article published in a book *partly* entitled, "GUMBO." In her wisdom, my momma never told me about the learning disability or the SSI check offer, until I graduated from the University of Texas at Austin and had thus well overcome it!

REFERENCES

Retarted. (n.d.). In Merriam-Webster's online dictionary. Retrieved from https://www.merriam-webster.com/dictionary/retarded

CHAPTER 35

FROM A REFUGEE CHILD TO SUCCESS IN AMERICA

Alex Sekwat

I was born in Sudan in the midst of one of the most brutal civil wars in Africa, that is, the first Sudanese Civil War. The conflict pitted the Muslim dominated government of Sudan against the predominantly Christian and indigenous Black Africans of South Sudan who demanded greater autonomy and a society free of injustice and discrimination. The war caused the death of more than half a million people and forced a million to flee their homes. It had adverse effects on me as a child and impacted the trajectory of my life. I first experienced the effects of the war at the tender age of five. It started when the Sudanese army bombed my village. It was late at night when I was awakened by an unfamiliar loud and frightening noise. It was the sound of gunfire and bombs raining on our village. I was gripped with fear and cried profusely. In the chaos that followed, my mother grabbed my younger brother and me and ran to the nearest bush. We sojourned for weeks in the bushes until we crossed the international border to Uganda.

Upon our arrival in Uganda, my family and other refugee families were rounded up by the Ugandan army and trucked to a remote forest turned into a makeshift refugee camp. As you can imagine, life in the refugee camp was very difficult. The most basic human needs essential for long-term survival were in short supply: Shelter and sanitation facilities were substandard, and food was insufficient. For survival, we relied on small food rations distributed by the World Food Program (WFP) and the United Nations High Commission for Refugees (UNHCR). We lacked access to clean drinking water and were forced to use untreated water from a nearby river. During the rainy season, outbreaks of infectious diseases such as cholera and malaria occasionally swept through the camp often causing high morbidity and mortality rates. Cholera is an acute bacterial disease spread by ingestion of contaminated food or drinking water. It thrives in overcrowded and unhygienic places and imposes substantial disease burden on refugees. The incidence of malaria infection was high in the refugee camp. As a child, I suffered recurrent malarial infections. Malaria is caused by parasites carried by mosquitoes.

After a year in the makeshift refugee camp, my parents decided to relocate our family to another refugee camp where some basic facilities and services were available such as schools, health clinics, clean water, and large arable land for farming. My parent's main reason for relocating our family was to ensure that I had access to educational opportunities. Upon resettling in the camp, I enrolled in first grade. The physical environment of the school was not conducive to learning: Classrooms were overcrowded and devoid of instructional materials such as chairs, tables, desks, and books. Moreover, the school was far from our home. Each day I walked at least six miles to and from school crossing a dangerous river susceptible to flash flooding. I vividly remember the day when the river overflowed its banks and swept away livestock and a couple of students from my school. However, these challenges and others did not deter me from attending school.

Education was neither free nor guaranteed in the refugee camp. Each semester my parents struggled to pay my school fees, uniforms, and supplies. My mother especially deserves most of the credit for financing my education. Although she had little formal education, she understood the significance of education and its potential positive impact on my future. She worked long hours doing farm work to support my educational needs. She invested the bulk of her resources in my education. To me, my mother was a supermom and the greatest person I have ever known.

We returned to Sudan after spending nearly a decade in refugee camps in Uganda. The warring parties had signed a peace agreement which resulted in a temporary lull in the conflict. When we left Uganda, I had completed sixth grade. Looking back at my journey through elementary and middle school at the refugee camp, it gave me a sense of pride and accomplishment. I studied very hard, and the rewards of my hard work paid off in the form of better grades. Most significantly, I was admitted to a public boarding high school. Although the school was under-resourced, that is, it lacked basic resources including textbooks, running water, electricity, and trained teachers, my strong desire to succeed motivated me to work harder. Again my efforts paid off, and I passed the college entrance exams and gained admission to the most prestigious institution in Sudan, the University of Khartoum.

At the University of Khartoum, I studied business and economics. My initial goal was to choose engineering as my major. However, subtle government policies designed to discriminate against non-Arabic speaking students like me made it difficult to be admitted in the fields of engineering, medicine, dentistry, and pharmacy. The Muslim majority government openly discriminated against ethnic minorities in virtually all aspects of society including employment, education, promotion, and more. While at the university, I met a Fulbright visiting professor from the United States. As it happened, this scholar assisted me in pursuing graduate studies in the United States. He helped me with the application process and loaned me money to begin my studies in the United States. I am forever indebted to him for his friendship and generosity.

I completed my undergraduate studies in business and economics in 4 years. Upon my graduation, I was lucky to find a job within 2 months. I was hired by CARE, a major U.S. based international humanitarian aid organization whose mission is to save lives, fight poverty, and achieve social justice around the globe. I was delighted to work under the tutelage of an experienced administrator. From him, I learned crucial lifelong learning skills which enhanced my understanding of the world around me. By the late 1980s, the political and economic conditions in Sudan had deteriorated drastically. Consequently, my supervisor encouraged me to pursue graduate studies either in Canada or the United States. He purchased the Test of English as a Foreign Language (TOEFL) and the Graduate Record Exam (GRE) study guides so I could prepare for the examinations. With his help and the friend, I met at the University of Khartoum, I began to explore opportunities for graduate studies in the United States and Canada in the late 1980s. I was eventually accepted to the masters of public administration (MPA) program at Arkansas State University.

I was in my mid-20s when I came to the United States. I arrived in early January, snow covered the ground and I was awed by its beauty. It was the first time in my life I had seen snow! I enrolled in the MPA program upon my arrival. My journey through the program had not been without trials and tribulations. I did not have sufficient resources to cover all my living expenses during the first semester of my enrollment. At times I relied on my roommates to make ends meet. As I stated earlier, the generosity of the visiting Fulbright scholar I met at the University of Khartoum, made it possible for me to complete my first semester in the program. He loaned me sufficient money which I agreed to repay him after I graduated. I earned a high GPA the first semester. As a result, I received a graduate assistantship which enabled me to complete the MPA program.

Due to the raging civil war in Sudan, I was unable to return home. I decided to pursue doctoral studies in the United States. I applied and gained admission to three PhD programs. I elected the PhD program in public administration at Florida Atlantic University because it offered me a generous 4-year graduate assistantship package. My first semester in the doctoral program started well. I adjusted quickly to the rigor and expectations of the program. However, the following semester the unexpected happened: I received a sad message from home. My brother called and informed me that my mother had passed. As you can imagine, I was devastated and heartbroken. My mother, more than anyone, had a profound and positive impact on my educational journey. I felt lonely, sad, and empty for the rest of that year. I learned that my mother, her younger sister, and my maternal grandmother all perished after artillery shells rained on their residence. They were victims of the Second Sudanese Civil War which raged for more than two decades (1983–2015).

Looking back, my life's journey has been replete with challenges, losses, successes, and triumphs. As a child I, saw the world as nothing but a violent, chaotic, and a brutal place. My early childhood experiences often evoke memories of poverty, loss, discrimination, despair, and hopelessness.

Drawing from my experience as a refugee and an immigrant, I would like to share with the reader how I overcame the hurdles and obstacles I encountered in life's journey. First, I credit my parents who supported me unconditionally in all my endeavors. They embraced the cardinal rule that the family is the most important influence in a child's life. Second, despite encountering war trauma, prejudice, and discrimination, I credit myself for not being distracted by protracted problems and hardships. Rather, I took proactive action and had the drive and belief that with determination, tenacity, and hard work, success was possible. Early in my life, I learned that success required hard work, discipline, dedication, and perseverance. I further learned that in order to succeed, I must set higher goals, trust myself and be prepared to overcome any unforeseen challenges. I figured out that education was my best ticket to success and that success itself is a product of my mindset. Finally, I overcame many challenges as a refugee and an immigrant with the help and generosity of friends, faith-based groups, and international institutions (such as United Nations, WHO), host nations, and universities. These groups provided significant assistance to me (and my family) throughout my life's journey.

In sum, overcoming the challenges faced by any refugee or immigrant requires collective and individual efforts; institutions, families, and generous individuals are critical to any success. Today with the help many support groups, coupled with my sheer determination to succeed, I can say with pride that I beat the odds.

CHAPTER 36

I AM NOT SUPPOSED TO BE HERE
Why Numbers Sometimes Lie

Stuart Rhoden

> I keep my head high
> I got my wings to carry me
> I don't know freedom
> I want my dreams to rescue me
> I keep my faith strong
> I ask the Lord to follow me
> I've been unfaithful
> I don't know why you call on me
> —J. Cole, *Apparently*, 2014

As a young person growing up on the south side of Chicago, I always had the goal of becoming a civil rights lawyer. I wanted to be the first Stuart Rhoden, but I also wanted to follow in the footsteps of Charles Hamilton Houston, Thurgood Marshall, Arthur Fletcher, and so many other lawyers of color who advocated for civil and social justice issues in this country. To this end, as a college student, I majored, first in diplomacy and world affairs, and then politics at Occidental College in Los Angeles. When I first heard of Occidental (Oxy), it was not because of an individual who would eventually inhabit the

White House (Barack Obama). I had heard of the reputation of Occidental through my college counselor who said it was a great school for liberal arts, was in a major city (with warm weather no less), and there was the chance that I could compete to be on the tennis team. I was in.

In terms of my growth and maturation as a person, moving to Los Angeles for college was one of the best things I ever did. This was an era, long before cell phones, helicopter parents (parents' who hover over their children 24/7 like helicopters, or more recently drones) or FaceTime. I recall having to wait sometimes up to an hour to use my calling card to make a weekly, sometimes bi-weekly call home to Chicago from one of the four to five pay phones in the lobby of my dormitory. Once my roommate and I eventually got a landline phone in our room, the long-distance rates were so high, that the frequency of calls essentially remained the same. I was on my own, 1,600 miles away from home in a large urban city. The choices I made, were predominantly my own. And so were the repercussions of those choices. I can safely say that I experienced college to the fullest and indulged in many of the pleasures southern California had to offer. While I was a good to great student in my major, I had problems focusing on the rest of the liberal arts curriculum and felt it was unfair that I was penalized for those poor grades in my collective GPA.

The stress of balancing emerging adulthood and college came to a head during the spring of 1990. My 90+ year old grandmother was slowly dying in a hospital in Chicago. As the son of a single mother, my emotions were 100% with my mother who was in the process of saying goodbye to her mother who was dying of diabetes. In my mind, college be damned, I wanted to go home, but I also did not want to "quit" or let others down. Consequently, at the young age of 20, I did not know what to do. Rather than reaching out for help from my advisor, professors, or friends, I retreated into my shell—only to emerge to rarely attend class. By the end of the semester, I was anxious to go home, and Occidental College was equally anxious for me to "take time off." I was placed on academic probation for failing two of my three courses (we were on trimesters back then in which we took three courses each of the three semesters).

This is the first time I have ever written those words, and although failing those two courses molded me into the intellectually curious and humble person I am today, it is still upsetting and angers me. I am equally still searing about what I perceived as a lack of institutional support. As a professor, I can now see that there were signs the college was reaching out to me, but I did not respond. For example, around week six or seven (of a 10 week semester), I was informed by the dean of students that I needed to go to counseling services. I was curious as to why when I felt I didn't need psychological counseling. Like many males, and Black males in particular, I wrongly thought that all I needed to do was to put my head down, grind it out, and pass the two courses I ultimately failed. The third course I was enrolled in, was the most difficult but it was part of my major. I received a B+. I knew my problems were not one based on competency or intellectual skill. I think, even to this day, the reason I feel betrayed by the institution is that my advisor at the time, did not make me aware that I could take two incompletes in courses I ultimately failed. Those marks to this day have been at times a roadblock to my professional advancement—first to become a teacher, and second to enter graduate school. However, I have been able to overcome these quantitative barriers by virtue of the strength of the recommendations from my advisor, my ability to utilize my social capital, and my strong faith.

To some, perhaps my dean included, my intentions to get back on track appeared to be overly ambitious. I registered to take summer courses at two separate universities in Chicago, spent time with my family mourning our matriarch, and intended to return to Occidental College in the fall to continue my studies and stay "on track" to graduate. That summer, my grandmother passed away peacefully, and I accomplished what I set out to do, receive As/Bs in my summer coursework and return to Los Angeles. Unfortunately, when I returned that fall, the dean did not feel that I was "ready" to return, which infuriated me. Rather than sulking at home and dropping out, I doubled down by staying in LA and enrolling in two courses at the University of California, Los Angeles (UCLA). Most importantly, in a move that humbles me to this day, I changed advisors to the person who is still one of my most influential mentors, Dr. Larry Caldwell. Eventually, with his brilliant guidance and assistance, I was reinstated and graduated only a semester "behind" in December of 1992.

I would love to say that was the last time I "failed," but there is another key moment in my life where I was challenged to demonstrate resilience and, as Bourdieu (1986) articulated, demonstrate "social capital." After years of moving around from job to job in politics, and spending one semester in law school, I realized that I needed a "career," and that it was time to "grow up." I decided to become a teacher because it seemed to me that I was best prepared for that profession, and I enjoyed helping young people learn about history and social justice. Of course, nothing with me is easy, so rather than staying in Chicago, I decided to embark on my journey to my own classroom back in Los Angeles.

In the Spring of 2003, I was chosen to be a member of the L.A. Teaching Fellows (LATF) for their intensive 6 week summer program in May of 2003. After completing the program, I returned to Chicago to gather my belongings and make the long drive in my "new" used 1999 Jeep (my first vehicle ever), purchased just one day before the move. Much in the same way I did at 18 when I flew west to begin college, at 33 years old, I drove cross-country alone to Los Angeles to begin the journey towards becoming a teacher in the inner city. I had not secured a job, a place to live, and had very little money. I placed my belongings in a storage facility near Echo Park, opened a post office box in Pasadena to collect my mail (and have a California mailing address to put on resumes), and thought I had secured a room in the YMCA down the street from my P.O. box. Unfortunately, when I arrived, I did not have a room in the YMCA (and upon further inspection, that may have been a blessing) and ended up being dependent on the kindness of friends and relatives of friends to give me shelter until I finally found a network of youth hostels (before Airbnb, these were an inexpensive option for long term lodging) in and around Hollywood, where I lived from August 2003 until December 2003.

Moving to Los Angeles, in the manner I did, was one of the most challenging endeavors I have undertaken in my life. The uncertainty of where I was going to sleep nightly coupled with the high stress of first the L.A. Teaching Fellows, the teacher induction graduate program at UCLA, TeachLA, as well as the demands of trying to secure a full-time teaching job was almost too much to bear. Trying to overcome all of these stressors simultaneously while facing dwindling finances and patience of friends, left me exhausted, frustrated, and discouraged. But once I set the goal of becoming an educator, I was determined to push ahead to make that happen. I have often thought of why I put myself in this position. It would have been so much "easier" to become a teacher in Chicago, because I had a support network, as well as contacts within both CPS and a number of charter schools who would have loved for me to be a part of their faculty. However, something inside me has always driven me to take the road less traveled. Much in the same vein as going to college on the west coast when most of my friends from high school went east, or stayed in the Midwest, I believed that being in California was in my spirit. I had to follow my gut, results be damned.

Eventually, in December of 2003, I was hired to take over the social studies classes for a friend (who already had a PhD and a JD) in my UCLA program who decided that this particular inner-city school and population of students was not for her. Eagerly I went into the classroom, as a long-term substitute. Even at 33 years old, just like many early career teachers, I entered the classroom thinking I was prepared, and that I could mold students into obtaining positive academic achievement. One of my biggest impetuses to wanting to be a public school teacher specifically was that I feel that my educational background was something I valued and appreciated from a young age. Being one of the few Black students, and Black males in particular, in both my private grade school and high school gave me a social and cultural capital that I wanted to instill to every child of color. Teaching them the agency and resilience that I oftentimes took for granted as obvious, was paramount to my classroom pedagogy.

Without going into too great of specificity, the first few months of my tenure were emotionally, physically, and mentally exhausting. Daily, I was verbally challenged by the students with one even saying, "When you gonna quit like the rest of them, Rhoden..." Little did they know I was too stubborn, and had too much to lose (pride, ego, a long painful trip back to Chicago) to "fail." Failure was not an option.

Considering my inauspicious beginning, I was surprised to be hired by the department chair to return the following school year to continue working full-time as a social studies teacher. As in many urban schools when talent is identified, I unexpectedly, during my 4-year tenure at the school, rose from a long-term substitute to the co-chair of one of the Small Learning Communities as well as a member of the School Site Council which oversaw the multimillion-dollar school budget and helped manage the school. However, in the spring of 2007, I ended up getting married and relocated to Philadelphia where my wife received a tenure-track position at Temple University.

At this juncture, once we arrived in Philadelphia, I reached another crossroads. I decided that I did not want to immediately re-enter the battleground of urban public school life. So, in January of 2008, I began taking graduate level courses at Temple as a "non-matriculating" student. I fell in love with being back in graduate school, and with being a student instead of the teacher. The following year I earned my master's degree in Urban Education and began teaching as a teaching assistant. I also decided to continue into the PhD program also in urban education. Finally, in December 2013, I defended my dissertation and became Dr. Stuart Rhoden.

The challenges that I experienced as the husband of a tenured faculty member, an older student, and at times, a male student of color, were immense. Similarly, to my entering public education at an older age, being in my 30s, prepared me to withstand those who challenged my abilities, my intellect, and sometimes, my Blackness. There were long days of teaching as a teaching assistant of a Youth Cultures course and nights of taking courses coupled with being newly married and living in a new city. The strength to take on challenges and see them as opportunities is a characteristic that many persons of color must learn from an early age. It is not the stressors, the systemic, or institutional barriers that prevent many from achieving, it is how they respond to them that stops people in their tracks. I was fortunate to learn, even if it was a false reality, that there wasn't anything I couldn't achieve, or any place where I couldn't belong. And while the realities of race, class, and gender barriers are real, equally as real is the ability to persist in an unjust world.

I strongly believe my story is not unique. I have to resolutely believe that. As a college level instructor teaching academic success to students who have "failed," and as a father of two children under the age of 7, I have to believe that, despite what social and mainstream media highlight, there are many persons of color, both male and female, who have a similar narrative. However, if I had to isolate one of the things that continued to drive me not towards success, but excellence or the being the best me, is the tremendous amount of faith my mother instilled in me from an early age.

Soon after I became a father, my mother told me that one of the hardest things she'd ever done was to allow me to think for myself. The best gift we can give our family members, and dare I say our, students or mentees, is the ability to be both humble and driven at the same time. Sometimes this combination is perceived as arrogance, being aloof, or over confidence. Yes, all of those traits can manifest themselves outwardly, and early in my life, I can see now that there were far too many times I tilted the scales towards those negative characteristics. However, what I have been able to consistently demonstrate is my persistence and adaptability whether it be—a failed relationship, a rejection letter(s) from a university, rejection from a potential job, peer reviewed journal, or conference. I have learned to fall down seven times, stand up eight. Most importantly, I have learned how to listen to that "still small voice," and meticulously execute the lessons taught in my childhood. As the 2013–2014 NBA MVP Kevin Durant affirmed in his acceptance speech acknowledging his mother's influence on his accomplishments: "We weren't supposed to be here. You made us believe, you kept us off the street. You put clothes on our backs, food on the table. When you didn't eat, you made sure we ate. You went to sleep hungry. You sacrificed for us. You're the real MVP."

REFERENCES

Bourdieu, P. (2011). The forms of capital. (1986). *Cultural theory: An anthology, 1*, 81–93.

Durant, K. (2014, May 6). 2013–2014 MVP Acceptance Speech. Retrieved from https://genius.com/Kevin-durant-2013-14-mvp-acceptance-speech-annotated

CHAPTER 37

SOCIAL CAPITAL AND ITS IMPACT ON MY PERSONAL AND ACADEMIC SUCCESS

Solomon Tention

My name is Solomon Tention, director for student engagement and Title IX coordinator at a local community college within the state of Louisiana. My education credentials include a bachelor's in sociology with a minor in child and youth advocacy, master's in educational leadership and instruction, and finally a doctorate in higher education leadership. I will start this chapter by stating that life can become very interesting when individuals make the all important decision that success is the only option. You will find as you read throughout this chapter that in no way will I tell you that my journey to even a small portion of success is a fairy tale, or a one size fits all approach. It's that thing we call life. You learn to adjust as life deals you its deck of cards. As men of color, at some point we have to make a decision that we will not be a product of our environment or become another statistic. We have to make decisions that we control our success. Our past feelings of hurt, abandonment, betrayal, and other challenges were meant to help build us into stronger men. Men of color must understand that our destiny and purpose is ultimately tied to our story.

Early on in my life, challenges occurred with my family setting that would suggest that perhaps I would take the path that all too often many men of color go down as a result of instability and other challenges within the home setting. Challenges forced me to grow up and mature well beyond my time, but ultimately shaped me into being the man I am today. You may be wondering at this point what some of those challenges were. To give you a brief overview, I will list a few: absentee father, absent mother who suffered with mental illness, unstable home environment, first generation college student, and *almost* high school drop-out. Again, these are just to name a few.

Once men of color make that critical decision and begin to engage in the necessary steps towards that success, while understanding that the journey will be difficult, the universe will provide you with what I like to refer to as the "third eye." The third eye is not like your right or left eye. The third eye is largely unseen. It is designed to help you strategically identify people and relationships that have been placed in your path with a goal of helping you accomplish goals along your journey to success. Those relationships are critical, and can range from the expected to unexpected. As an African American male currently working as a student affairs professional in higher education, I will tell you that there is no secret code or guidebook for success. My story is simply a testament of hard work, determination, and sacrifice. My life is a true testimony to how social capital (people and relationships) positively impacted both my personal and academic success.

However, before I share my story, many of you may be wondering, "What is social capital..." I have provided both a theoretical and conceptual explanation in the next section of this chapter.

WHAT IS SOCIAL CAPITAL...

Theoretical Framework: James Cohen is also known as the developer of the social capital theory (Acar, 2011). Cohen's social capital theory suggests that social capital resources must include norms, trust, and networks of associations representing groups that gather consistently for a common purpose (Acar, 2011).

Conceptual Framework: According to Cohen and Prusack (2001), social capital is "the stock of active connections among people; the trust, mutual understanding, and shared values and behaviors that bind the members of human networks and communities and make cooperative action possible" (p. 4). Secondly, the literature also suggests that there are various elements of social capital. OCED Insights: Human Capital (n.d.) indicates that social capital can be divided into two major categories, bonds and bridges. Bonds are relationships with people of which have a common identity. Bridges are relationships that extend beyond a sense of identity (OCED Insights, n.d.).

BONDS AND BRIDGES ALONG MY JOURNEY OF PERSONAL AND ACADEMIC SUCCESS

Bonds: When writing this chapter, I must say that it was difficult to choose a few of the bond "relationships" that had the greatest impact both personally and professionally. Over the years, there have been so many people that have come into my life and imparted various levels of wisdom and guidance needed along my journey to success. When I think about bonds, I think about a group of men that I met my first year of college. During several days after freshmen "move in" we became close friends and knew then our relationships were the beginning of life-long friendships. These individuals were from around the country while also having a diverse set of backgrounds, cultures, and beliefs. While we were inheritably different, we shared some common interests; we were all working towards the ultimate goal of academic and professional success. We all endured some type of struggle to make it to our freshmen year of college. We endured some normal challenges associated with students within their first year of college, from financial issues, academic, and navigating our way through growth challenges. During our freshmen year we also faced issues that challenged and cultivated our growth toward "manhood" and even issues that tested our friendship. We also knew that as men of color, our journey to success would look much different than our White peers. These individuals encouraged me, provided me with advice, and even were strong enough to tell me when I was wrong. It is much easier to work towards success with a team of people as opposed to alone. These individuals served as my first support team. They challenged me and held me accountable throughout my personal and academic journey. As a student, my dissertation committee served a form of bonds; as a professional, I have a circle of professional mentors within higher education who also serve as a form of bonds who help me navigate my professional career and make critical decisions that ultimately promote my growth as an administrator. As men of color we need to develop bonds with like-minded and progressive individuals who can help us "navigate" our journey.

Bridges: One of the first relationships that impacted my overall *identity* would have been throughout my time serving as an intern within the Louisiana Governor's Office of Women and Children's Policy. When I began my college career, I thought I had it all figured out. I started with a plan to become a family attorney. I often tell my current students that I thought I had it so figured out that even during my elementary experience, during an activity of which I was tasked with creating a visual of my career path, I vividly remember drawing a judge with a mallet. Fast forward more than a decade, during my undergraduate experience I chose to participate in this internship because I believed that it would be an opportunity for me to engage a variety of state-level leaders, while also engaging in activities that would provide me with a macro-view of issues relative to family and policy within the state of Louisiana. However, while this experience was rewarding with 12 hours of credit from the college, a paid stipend, and covered living expenses, it also revealed to me that perhaps law was not who my identity truly was, it caused me to pause and rethink my career path. Would this be a lifestyle I would be comfortable with...Would I enjoy this network...Would I be able to manage some of the emotional stress attached to work in juvenile and family law... These were all questions I pondered near the end of my internship experience. However, I continued to persist in being reluctant to acknowledge some of the signs of the universe, I decided to continue into my senior year with still a plan to pursue a law degree. I visited several law schools, and decided that becoming an educator would be my backup plan.

The next summer I was offered an opportunity to participate in an internship within the University of Tennessee at Chattanooga-Upward Bound Program. It provided me with the opportunity to engage and mentor students placed at risk. It was this experience that ultimately exposed me to the field of education, its endless possibilities, and the potential power to impact students, while also changing the trajectory of their lives. It was because of these types of "bridge" relationships and experiences that I realized that education should no longer be my backup plan, but my career of choice. My experience as an intern allowed me to positively associate my personal identity as an educator—this internship experience and working with students who saw me as a model for their success. They embraced my instruction and guidance readily integrating the change in their lives, while also demonstrating to me the potential impact I could make on the lives of students within a career in education. Through this internship, I engaged with higher education leaders of color. These individuals not only served as positive affirmations of myself but also revealed to me the type of impact I could potentially make as an educator.

Experiencing bridge-focused relationships and engaging in bridge-focused experiences are vital elements of growth that all men of color should experience. Bridges impact your overall identity as a male of color through either exploration or validation. Social capital that serves as bridges help build our self-efficacy or how we feel about our ability to achieve success and ultimately impact our motivation levels and goal attainment.

INCREASING SOCIAL CAPITAL AMONGST MEN OF COLOR

Men of color can obtain social capital by first positioning themselves for success. So often men of color aren't successful because they simply haven't positioned themselves as such. Men of color who are "out of position" often miss opportunities to develop *bonds and bridges*. For example, you are a criminal justice major, and you decide to miss class because you are tired. That day your major professor has invited one of their former students who works for the Federal Bureau of Investigation (FBI) to speak to the class. Within this presentation, the agent has informed the class that there is a partnership with the institution and the FBI to provide summer long paid internships to 30 students enrolled in the criminal justice program. Remember, you decided to miss class that day. You were "out of position" thus you missed this invaluable opportunity to build bonds, bridges, and linkage type relationships. Men of color are often not only out of position when attempting to pursue academic and career goals, but we are also "out of position" in our homes, places of businesses, and the church.

I challenge you to adopt the mentality that you will not wait for an opportunity to present itself before you plan for success, but you will "get in position" to become successful. By doing so when the opportunity comes you will be ready. So many of the opportunities for success presented themselves to me because I was simply positioned for success.

Whether you are a college student or reading this chapter a year after your college graduation, the vitality of bond and bridges, remains consistent. Men of color who are in college can develop "bonds" through joining various academic organizations, special interests, or Greek lettered student organizations. Bonds for college men of color can also be formed through various mentorship or student leadership opportunities, that is, student ambassadors, orientation leaders, student government association, and so on. Bonds for men of color post-graduation can be cultivated by engaging in professional organizations aligned with your profession at the national and state level. Secondly, regional professional organizations that focus on empowerment, community involvement, and social interaction can also be critical in the development of bonds.

Bridge focused relationships serve as a vehicle to stretch your identity as a man of color. Bridge relationships can be developed through researching volunteer opportunities and internships within your specific career field. These experiences will not only impact your identity, but also either validate your career choice and/or help you think deeper about other career choices.

Bridge-focused relationships are also developed through your willingness to immerse yourself in the journey towards success. After you have identified your potential career field, research career entry and leadership paths. Develop bridge-focused relationships as you engage in these opportunities; ask current leaders in your field career focused questions. Those bridge relationships may develop into future mentorship opportunities, and/or job recommendations/opportunities.

These experiences can be recorded on your professional resume and are invaluable to your personal and professional development. I recommend readers engage in professional social media profiles such as LinkedIn and Facebook groups designed to provide a space for men of color to develop a professional identity by connecting with other professionals of similar interests and backgrounds, engage and discuss best practices for implementation with their respective workplaces.

How do we identity a bond or bridge relationship... Think about the role that person plays in your life, does this person add-value to you, does this individual hold you accountable, and is this person in a position of which you desire to be along your academic and career trajectory... Can you trust this individual... What are some of their current existing relationships like... Could this person sponsor you... These are just a few questions that men of color should ask themselves along their journey of building bridge and bond relationships. Your "third-eye" as referenced earlier in the chapter will be critical in the decision-making surrounding these relationships.

FINAL THOUGHTS

At the time of writing this chapter, I can honestly say that with the help and prayer from others, I am blessed to have achieved many accomplishments. When you read the beginning of this chapter, note that some of my personal challenges are some of the same that we hear many men of color are faced with today. What was the difference between my story of one who has achieved success as opposed to others who may have fallen victim to their environment and or circumstance... It is my ability to embrace and cultivate social capital or relationships.

After reading this chapter about the experiences from my life, I now challenge you to examine goals you would like to accomplish in your personal and academic career. What will be the path you must take to achieve those goals... What will be the plan to help you develop social capital needed for success along the way...

REFERENCES

Acar, E. (2011). Effects of social capital on academic success: A narrative thesis. *Educational Research and Reviews, 6*(6), 456–461. Retrieved from http://www.academicjournals.org/article/article1379690850_Acar.pdf

Cohen D., & Prusak, L. (2001). *In good company. How social capital makes organizations work.* Boston, MA: Harvard Business School Press.

OCED Insights: Human Capital. (n.d). *What is social capital?...* Retrieved from https://www.oecd.org/insights/37966934.pdf

CHAPTER 38

NOBODY TOLD ME THE ROAD WOULD BE EASY

Dante Pelzer

With sweaty palms, I held hands with my colleagues and classmates. My legs shook and my mind raced, thinking about the announcement that awaited me. In the middle of the hallway on this fateful day we stood in a circle as passersby attempted to maneuver around this collection of melanin, intelligence, resistance, and perseverance. My eyes followed the contours of the circle as I nonverbally acknowledged the presence of each individual standing there. Half of the people in this huddle I had known for years; we laughed, cried, and toiled together along this academic journey. The others present had just started their own doctoral march, but for whatever reason felt connected to my journey. As we stood in solidarity with our eyes closed, hands and arms linked, a calm came over me when I heard the words, "In this moment, Lord, please cover brother Dante..." As the prayer concluded I felt a rush of energy, my body felt warm, and my mind was at ease. The next sound I heard was, "Dante the committee has reached a decision, you may reenter." We filed into the tiny conference room one by one with me bringing up the rear. As each person entered the room, I knew I was inching closer to hearing a phrase no one in my immediate or extended family had ever heard. My last few steps were strident and bold. As I closed the door behind me I heard the words, "Congratulations, Dr. Pelzer!" At that moment, the dreams and aspirations of a Geechee-talking, Charleston boy had come true.

As my peers and the committee cheered, applauded, and chatted around me, I sat there silent, almost in a catatonic state. I was still overwhelmed by the gravity of this moment. In this emotional mental space, I started to reflect on the journey that led me to this accomplishment. My first thoughts took me back to my childhood home. Situated in a neighborhood indicative of the late-1980s/early-1990s crack epidemic, the three-bedroom, one-bathroom brick house that served as the epicenter of my childhood was not immune to the derelict of our community. Drug dealing, gun violence, and prostitution were elements of everyday life. The crack house was next door to where we lived, and the street that ran in front of our home could have been mistaken for a catwalk judging by the way women strolled and strutted back and forth looking for Johns. At times, the carousel of activity in and around our house was dizzying.

During the early parts of my childhood my mom and I stayed with my granny. As the matriarch of our family, granny's house served as home for anyone needing a place to stay. In addition to my mom and me, granny took care of her youngest brother who has a severe learning disability. Granny was also the legal guardian of one of my first cousins. At one point during my youth as many as eight people were crammed into granny's shotgun house. Some of those housemates were street pharmacists, servicing the community with the same addictive beige rocks that ravished Black communities around the country. It was not uncommon to be woken up in the middle of the night by constant tapping on my bedroom room window. The syncopated beat was a signal that a customer needed a fix.

The vices that surrounded my home life were distant memories when I went to school. First through fourth grade, I attended a private Catholic school. I was not Catholic and my mom was not wealthy by any means, but she worked two jobs and scraped together enough money each month to pay tuition. The school was fairly diverse with many students belonging to military families who lived in the nearby, now-defunct, naval base housing community. In this educational setting it was okay to be intellectually curious, spontaneous, and hopeful. While at school, I was able to dream about what could be. I dreamed of a life void of sirens, house raids, and sharing a twin-size bed. I quickly realized with education I could have a life my granny and momma only dreamed about having. At school, the environmental trappings of my neighborhood felt so distant. Then each day the bell would ring with my mom waiting outside the large, wooden schoolhouse doors, ready to take me back to my other reality.

The summer before fifth grade, my mom told me the tuition at the Catholic school had gone up to $215 per month and she could no longer afford it. I was now forced to attend public school. It was during my public school experience when I realized vigorously pursuing education was not seen as normalized behavior for Black boys. My curiosity, which was once celebrated, was now met with opposition. My spontaneous behavior and talkativeness was now problematized. I went from teachers telling me I could be anything, to teachers telling me, "You just like the rest of them; you ain't gonna amount to nothing." The low expectations teachers and administrators often levied upon Black males were my new benchmarks. Let them tell it, I was destined for jail or early death by bullet.

My peers did not make the transition to public school any easier. I was ridiculed for the way I dressed (e.g., collared shirts and boat shoes), the way I spoke, and how I participated in class. As I completed a rough fifth grade year, I began to think my dream of making it out of my neighborhood was a foolish thought experiment.

Probably the lowest point of my public school years came in eighth grade. At the start of the school year I sat through a presentation about an academic magnet high school. The school was managed by Charleston County and students were admitted through an application process. The magnet school required that all incoming freshmen complete Algebra 1 prior to enrolling. Math was my kryptonite so my seventh grade standardized test math scores placed me in pre-algebra for eighth grade. But after sitting through the magnet school presentation I knew I needed to weasel my way into a section of Algebra 1. I begged and pleaded with the guidance counselor to place me in the more advanced math class, telling them my future depended on it. To my surprise the guidance counselor granted my request. Despite making an "A" in algebra and having an honor roll record throughout my middle school years, I was declined admission into the magnet school. As I read the rejection letter I sank in my desk and cried as my other classmates pranced, slapped-five, and celebrated their acceptance into the premier academic high school in the city. That rejection letter was another indicator that my dreams to have a new and better life was slowly slipping away.

I was zoned to attend one of worst high schools in the city, so I was not optimistic my high school experience would be any different from what I endured in middle school. My feeling of dread and despair changed after attending my first day of freshman, honors world history class. The teacher, Mr. Richards, was engaging, personable, and excited about the course content. His enthusiasm for the material inspired a part of me that had been dormant since my days at Catholic school. I began to speak up in class and raise my hand to answer questions. My intellectual curiosity was rewarded with positive affirmation and encouragement. Furthermore, Mr. Richards saw my potential and knew college was in my future. He got me plugged into various afterschool activities, ranging from speech and debate to community service. Mr. Richards, a White male, became the father figure I never had. He was my quiz bowl team coach, my unofficial academic advisor, my ride to and from extracurricular activities, and the person who helped me navigate my first serious crush. I owed a lot to Mr. Richards; he was a lifeline during a time when I was drowning in pessimism, depression, and rejection. Mr. Richards, my mom, and my granny were the pillars who held me up during my high school years. They let me know, in spite of "Black male crisis" pathology, that I was not a criminal-in-waiting. Moreover, these individuals plus my guidance counselors and church family helped me realize the power of having a village supporting you. With proper support and love, dreams live on, goals are achieved, and cycles of criminality are broken.

As my dissertation chair passed me the degree completion paperwork, I snapped back to reality. What seemed like hours in personal reflection probably lasted all of 15 seconds. Yet the mental journey from granny's house, through the educational pipeline, and finally to the conference room where I had just successfully defended my dissertation was too vivid and real. I got up from the table, took photos with my committee and friends, packed my bookbag, and exited the room. As the conference door closed behind me, I knew simultaneously more doors were opening in my future. Walking to my car I realized the magnitude of what I had just achieved. I achieved something that would not only change the trajectory of my life, but the life of my 2-year-old daughter and the generations that will follow her. She will not have to live the life I lived or see many of the things I saw; the success of her parents will ensure her life is better. But her reality is a stark contrast to the life lived by many young Black men in our country; Black men who live in impoverished neighborhoods, navigate oppressive educational systems, and constantly fight against the criminalization of their Black bodies. To those young men, I offer this advice:

1. Be dogged about achieving your dreams. Chase them with tenacity and vigor, even when the outlook appears bleak.
2. Find a village of support. Identify individuals who believe in your educational dreams as those folks will pour love, affirmation, and positivity into your life. They will give you the inspiration you need when you feel you cannot go on.
3. Be you. Black men are not a monolithic demographic bloc; there is no universal blueprint or definition for Black masculinity. We may share a racial identity, but we also have intersecting social identities, personalities, beliefs, and aspirations that make each of us unique. Be the author of your own life; let your voice be heard.

CHAPTER 39

I'M NOT MY CHAIR

Michael S. Washington

I became a wheelchair user in my early fifties after suffering from gout the majority of my adult life. I can remember like it was yesterday that morning awakening with a throbbing pain in my big toe as if someone had stuck a giant needle in it without anesthetic. I was 27 and had no idea what gout was and how it would change my life. When I think about it, long before I needed a wheelchair, I had some experiences that were figuratively disabling or could have been. Sometimes how you see yourself is most important; other times, how others see you may matter more. For me, how I see myself and move through life all begins with family. Growing up in the 1960s in a lower-middle class neighborhood exposed me to a wide range of people and situations: the importance of community, neighbors looking out for each other, and taking pride in what they had, however modest. I felt loved as a child by my parents and extended family.

Back then, it was common in African American communities to grow up in a multi-generational household like mine. Three generations lived in my house. My mother was loving and kind, but a strict disciplinarian. By contrast, my father a man of few words, taught more by example through his strong work ethic. He really knew how to manage money on a tight budget. Neither of my parents graduated high school; mom finished eleventh grade and dad the third grade. Yet, I've never known two smarter people with incredible common sense and wisdom. As I think back, more-than-likely my father was functionally illiterate. But when he died, he had no debt, left two mortgage-free homes, and a small monetary inheritance.

What my parents lacked educationally, my aunts made up the difference. Three of them graduated college and were elementary school teachers. They really pushed education and I caught the bug. They also exposed me to the love music, the arts, religion, travel, and the importance of family traditions. While all families have some dysfunction, including my own, I wouldn't trade mine for any other.

There were many positive things about my neighborhood growing up, though it was not devoid of the fragilities of the human condition. Some of my childhood friends succumbed to those pitfalls by dropping out of high school, going to jail, or simply not realizing their full potential. One thing or another got them off track. However, the influence of my family was always greater for me. Having strict parents was my saving grace! I remember having to be in the house before sunset or my mother would get in the car with switches (a bunch of small, long branches from a tree) in the back seat looking for me and would whup me on the spot wherever she found me. While still living at home at 23, I had a 3:00 a.m. curfew.

Although disabled now, I believe other challenges early on prepared me to face my new reality. In eighth grade, I recall asking my math teacher to be in the accelerated math group and she said, "Michael, the problem is some people think they are smarter than what they are" and I replied, "And some of them are teachers." Though shocked by her response, I couldn't resist giving her a taste of her own medicine. Fortunately, her words didn't break me. By the way, she sent me to the office to get paddled.

The summer before ninth grade, my mother gave me one of her famous lectures, which usually followed a whupping. She told me I could do better in school if I made up my mind I wanted to. That conversation stuck with me and I made the honor roll the first two report periods. Being inducted into the national junior honor society seemed within reach.

Adding to my momentum was having a substitute math teacher who told me I was too smart to be in her general math class. She told me I should be in Algebra I instead, even though my grades placed me in her class. Somehow, she got me into algebra. I have never forgotten her kind words and how she looked at me when she spoke them. She saw my potential and not simply my transcript. That was a life-affirming moment, one that boosted my confidence immeasurably.

Unfortunately, shortly thereafter, something happened that dashed my hopes of being inducted into the honor society. Just before the third report card, I was bullied by a classmate from my neighborhood and was threatened not to come to gym class. He said he was going to "kick my a**" if I came. And I believed him. Not being the fighting type, I stopped going to gym class and failed gym that term. Consequently, I was not inducted into the honor society. In some ways, I never got over that disappointment. It took something from me that affected me even in high school. Eventually, it came out that I had been bullied, but nothing ever happened to him.

In high school, music continued to be a source of joy that kept me connected in positive ways, but I was still disconnected academically. My junior year I got involved in speech and drama on a fluke by going to a meeting with a friend. I left the meeting a member and vice president of the club. Music, speech, and drama were my lifelines. Senior year I was asked to coach the class salutatorian to give the invocation at graduation. Public speaking made him extremely nervous. After working with him for weeks, we both concluded he couldn't do it. Our teacher suggested I give the invocation instead and the guidance counselor immediately said no, citing my grades were not good enough. I remember thinking what did grades have to do with saying a prayer, and if they did, why was the salutatorian failing so miserably. They asked me to work with him again and I did so in earnest, but ultimately, the salutatorian backed out. In the end, I gave the invocation at graduation even though I graduated in the middle of my class. That was a moment when talent trumped tradition.

After high school, I attended community college and reflected on my mother's conversation years earlier about making up my mind to do better academically, and I did. Sophomore year I transferred to a university but returned to my old habits of not performing well academically, which led to me dropping out and working full time instead.

At 32, after being promoted on my job, away on a business trip in New York, I wanted to go to a Broadway musical but couldn't afford it. In that moment, I saw my life flash before me thinking 40 was just around the corner and I had no degree. I knew I had to do something about it. As a Black man I felt having a degree was critical to my future success. Right then and there, I decided to go back to school full time and made the decision to quit my job to focus on my studies. I sought affirmation from family and friends with mixed results. Some encouraged me to go for it, while others told me to play it safe and work and go to school part time. One mentor told me he knew someone who quit their job to go to school and never got back on track. Yet, something within me was saying it was an all-or-nothing proposition—that I would never finish college on a part-time basis. So, I quit my job and enrolled full time. I give credit to my girlfriend, who is now my wife, for encouraging me to follow my heart. Her support made me feel secure about my decision. Two months after quitting my job, I got a full-time job on campus at half my former salary but enough to make ends meet until I graduated 2 years later, with highest honors. Going back to college full time to complete my degree was one of the single best decisions of my adult life, one that has been the catalyst for moving my career forward until this day. As of fall 2017, I began my doctoral studies.

Although I did not become a wheelchair user until later in life, challenges I experienced earlier could have stunted my personal and professional growth. Metaphorically speaking, those experiences could have crippled me. Sometimes it was my own determination that got me through, other times it was someone else who saw my potential. Every challenge along the way prepared me for what some would consider an ultimate challenge, losing a major life function like the ability to walk.

Around the time I began using a wheelchair, the president of the college where I worked gave his fall convocation speech that focused on some of his personal heroes. He recognized me as one of his heroes because of my positive outlook. He shared how he marveled at my upbeat attitude when I talked about my aspirations because I never focused on my disability, like it isn't a factor. Certainly, flattered by his public acknowledgment, I sat there thinking then as I do now—*What I can't do* is so immediately apparent that I simply focus on *what I can do*. After all, I'm not my chair.

More recently, sometimes when I go for medical treatment, medical personnel will ask my wife questions about me as though I'm not sitting there. She either defers to me or I simply answer the question. When this happens, it's like they cannot see beyond my wheelchair, as if they assume if I can't walk, I can't talk either. Those moments cause me to think about why I maintain an upbeat, positive attitude. They cause me to more fully appreciate I'm not my chair!

Remember, don't let challenges define or limit you. Whatever your circumstances, stay optimistic, knowing sometimes you'll have setbacks. Understand that the path to achieving your goals is not always logical or linear. Sometimes, you just have to follow your heart.

CHAPTER 40

ON STUTTERING AND SPEECH IMPEDIMENTS

Stepping Stones Not Speed Bumps

Charles A. Barrett

> ... O Lord, I'm not very good with words. I never have been, and I'm not now, even though you have spoken to me. I get tongue-tied, and my words get tangled.
> —Moses, Exodus 4:10–14 (NLT)

Since the beginning of time, men have been making excuses for why they could not accomplish what they have been called to do. The epitaph above was Moses' plea to avoid a task that had life-changing implications for an entire nation. An Israelite, Moses was chosen to liberate his brothers and sisters from Egyptian slavery. Despite receiving very clear instructions about his assignment, because of an inadequacy that he perceived within himself, Moses focused on what he felt disqualified him from being a part of something great.

Like Moses, everyone has something to overcome. Too numerous to name, each of us will face situations that are seemingly insurmountable. While some brothers live with the reality of mental illness, others wonder how they will rise above poverty, homelessness, illiteracy, drug and alcohol addiction, or physical, psychological, and sexual abuse. But as challenging as these circumstances may be, we should always be encouraged with two fundamental truths. First, these things will not get the best of us. Second, they exist to propel us toward our purpose, which will positively affect the lives of others, especially those like us. Regardless of what we may struggle with today, these temporary setbacks and moments of adversity cannot be compared to all that we will achieve as we, and after we, emerge as more than conquerors.

Like many others, my life was far from picture perfect. However, I am grateful for everything that I have experienced and encountered. Albeit cliché, my four brothers and I were raised in a loving and supportive home in Freeport, a Long Island suburb east of New York City. Although my parents both worked full-time jobs to provide for our family, they did not always have the financial means to give us everything that we wanted. Nevertheless, mom and dad made tremendous sacrifices to provide everything that we needed. They were fierce supporters of our educational, athletic, musical, and extracurricular activities. Perhaps because I serve children and families as a school psychologist and have intimate knowledge of the importance of parental involvement, I am especially grateful for the childhood that my parents gave me.

Despite how much I enjoyed growing up in Freeport, attending great schools in a diverse middle-class community, and my parents' unconditional love and support, these things were not protective against something that seemed to be a thorn in my flesh: stuttering. While anxiety and trauma have been implicated as causes of some individuals' stuttering, these explanations were not applicable to me. Having stuttered since I was a young child, my dysfluency of speech was the result of a biological predisposition as my father and some of his siblings stuttered as well.

STUTTERING: THE EARLY YEARS

My earliest memory of stuttering was in first grade. I was in Mrs. Keyser's class at Leo F. Giblyn Elementary School. Although the exact details escape me, I remember crying at school and my father talking to me about it at home—I am pretty sure that Mrs. Keyser called to tell him what happened. Shortly afterwards, I began speech therapy with the school's speech pathologist, Ms. Valerie Schwinger. Parenthetically, I loved—whatever that meant for a 7-year old, impressionable boy—Ms. Schwinger! She worked with me through elementary school until I met another speech pathologist in fifth and sixth grades.

Formally known as Childhood-Onset Fluency Disorder and classified as a Communication Disorder in the Diagnostic and Statistical Manual of Mental Disorders, Fifth Edition (DSM-5; American Psychological Association, 2013), for the estimated 3 million Americans who stutter (National

Institute on Deafness and Other Communication Disorders, 2017), it affects our lives in myriad ways. For me, although I am naturally quiet and have a reserved disposition, stuttering certainly exacerbated these qualities. Especially in school, because I could not always predict when I would stutter, it was easier to simply not speak as much during class discussions. Rather than raising my hand to ask or answer questions, I became very comfortable observing and listening to what the teacher and my peers were saying. Although I could read, being called upon to do so was uncomfortable. Would I stutter... Would I be able to read the passage fluently... Would my peers laugh at me... While sitting in class, these thoughts occasionally occupied my mind. As a result, and somewhat subconsciously as I matriculated through elementary, middle, high school, and even undergraduate and graduate school, I became very comfortable with not using my voice to avoid the embarrassment associated with my potential dysfluency.

Stuttering is characterized by speech that is not fluent. Rather than saying words smoothly and efficiently, those of us who stutter struggle with articulating various sounds or expressing our thoughts despite knowing exactly what we want to convey. Although I did not realize this as a child, for me, stuttering was more than a speech impediment. It was an attempt to silence my voice and perspective.

DISTRACTION AND DISCOURAGEMENT

Before his passing in January 2015, legendary Gospel singer, songwriter, musician, and composer Andre Crouch (1997) penned these opening words to "Distraction," which was released on his 1997 album, *Pray: I Met a Man the Other Day on the Road of Good Intentions*. After providing a few more descriptors, Crouch identifies this character as *Distraction* whose ultimate purpose was to prevent him from reaching his destination. Metaphorically, this is what stuttering was for me—a distraction. Similar to the distractions that we encounter in other areas of our lives, stuttering tried to shift my focus from fulfilling my purpose, which I later realized was to minister hope and wholeness to people. The danger of distraction is captured in a statement that I created and live my life by:

> If we can simply lose our focus, sometimes this is enough to prevent us from accomplishing everything that we are destined to achieve. As one who stuttered, could I encourage others and minister hope and wholeness without speaking...

Like Moses, stuttering tried to discourage me by making me feel less than others. Fundamentally, I have learned that those who are quiet are often misunderstood. Because people are generally uncomfortable with ambiguity, in the absence of certainty, we formulate our own conclusions, although they may be inaccurate, to lessen the uneasiness of cognitive dissonance. In trying to understand quiet people, others likely form impressions that are premature, misinformed, and quite honestly, wrong. Especially in graduate school, because I was generally quieter than the other students were, both peers and faculty misunderstood me. Coupled with my quiet demeanor, I was also the only Black male in a PhD program with no faculty of color. Rather than reserving judgment about my reluctance to speak, some felt that I was less capable and/or disinterested in the subject matter. Although both of these ideas were untrue, I experienced fleeting "Moses moments" in which I questioned whether I was smart enough, qualified enough, or simply enough to occupy the mostly White space of higher education.

FINDING MY VOICE

As I mentioned earlier in this chapter, obstacles and challenges are only seemingly impossible. While they try to discourage and distract us, more importantly, they propel us in the direction of our destiny. Although stuttering tried to impede my meaningful participation in, and contribution to, issues that are relevant to me, others who are like me, and the field of school psychology, it also helped to develop other areas of my life.

It has been said that for those who have lost or limited use of one of their senses—seeing, touching, tasting, feeling, smelling, or hearing—another develops more keenly. For example, despite Ray Charles Robinson (Ray Charles) and Stevland Hardaway Morris (Stevie Wonder) being blind, they had a supernatural ability to hear and create timeless melodies that inspire countless millions. In some ways, their inability to see strengthened their ability to hear.

Because we are never expected to use what we do not have, similarly, my discomfort with speaking due to stuttering helped me to use my voice in other ways. Having been a musician for more than 30 years, I have always expressed my innermost feelings without saying a word. Inspired by my pre-kindergarten and kindergarten teachers, Mr. John Schreiber and Mr. Ned Decker, who incorporated music into virtually every aspect of the school day, music has always been a powerful medium for me to convey sentiments that could not be uttered or that I was too reluctant to communicate with words. Without lyrics, I have used instrumental offerings that are transformative for others' hope and wholeness.

Equally significant has been my ability to express myself through writing. In both professional and personal arenas, writing is not only something that I enjoy, but a gift that I have been given to speak truth to power related to school psychology, social justice, and equitable educational practice. Ironically, while in graduate school, a professor who did not understand me, and was somewhat critical of my style, also told me that I had a perspective that was worth sharing. Although I did not fully appreciate the depth of this statement years ago, it has proven to be one of the most empowering affirmations of my career.

Like Moses, I know that it is easy to make excuses because we feel inadequate to accomplish great things. After all, we may stutter. We may not read very well. We may have been abused. We may be poor. But ultimately, these things do not disqualify us from making meaningful contributions to the world around us. In fact, they are exactly the things that the world needs. Because we have a perspective that is worth sharing, we can overcome the discouragement and distraction that are associated with stuttering or any other speech impediment. If you are struggling with finding your voice and the manner in which you can rise above challenges that are trying to silence you and your perspective, be encouraged. Below are a few suggestions that can help you in your personal journey to succeed despite facing an obstacle in your speech.

YOU CAN OVERCOME, TOO

As I mentioned earlier in this chapter, I am grateful for my life. No doubt, things could have been worse for me. Stuttering, an impediment to slow my momentum and prevent me from pursuing and fulfilling my purpose, has actually been instrumental in my development. And because I overcame this, you can too!

The Importance of Early Intervention

If possible, participate in speech and language therapy with a certified or licensed provider. For parents and guardians of young men who stutter or have other speech impediments, early intervention is critical to their success. When I participated in speech therapy at school, it was with other students who had a variety of speech and language weaknesses. In other words, I was not the only one. The normalization of young people's speech impediments in a supportive therapeutic environment is tremendously helpful because they may feel self-conscious about their respective conditions. Although stuttering and other speech impediments might not be curable, with the proper support and interventions, children are able to learn effective strategies to manage their speech conditions and minimize academic, social, emotional, and behavioral impact in school and with their peers.

If you have questions about securing these support services for your child, contact your local public school or school district for more information. In many instances, there is a building administrator (i.e., an assistant principal) who is responsible for overseeing these services. Additionally, if you have concerns about your child's speech and language development, share them with your family practice physician or your child's pediatrician as they can provide referrals for more specialized assessments. Lastly, to find a certified speech-language pathologist (SLP) in your area, please visit the American Speech-Language-Hearing Association (ASHA; www.asha.org).

Combatting Discouragement and Distraction

Perhaps most importantly, do not allow any situation or person to steal your voice. Because your perspective is important and has life-changing implications for others, especially those who are like you, nothing, not even a speech impediment, can silence what you have to say. If necessary, find an alternative method to speak truth to power. For me, my message of hope and wholeness is primarily communicated through music and writing. For others, it may be through singing, rapping, or dancing. Especially for parents and guardians, exposing your children to various outlets of creative expression is one of the most meaningful contributions that you can make to their lives. Although this often involves sacrifices of time and financial resources, affording them these opportunities is not only critical to their development as individuals, but they can also be therapeutic as they face current challenges, and protective against future obstacles.

It's Really Not About You

Focus on something that is greater than you. As we experience myriad challenges, perspective is critically important. In other words, although it does not change the reality of what we are facing, it helps to know that there is purpose behind and beyond what we are currently going through. As a school psychologist and adjunct professor, an ancient parable that refers to *the least of these* has informed the manner in which I serve students and families. Somewhat unexpectedly, the child and young adult who preferred to not speak in class, regularly lectures and presents to local and national audiences. Why... Because my perspective matters. As a Black male school psychologist in a field that is disproportionately White and female, my voice needs to he heard—especially by the boys and young men who look like me.

Through the lens of social justice, although my speech is not always perfect, I cannot allow this relatively insignificant impediment to discourage me from speaking up and out against inequity and injustice. I cannot allow this inconvenience to distract me from the necessity of speaking on behalf of those who have been marginalized by systemic racism. Even with its flaws and imperfections, my voice is perfectly suited to speak for those who have been silenced and to empower those who are unsure of how to speak for themselves. Young brother, you are in excellent company. Like Moses, you will be instrumental in the liberation of an entire nation and generation. Do not allow your speech impediment to cause you to second guess your fundamental right and authority to speak to situations that must be changed for the advancement of others.

The Importance of a Supportive Network

Find a supportive network of individuals who will encourage you and be patient with you during your moments of dysfluency. I remember my parents, especially my father, telling others that I stuttered so that that they would be patient with me. A few years ago, I was visiting a former teacher and saw one of the secretaries at my elementary school. Not only did she remember me, but she also told me about a conversation that she had with my father. Although it was more than 20 years ago, she remembered that he told her about being patient with me because I stuttered. Similarly, when I was 11 years old, I was going to play in California with a church choir. Because it was my first time traveling with this group, my father told one of the musicians about my stutter. Although somewhat embarrassed, it helped to put me at ease.

Stepping Stone Not a Speed Bump

Rather than viewing your speech impediment as a speed bump, it is a stepping stone. In other words, because of this you will be more sensitive to others, not only those with speech impediments, but those who are different for a variety of reasons.

In my undergraduate and graduate courses, I require my students to speak in every class session. But because I stutter, I also intentionally, and quickly, create a supportive environment that is conducive for students to feel comfortable sharing their ideas, asking questions, and responding to their peers and me. Because I stutter and know what it feels like to prefer listening rather than contributing verbally, I am sensitive to my English language learner (ELL) students who may be self-conscious about their English proficiency. I am sensitive to shy students whose anxiety makes it difficult to present to their peers. Without a doubt, my perspective as a Black male who stutters has made me more patient because I wanted others to be patient with me. It has made me a better listener because I needed others to listen to me more intently when I was a youngster. It has made me a better psychologist—one who is slow to form impressions because all students deserve this from the adults in their lives. Having met with parents and students who stutter, I understand that they are quiet, not because they do not know the answer or want to contribute, but because they may be nervous.

Be encouraged. It is a stepping stone, not a speed bump.

REFERENCES

American Psychiatric Association, DSM-5 Task Force. (2013). *Diagnostic and statistical manual of mental disorders: DSM-5* (5th ed.). Arlington, VA: Author.

Crouch, A. (1997). Distraction. On *Pray: I Met a Man the Other Day on the Road of Good Intentions* [CD]. United States: Qwest Records.

National Institute on Deafness and Other Communication Disorders. (2017). *Stuttering*. Retrieved from https://www.nidcd.nih.gov/health/stuttering

CHAPTER 41

KEEPING MY HEAD ABOVE WATER IN A RIVER OF WHITENESS

LaMarcus J. Hall

I must say that I am thankful for all things and everything that the Lord has blessed me with. However, my life has been far from easy. As I reflect back to my childhood days, it all starts at the home of my grandparents, Hattie and the late Y. M. Hall, in Elberton, GA. This is where I gained much of my foundation. Until the age of nine, I really did not know much about my biological father. I attended Blackwell Elementary School while living with my grandparents because, my mother was away in college. When my mother returned, she dated my step-father and he's been in my life since the first grade. Eventually, they got married when I was in ninth grade. While attending Blackwell, I gained knowledge from a wealth of stellar teachers who really had my best interest at heart. Along with attending school, I was very involved in my church, Mt. Calvary Baptist Church. As I made the transition to middle school, I had the opportunity to learn about music. That's where my love for playing the drums started. I became a decent player of the drums and also played for church choirs.

MIDDLE SCHOOL

The transition to middle school was definitely one that I will not forget. For the most part, middle school was full of adventure, making new friends, and learning more about myself. During this stage in life, I dealt with "puppy love," hormones raging, and trying to stay balanced. I was very sociable and had two close friends. We became very close from playing drums/percussion for the middle school football games and concert band. My "crew" was not the popular bunch in school. We were not the jocks or the boys all the girls thought were cute. We were called names such as nerds and accused of "acting White," due to not fitting in with the other guys. Outside of band and church, we stayed within our crew and hung out together. My close friends were very smart and took many accelerated classes.

Mathematics was a struggle for me. I remember being told that I had to take remedial math in the eighth grade. I felt defeated, beneath my friends and everyone else around me. It was God's grace that kept me during such a difficult moment. Band and church were a distraction, but they were also a place of refuge. One of the key moments I remember in middle school was trying out for the high school marching band drumline, specifically for the snare drum. This was a difficult task. After several weeks of practice and going over fundamentals, I made the drum line as an eighth grader.

HIGH SCHOOL

High school was the educational place where I was beginning to find myself. I hung out with my best friends and eventually became cool with other classmates as well. This was also the time where I needed to figure out where I would like to be after graduation; I thought often about my future career. I knew that I wanted to go to college but was very unsure what college would accept me. I continued to struggle with mathematics. I remember crying many nights because of not being able to grasp the concepts. I earned a "C" in all of my math courses in high school. Along with the stress of school and trying to keep up with everything else, a life changing event occurred. In April of 1999, my grandfather, Mr. Y. M. Hall, died. I thought that the world actually stopped rotating, and my life was over. He was everything to me. This man who taught me how to pray, learn about church and World Champion Wrestling, and raised me was gone. Following his death, things were not the same for me. I miss him dearly and wish he could be here in my life today.

My junior year, I joined the TRIO-Educational Talent Search program. I learned the college admission process, requirements for colleges/universities, and had the opportunity to go on several college tours. At the time, my mother did not have the finances to send me on many college tours or pay for college application fees or SAT/ACT tests. The TRIO-ETS program provided me with the resources to progress forward.

As I approached my senior year, my close friends were accepted into the colleges of their choice. At this time, I absolutely had no idea where I was going. As the last semester of high school approached, decisions had to be made. I had been accepted to several Historically Black Colleges and Universities (HBCUs), but my heart was set on Georgia Southern University. In March, Georgia Southern informed me that I was not accepted but offered me the opportunity to go to the community college on their campus, East Georgia College. If I successfully completed 30 hours at East Georgia College, I would be allowed to transfer into Georgia Southern. This was a hurtful moment for me, but I refused to let this stand in my way. I embraced the opportunity and moved forward.

COLLEGE DAYS SWIFTLY PASS

I remember being so excited to move to Statesboro, Georgia to begin my collegiate journey. I woke my parents up early that morning so that I could get to Georgia Southern University or GSU as soon as possible. Although I moved to GSU to begin the journey of college, I realize now that I was in a stage of self-doubt. It was tough taking courses and not feeling competent as your peers around you who were accepted on their first try. Somehow, I had to "suck up" this shame and make the best of it. During my first year at East Georgia College from 2002 to 2003, I maintained a GPA over a 3.0 and was able to transfer to Georgia Southern University the next fall.

Becoming a Georgia Southern University student meant the world to me. My best friend was there. He began his studies at GSU the previous year. I was exposed to various cultures, religions, and opportunities. I was presented with a life changing opportunity after becoming a GSU student. I was eligible to seek membership into the Xi Tau chapter of Alpha Phi Alpha Fraternity, Inc. I took a journey that I will never forget. From that moment on, I was surrounded by members of my fraternity who had similar beliefs, goals, and stood for something. After going through a phase of choosing the right major, I found that child and family development (CHFD) was the best degree option for me. CHFD gave me the opportunity to be creative in teaching, which meant not being forced to teach in one way mandated by the local and state government. I was often criticized, due to being only 1 of 3 males in the program. When people hear the term child and family development, many think of young females working with babies. I could have cared less what people thought about my passion for children. I was going to see this degree through, regardless of misperceptions.

As my senior semester approached, the dean of students pulled me in his office. I'll never forget this day because I literally believed that I was about to be expelled or was in trouble. Instead, the dean put the idea in mind to consider working in the field of higher education. He told me to think about working in the field, the multiple career opportunities, and how he knew that I had the ability to impact students by the 100s. I took in his advice and applied for the master's of higher education and administration at GSU. Through all of the adversity faced, I was able to finish my bachelor's degree in four years, majoring in child and family development. When there's a will, there's a way!

GRADUATE SCHOOL

It took quite some time to know if I got accepted into the graduate program at GSU. I began to panic. By mid-June of receiving my undergraduate degree, I became worried that my application was lost. I went to Wal-Mart one evening and one of the professors passed me while I was in line. She asked, "Son, have you found out if you got accepted into graduate school..." I said, "No, I'm patiently waiting." She told me to check my status late that night and a decision should be made. I did my best to be patient and wait. I went to get lunch with my line brothers to kill some time. I waited until about 7:00 p.m. to check my status. When I logged in, my status had changed from "undecided" to "provisional acceptance." I was in shock because I was accepted into the program by the grace of God! Provisionally accepted or not, I knew it was a sign from Him.

It was during graduate school when I noticed that I was the only Black male in most of my classes. Not only was I the only Black male, but in many cases, I was the youngest. During that time of my life, I began to observe how Black males are highly observed in everything we do. I learned quickly that there is very little room for error and that perception always overruled reality. After the first semester, I was taken off provisional acceptance. That was only the beginning of a tough graduate journey. The next semester, I had to take a theory and application course online. I was very skeptical about taking an online course in graduate school. The class did not turn out well and I was kicked out of the program. I was very disappointed in myself, but reapplied to the program. I was accepted again and progressed through my courses. By God's grace, I finished that summer of 2008 with my master's of education degree.

DOCTORAL STUDIES

As a doctoral student, I've come to realize that much of the pressure experienced by Black males has not changed in the realm of academia. We are often expected to produce more work than our counterparts. We have to get accustomed to being isolated in White spaces. In those spaces, there is a light of critique that is shined upon us, whether we want it or not; like being under a microscope, like being profiled.

Although we face a different journey than most, we must continue to progress forward, creating a pathway for the next Black male to come behind us. I also believe that we should not indulged too much in the luxury things along the way. For example, it's okay to have a nice car and a home for your family (if you have one during graduate school). However, that should not be your only identity. As one who is aspiring to one day join the academy, I refuse to be defined by the tangible things I possess. When I leave this world, I want my work for family, students, and friends to speak for itself. Stay encouraged. Ask for help. Find friends and allies. We as people of color are more than capable of being successful. It takes time, commitment, and determination, along with faith!

CHAPTER 42

RISING ABOVE A TRACKED SYSTEM

Brian K. Williams

Do your best. Make good choices. You have to make it. These words, said to me before each school day as a child, are still cemented in my mind. Their usage placed emphasis on the importance of education in my household growing up. My mom was a teacher and my dad's side of the family was deeply rooted in the education system. I learned at an early age that doing well in school was the pathway to opportunity, success, and a prosperous life; at least that was the message in my home. Unfortunately, school was sending a different message that I did not quite understand. I learned quickly that opportunity and success were exclusive and predicated on one's academic group. It was the concept of tracking students based on standardized tests. The strategy of tracking required teachers to place students in different classes based on their standardized test data, and not on their daily academic achievements or quarterly grades. I was dismayed at the thought of being one of the students stuck in a track not conducive to personal or academic growth. My track placement, however, became one that I was forced to endure while in middle and high school. Nevertheless, I had to make the most of what school had to offer and translate the lessons learned from my educational experience to success. I did this by not allowing tracking to become a hindrance, but a stepping-stone to an even greater pathway.

A STRONG START

My love for school started at the elementary level. I cannot recall anything I enjoyed more than learning. School was like a big playground for me. Every class was a new, fun way to do mental exercises. I was eager to explore new concepts, collaborate with my peers, and conquer new challenges. The best part of my day was going home to tell my parents all that I had learned at school. During this phase of my life, I excelled in all subject areas and teachers considered me a star student. My parents and teachers believed I had a promising future and I was determined to create one. As my parents expected of me, I did my best and made good choices. I was on the pathway to success!

GETTING OFF TRACK

Unfortunately, my passion for school started to waver in middle school. It was a period when I encountered the state mandated end of grade test. The emphasis on this exam was massive and the power of it was unmatched. I could not believe one assessment could derail my academic career. Well it did! My less than proficient score on the sixth grade end-of-grade test was a blow to my academic reputation and confidence. It seemed everyone's conversations changed about me being successful in school. Because of my poor performance, my track placement was determined to be at the remedial level. I went from being a gifted student to a remedial student within a blink of an eye. Although my track placement served as an intervention to produce better test scores, I did not feel as though I was growing academically. Consequently, I regressed in my learning because the expectations of me were so low. My education began to be mostly confined to textbook work and worksheets, finishing one and getting handed another. The basis of learning was primarily concept memorization and recall, nothing exciting or worth going home to share. Nevertheless, I continued to excel in my courses and endured the changes, trusting it was for the best.

Reaching my maximum potential of learning was more challenging than ever. I had never been so displeased and disengaged in school than when I got into high school. I dreaded going to class and only did my best because college was the end goal. Academic challenge was nonexistent, my teachers did not build authentic relationships, and most of the students in my courses did not want to be in school. I could not blame them. They were a product of low expectations, poor classroom relationships, and learning that was not rigorous, causing them to underperform. We were all traveling down a road to ultimate failure based on our academic track. My friends on the other hand, were in all types of advanced courses, classes I would soon realize were necessary to attend high ranked universities.

As I read the admission requirements of the top universities I wanted to attend, I quickly noticed I did not measure up to their standards. I gave school everything I had to find out I was not good enough for the next stage. I felt excluded and unwelcomed by the very thing that was supposed to provide me with endless opportunities. I was not enrolled in the required courses, I did not take on the sought after leadership roles, nor did I get the requested community service hours required for admission. I was confused and filled with anger. No one ever told me the courses I needed to take, what extracurricular activities I should have been involved in, or the type of experiences I should have had in high school to receive acceptance to the most competitive universities in my state. It was clear my high school offered college-ready courses to some of the student body and counseled them toward their goals. The education tracks they provided, however, placed numerous students on a path to endless opportunities, while others like me had to figure out where we belonged in education and the world outside of high school. When I realized how my track placement molded my future, it was too late. I would need to start high school over to meet the requirements of the top universities I wanted to attend. I did not know what to do. I felt defeated.

I had countless conversations with my parents about my future and they assured me my hard work was not in vain. They reminded me that going to college was my only option and I would find the perfect university. While feelings of defeat did not easily subside, they were right. I worked extremely hard to make it to college and that is where I was going. Besides, I could not let a system designed to fail me win. I mustered up the strength and started researching potential universities to attend post high school, none of which was on my original list. After several days of researching, I found a few universities in which I met their admission criteria. I applied, and the waiting game began.

REDEMPTION

While I impatiently waited for an acceptance letter, I reflected on my high school career and thought about all the things that I could have done differently. I thought about how I could have advocated for myself to be more prepared to reach my goals. There had to be some way I could have been in control of my courses, the material exposed to me, and the information I received pertaining to life post graduation. I am sure there was, but I did not seek that control or fight for it. I went on with my high school career naïve, trusting that my school was going to do what was best for me.

The wait was officially over. I gained acceptance to a nearby university, the only university I received an acceptance letter from out of the few schools I sent applications. While overjoyed to be going to college, my acceptance solely from one university was a reminder of how my track placement limited my options. Either way, I was excited to change the narrative of my story. I was determined to erase the disappointment and change my trajectory with this fresh start, a fresh start to advocate for myself and not let any system decide the outcomes of my future. I was going to be in control. From the day of my college acceptance, I decided to approach my education with a critical outlook and plan. I was going to be informed and prepared for the road ahead. My decision to advocate for myself led to graduating undergraduate school in three years, obtaining a masters and doctorate degree, and securing the job of my dreams. As my parents hoped, I made it. I defied the odds and created a future not probable for a student in my track placement.

While I did not advocate for myself or take a proactive approach to my education early on, I was still able to make critical adjustments that would positively affect my future. It is important to understand that at any stage of your education, you can work to change the outcomes of your academic trajectory. I encourage students feeling trapped in a tracked system to:

- *Embrace curiosity and constantly seek to understand*: Ask questions and do research on your placement to determine if it is conducive to your academic and personal growth.
- *Set goals and identify strategies for achieving them*: Be intentional about your path and the steps necessary to accomplish the desired results.
- *Build a strong network*: Collaborate and build relationships with peers headed toward similar goals, teachers, and administrators.

The abovementioned recommendations were a lifesaver for me. They allowed me to be informed and in control of my educational career, setting the foundation for a prosperous future outside of school. My curiosity solidified my path to success. I questioned every advising appointment, course selection, and academic opportunity extended to my peers which I was unaware. At this point, I never naively accepted what another person had planned for me. The goals I set allowed me to be intentional about my decision-making, carefully identifying the strategies necessary to create a clear path to success. With this approach, I minimized distractions, meaningless detours, and roadblocks. Moreover, the people in my network held me accountable and pushed me to my full potential. Through them, I experienced diverse perspectives and stayed abreast of important developments on my academic journey. I firmly believe if students use the recommendations I propose, they will reach their goals and rise above a tracked system designed to block their progress.

CHAPTER 43

EVEN TODAY I REMEMBER THE PAIN

Gregory Washington

This chapter includes reflections on how I have to daily overcome the systemic challenges many men of color face in the United States of America and the last two sections include keys for thriving. Today I appreciate my role as a scholar practitioner in the social work profession with over 25 years of professional experience. It was a challenge to get out of the Robert Taylor Housing Projects on the southside of Chicago and transition to middle-class neighborhoods. It has been an adventure in utilizing my family's resilience and the love of my parents.

My parents migrated from rural sharecropping communities in Mississippi and established a family that included my brother and I during a time where hope for inclusion and opportunity was blooming. We were all connected to the family members that preceded us and were able to benefit from the work ethic, lessons, and networks my extended family established. Much of this information was shared via the verbal Griot tradition of storytelling and I was fascinated by the colorful episodes of struggle, survival, and triumph shared during family gatherings over Bid Wisk games, southern delicacy meals, and family reunions.

Multiple levels of trauma were a part of these stories but the laughter during the storytelling taught lessons of survival, how to navigate extreme poverty and tremendous suffering by staying intimately connected. I now know today what I did not understand at that time about the pain and frustrations omitted or humorously recounted in various ways by my family. The African American legacy of mutual aid and maximizing cultural strengths served to ease the pain and was integrated into stories about migration from Mississippi to Chicago in ways that linked them with housing, jobs, and education. The brutal oppression my family experienced in the Jim Crow environment of Mississippi, and the slave plantations before that, left deep scars in their psyche and that of their born and unborn children. The "New Jim Crow" system modifies the past oppression mechanisms with disproportionate minority confinement systems that control the freedom of African American men (Leary, 2005; Alexander, 2012). Systematic oppression was combined with very overt visible violent events that exist in my memory.

PSYCHOLOGICAL TRAUMA AND CONSCIOUSNESS

Memories and memoirs can be painful and one that stands out from my childhood was the day Dr. Reverend Martin Luther King Jr. was killed. I was 10 years old at the time, with pain mixed with confusion; I remember asking my father why "they" killed him. I do not remember what he said, but I do remember the pain on his face. Even then, I somehow knew it was more complicated than a single crazed lone gunman as presented by many in media and throughout historical recollections. I understood White people hated Black people and killing the most important Black man in the nation was a way to hurt all Black people. This understanding or "consciousness" about how the world worked and the related pain was something I would experience repeatedly as I progressed along my educational journey. Education provided an opportunity to gain a detailed understanding about centuries of systemized dehumanizing slavery, terrorizing Jim Crow codes, and oppressive social policies. This awareness of the death and torture of Black people can be difficult to process and handle in productive ways. Black consciousness can contribute to the production of an educated Black man with collective pain, anger, and sense of helplessness from generations of Black people.

Awareness of the enslavement, rape, torture, and murder of my ancestors is something I had to learn how to tolerate. Although rarely discussed in scholarly literature in its totality, this awareness of the science of White supremacy and its contribution to millions of deaths and torture of Black families can be painful and difficult for men to process and handle in healthy ways. I am aware of how it contributed to my experiences with bouts of depression and related self-destructive behavior that required culturally sensitive intervention. Continual healing provides awareness of why I have periodically operated as a tortured soul and lights a focus on the science and art of promoting the healthy development of young Black males.

BLACK MANHOOD IN THE ACADEMY

I identify myself as a conscious Black man that has slipped through the marginalization socializing mechanisms of U.S. education institutions. It has been important to learn that men of color in academic institutions can leverage resources to empower and liberate their people. Many men of color understand they have been allowed to participate in a majority of academic institutions because they do not threaten the power elite. This allows a focus on saving our children from the impact of biased and under resourced systems by learning to utilize cultural assets. Integrating culturally specific methods of empowerment into systems is a significant challenge that is frequently under appreciated. I have embraced my role as a scholar practitioner that has focused on culturally centered group interventions for young males of color. I have learned that the social work profession, inside and outside the academy, can sometimes be a nurturing place for a conscious Black man that understands history, culture, politics, and the economics of exploitation. Part of the challenge is that many if not most men typically consider teaching and social work a field that is specifically geared towards and best handled by women in part because it emphasizes nurturing, self-awareness, sharing vulnerabilities, and feelings. Particularly, men of color, from dangerous poverty-stricken urban neighborhoods, are taught that sharing feelings, fears, and insecurities can make you vulnerable to harm. But exploring emotions, trauma histories, coping skills, and vulnerabilities are frequently important tasks for men who are helping families raise their grandchildren, sisters, brothers, nieces, nephews, and so on, and in the teaching and social work systems. Focusing on this part of my identity and helping others to understand has been instrumental to my professional and personal mission.

UNDERSTAND AND THE "GAME"

Working as a scholar practitioner in Chicago, Atlanta, and Memphis has required me to have an understanding that in poverty stricken urban neighborhoods, which are sometimes referred to as, "the streets or the hood," boys and men survive by being "hard" and understanding the rules of the "game." By this, I mean the rules related to navigating the threats to life and freedom that exist in the "streets" or the "hood" include not showing you care, but showing you are "hard." Many successful men of color respect and understand the rules of the "game" and there is value in helping them respect ways to integrate a self-reflective nurturing side. It seems reasonable to believe successful men of color have learned to operate in society by strategically maximizing the educational resources available to them and the ways to navigate the racism and inequity within educational institutions. I believe this knowledge, "street knowledge," and the availability of nurturing cultural assets is also critical.

It is also important for men of color to understand the oppression "game" and how it is played in two consistent ways in social settings. First, education curriculums in all U.S. schools tend to minimize or omit the cultural assets and the contributions of people of color. Secondly, schools in communities where people of color live are not as well funded as those in White communities (Spatig-Amerikaner & Center for American, 2012). The result is the pedagogy of White supremacy consistently shows up in the U.S. school systems (De los Rios, Lopez, & Morrell, 2015). When working with young African-American males in school and community-based settings, I have been intentional about helping them understand the rich history of people of African descent that preceded the transatlantic slave trade. I feel it is also important to help them develop a critical consciousness about historical trauma and the current threats and assets related to being a Black man in the United States (Watts & Abdul-Adil, 1997). In addition to helping young males understand the systematic factors that disproportionately affect people of color, it is important to share love, care, and nurturance as strategies to help men of color have and help oppressed people.

UTILIZE ELDERS

I advise the recognition of "elders" as valuable resources for success. In many communities around the world, elders are given the task of protecting and educating young people in culturally specific ways such as African-centered rites of passage programs. Men of color need to be mentored and in turn, mentor others. As an African American social worker, I have found the African-centered or Afrocentric rites of passage approach a valuable resource in promoting the healthy development of African American males (Washington, Johnston, Jones, & Langs, 2006; Washington, Watts & Watson, 2008). I have designed and continue to refine as well as evaluate a mentoring approach called Pyramid Mentoring that integrates young men (junior elders) and middle age men (senior elders) as mentors. This approach allows the junior elders to be trained and mentored by the senior elders. Subsequently, all elders work together to mentor boys (Washington,

Barnes, & Watts, 2014). Culturally-centered group work is proving to be a valuable resource for influencing the pro-social behaviors of youth and it also contributes to elders being mentored and mentoring (Washington, Caldwell, Watson, & Lindsey, 2017; Washington et al., 2007).

CONCLUSION

The ability to overcome can be fueled by knowledge of how the White supremacy has contributed to genocide and mass incarceration. As uncomfortable as it is to speak about, we cannot afford to forget the lessons of the elders and ancestors that include mutual aid networks and reliance on cultural assets in our determination to dismantle the structure of White supremacy. It is critical to stay connected to elders and to continue to mentor boys. This contributes to processing our frustrations and sharing our successes. Recognizing that we are not alone and can connect with men like us who understand what we feel and are capable of successfully navigating life's journeys is a way that remains true to self, cultural identity development, and personal legacy gains; it is also a meaningful way to use our resource. When we share this skill with our youth, we help them understand their value and power.

RECOMMENDATIONS

1. Adult men need to stay connected to their elders to nurture their health and healing. In many cases the insidious effects of oppression can best be understood by those who have experienced and developed ways to survive and thrive. I believe older adult men (senior elders) in barber shops, churches, community centers, and drumming circles are a valuable resource for younger adult men (junior elders).
2. The interaction of those of us who are senior elders with the programs that mentor boys is recommended as a proven way to reduce the risk for the boys who follow in our path. It is important to encourage, and train junior elders to join us in a mentoring pyramid of energy that allows them to continue to be mentored.
3. Safe spaces and circles are important for continual self-reflection and growth. I recommend the creation of nurturing safe places in our homes to journal, meditate, and pray. The preservation of a life force often begins with being grateful for what we have and regularly reflecting on how to maintain and share our gifts. We can also take

advantage of drumming and rituals spaces that exist in most of our communities; these allow the spirit of communal reflection with ourselves and our ancestors to nurture growth.

REFERENCES

Alexander, M. (2012). *The new Jim Crow: Mass incarceration in the age of colorblindness.* New York, NY: The New Press.

De los Ríos, C. V., López, J., & Morrell, E. (2015). Toward a critical pedagogy of race: Ethnic studies and literacies of power in high school classrooms. *Race and Social Problems, 7*(1), 84–96. doi:10.1007/s12552-014-9142-1

Leary, J. D. (2005). *Post traumatic slave syndrome: America's legacy of enduring injury and healing.* Milwaukie, OR: Uptone Press.

Spatig-Amerikaner, A., & Center for American, P. (2012). *Unequal education: Federal loophole enables lower spending on students of color.* Center for American Progress.

Watts, R. J., & Abdul-Adil, J. K. (1997). Promoting critical consciousness in young, African-American men. *Journal Of Prevention & Intervention In The Community, 16*(1–2), 63–86. doi:10.1300/J005v16n01_04

Washington, G., Barnes, D., & Watts, R. J. (2014). Reducing risk with pyramid mentoring: A proposal for a culturally-centered group intervention. *Journal of Human Behavior and the Social Environment, 24*(6), 646–657.

Washington, G., Caldwell, L., Watson, J., & Lindsey, L. (2017). African-American rites of passage interventions: A vehicle for utilizing African-American male elders. *Journal of Human Behavior and the Social Environment, 27*(1–2), 100–109.

Washington, G., Johnson, T., Jones, J., & Langs, S. (2006). African-American boys in relative care and a culturally centered group mentoring approach. *Social Work with Groups, 30*(1), 45–69.

Washington, G., Watts, R. J., & Watson, J. (2008). Manhood seekers camp: A proposal for a culturally-centered camp intervention. *Residential Treatment for Children & Youth, 23*(1–2), 75–90.

CHAPTER 44

THE TEST OF A MAN

Verontae Deams

>The test of a man is the fight that he makes,
>The grit that he daily shows,
>The way he stands upon his feet,
>And takes life's numerous bumps and blows.
>A coward can smile when there's naught to fear.
>And nothing his progress bars,
>But it takes a man to stand and cheer,
>While the other fellow stars.
>It isn't the victory after all
>But the fight that a Brother makes.
>A man when driven against the wall,
>Still stands erect and takes the blows of fate
>With his head held high,
>bleeding, bruised and pale,
>Is the man who will win and fate defied,
>For he isn't afraid to fail!
>—Author Unknown

"It isn't the victory after all but the fight that a Brother makes." Life has a way of presenting a wide array of situations and circumstances that we must face. My belief is that we have within us the innate desire to win and overcome. Often, the victory is honored and celebrated but no one knows the process it takes to get there. But it's in the fight—the tenacity, struggle, grit, and self-motivation—where the invaluable lessons are learned.

Statistically, my circumstance should have led me to prison, poverty, or perished. Born to a single mother and raised by the elders of my family, I am the product of the saying "it takes a village to raise a child." I was the child of the community. My mother married and left to build a life with her husband, and my relationship with my biological father was nonexistent until I was much older. I was able to visit my mother on the weekend; however, the absence of my biological father left a void that I did not realize was there until my adult life. I convinced myself that I was unaffected. Although I had father figures, the residual effects of my father's absence (abandonment, rejection, low self-esteem, low self-worth, and a sense of belonging) existed heavily. Being a "child of the community" is honorable and gracious. However, the antagonistic side of having several authoritative voices and opinions allows for over trust and indecisiveness. There was little opportunity to fail and learn. Everyone's opinion and perspective was the gospel that could not be altered. There was never that single person who had the final say on a given situation or circumstance I encountered. This had a vast impact on my psychosocial development.

"A man when driven against the wall, still stands erect and takes the blows of fate." In 1990, my world was shaken when my grandmother suddenly passed away. Not only did she instill values and morals in me, she also introduced me to faith and love. My grandparents were my safety net. The devastation I experienced after her death was heartbreaking and traumatic. My grades dropped tremendously, and I became withdrawn. The saving grace was my mother, who became a constant presence. She helped me to regain a sense of familial normalcy and support.

Throughout my elementary and secondary years, I was an average student, attended average schools, and made average grades. School was not difficult for me, but I was never motivated to go beyond average. Therefore, I did just enough to get by. The majority of my teachers were White females who, some by ignorance and others by choice, really did not understand how to teach or reach Black male students. Consequently, there were not many Black males who were scholastically motivated by teachers or administrators. Few were screened for gifted education and many were screened for special education. However, we were dominant and well represented in sports and behavioral modification programs. Not only did this have an effect on our interest in academics, it affected self-esteem, self-worth, and self-efficacy. This is the culture I was taught in and struggled to overcome.

While I was a senior in high school, a Black male teacher, one of the few I had, said in front of the entire class, "Mr. Deams is extremely smart. But he is also extremely lazy!" I was embarrassed and also insulted. I could not believe that this teacher not only criticized me, but he did it publicly! By no means did I consider myself a lazy student. And, after much thought, I did not consider myself a smart student. This was a cognitive struggle for me as

I rehearsed what he said and what I believed. I never had a teacher to call me "smart" or challenge me academically. I later realized that my anger was rooted in fear. My subconscious thoughts were, once a person is identified as "smart," there is a certain expectation to be profoundly wise and always perform well academically, which was a standard I could not meet. Thus, I shied away from the title and all of its associated outcomes.

After high school graduation, I attended Southern University and majored in microbiology with the hopes and expectations of becoming a medical doctor. Southern University is a Historically Black College and University (HBCU). There were many students, instructors, and administrators who looked like me and identified with me. It was during the years spent at Southern University that I grew as a student and developed critical thinking and social skills. My academic advisor, Dr. Bryan Lewis, was instrumental in encouraging me to take challenging courses and perform optimally. Not only was he a mentor, he was living proof that it was okay to be portrayed as "smart." Dr. Lewis shaped my perspective of an intellect and a professional.

My life changed dramatically, again, when my grandfather passed away. He was my provider, protector, counselor, teacher, and my dad. "Dobey," as he affectionately called me, was the apple of his eye. He was essential in my upbringing. His death was a reminder of the pain I experienced during my grandmother's transition. Old wounds and hurt were exacerbated, and I did not know how to handle them. Once again, I felt abandoned and rejected. This time of my life was filled with depression and indirection. I fought, daily, for sanity and a peace of mind. I was merely existing but not living; here but not present. It was only through prayer and the grace of God that I was able to recover from the sunken place, regain my composure, and live again. The memories and the invaluable life lessons, both spoken and unspoken, keeps him alive within my heart.

I married my high school sweetheart and moved to Nashville, Tennessee. As a young married man, I had all the answers; unfortunately, they were all the wrong answers. It was during this time I was introduced to Amos L. Howard Sr., who was the pastor of a local church. It was here where my life was radically changed. I developed my faith and spiritual life and was able to confront and conquer the pains of my past. I viewed life holistically and was able to grow spiritually, personally, financially, and professionally. During this time, I discovered my passion for HBCUs and higher education. I was afforded the opportunity to become an administrator at a prominent HBCU and work directly with students. Additionally, I applied and was accepted into a doctoral program; which was imaginable but unrealistic to me as a young adult.

"*With his head held high, bleeding, bruised and pale, is the man who will win and fate defied, for he isn't afraid to fail!*" My faith has been instrumental in overcoming many situations I have encountered. I apply it to every area of life. It's the reason I am able to be a leader and a calculated risk taker. Every ordeal I have been through has shaped me into the man I am today. I take nothing for granted. I have experienced many war wounds, setbacks, heartaches, and disappointments. My trust has been betrayed, my friendship taken for granted, and my kindness has been exploited. There are several times when I get fearful and want to give up and retreat. But I am reminded that my journey is not my own; but it is designed to be a beacon of hope and a source of inspiration to someone else. On several occasions, I thought I failed only to realize that, in the end, I won. As a first-generation college student and doctoral candidate, I have beaten the odds of what society says of Black males with modest beginnings. During the process of becoming a member of my fraternity, Alpha Phi Alpha, Fraternity, Inc., I was taught that "excuses are tools of incompetence used to build monuments of nothingness. Those who use them seldom amount to anything." I recommend to any brother who has similar experiences to rid yourself of excuses, silence the voices of doubt and disbelief, and become resilient and focused on your assignment. For decades, Black males have not been seen in a positive light. We have to constantly be reminded of who we are and "whose" we are so that we can be examples for future generations. No longer can we let others who don't know us tell our story. Together, we must change the narrative for the good, one brother at a time.

CHAPTER 45

RISING THROUGH THE CONCRETE LIKE A ROSE

Nathan Stephens

Did you hear about the rose that grew from a crack in the concrete...
Provin' nature's laws wrong it learned how to walk without havin' feet
Funny it seems but, by keepin' its dreams, It learned to breathe fresh air,
Long live the rose that grew from concrete...

—Tupac Shakur

Being a Black man in a country whose foundations are rooted in racism and capitalism is difficult. That challenge coupled with being raised by a single drug-addicted mother in public housing, the odds against success increase exponentially. Black men from disadvantaged circumstances that work to change their life trajectory, can be compared to a rose growing through a crack in the concrete. The beauty within them is maintained while externally, an immense amount of effort that would cause many to succumb to failure, is exhibited and should be commended. In this chapter, I share some of the obstacles that I have faced in my life under the aforementioned adverse conditions. I conclude with recommendations on how young Black men can navigate their life circumstances and lead a productive life.

Early in my childhood, I learned what it felt like to now have a father in the home. My mother told me that my father left our home when I was 2 years old. Every so often we'd hear that he was in town and I would go to the crap-house to see him. For those unfamiliar, the crap-house is where people gambled, shooting dice or "craps" specifically but also a place where drinking, playing cards, and prostitution was common. This is where I would meet my dad. By middle school my mom had married, but my stepdad became incarcerated and occasionally I would accompany my mom to visit him. By high school, my mother and stepdad were addicted to crack cocaine. Initially they hid their drug habit from my younger brother and I, but eventually it wasn't something they could hide.

I graduated from high school and was set to attend college in the fall but before I could become a college student, I became a father. My first semester was successful despite my frequent travels back home to see my daughter. During the Christmas break, I was forced to take all of my stuff home because my scholarship only covered the fall semester. After being home for about a week, my mom said, "There ain't gonna be no Christmas, unless you want to do something with this..." I was confused and didn't understand what she was saying. She explained to me that I could go next door, buy some crack, and sell it for a profit. My neighbor was a former schoolmate and her boyfriend sold me the drugs. He showed me how to process it and explained that it had a $300 street value. Later that night I stood on the corner and sold the drugs. My customers made their purchases and left as if it was as normal as buying something at the mall. By 10:00 p.m. I had sold almost all of the drugs and began walking home. I noticed a car slowly approaching and I wanted to make one last transaction. As the car got closer, I realized it was a police car. Fearing being arrested, I tried to toss the crack discreetly. The police officers rushed me to the ground, placed me under arrest, and transported me to the county jail. In the jail were people that I knew including one of my uncles. Many of them joked, "'Joe College,' what are you doing in here with us..." They all laughed at the ignorance of a college student selling crack in an area with high police surveillance. After about 20 hours, my aunt and uncle used their home as surety for a bail bondsman to get me released from jail. I was assigned a public defender because I couldn't afford a private lawyer. He recommended that I accept a plea bargain for possession of drugs to avoid being charged with possession with intent to distribute. Because I was a first-time offender and a college student caught in a bad situation, I was sentenced to 5 years of probation. Probation is a suspended imposition of sentence but, all that I knew was that I was not going to prison that day. The judge insisted that I state that he was "doing me a favor."

Without housing, returning to school was not really an option. Eventually I dropped out of school and started hanging with my new homie next door. I sold drugs to family members, neighbors, and even a local preacher. I felt guilty for adding to the destruction of my community. But my guilt was eased by addicts known and unknown stating, "If we don't buy it from you, we'll buy it from someone else." Later in life I would describe my community as three populations. Those that sold drugs, those that did drugs, and the innocent people that are negatively impacted and caught in the middle. The emotional roller coaster that came from selling drugs took its toll on me. The financial and social benefits from dealing was offset by seeing family members, neighbors, and others addicted to crack. I witnessed young children tell their addicted parents that they were hungry, but the parents had traded the food stamps for crack. Mothers I knew traded oral sex to dealers in exchange for drugs.

In July 1990, I packed up and moved to Oklahoma. I was working at K-Mart and McDonald's with plans returning to college. While at work one day, I was called to the K-Mart customer service desk. My then girlfriend stood there by the customer service desk and burst into tears as I got closer. She told me that she received a call earlier that my older brother had been shot and killed back home over a dice game. This confirmed that my decision to move was the correct one. In August of 1991, I enrolled at Northeastern Oklahoma State University (NSU). Being back in school and attempting to improve my life felt good. I met people who became lifelong friends. My time at NSU was great but that changed when I learned that I was about to father my second child.

Despite wanting to raise my second daughter in a two-parent home, my daughter's mother and I broke up, and I moved into my own apartment. Reeling emotionally, I met new friends and began partying too much which led to several missed days of work. This created financial hardships for me and I couldn't pay my rent. Learning of my financial struggles, a guy that I had started hanging with told me about an upcoming robbery he was planning if I wanted in. I balked and stated that I had sold drugs before, but that I wasn't "Jesse James." He countered that the robbery would be an inside job, where we would run in grab the money bag and run out. No guns or anything like that. Against my better judgment, I agreed to participate. The night of the robbery, we were arrested and facing 25 years to life. After 8 months in the county jail, I accepted a plea bargain of 12 years for Robbery by Force or Fear. In the midst of my partying, I had started dating another woman. We were intimate earlier in the week of my arrest. She told me that she was pregnant as I sat in the county jail. We kept in touch and tried to maintain our relationship. In February 1995, as I was being transferred to the department of corrections, she went into labor and my third beautiful baby girl was born. On top of being locked up, it was painful to acknowledge that I was not in my children's lives, just like my dad was not in mine.

In March 2000, after almost 6 years of incarceration, I was released from the Missouri Department of Corrections on parole. I decided that the best option for me was to return to college and try to get a degree and avoid the streets. I enrolled in Columbia College, located just minutes from the crap-house where I used to meet my dad. Columbia College is also near where I used to live and sell drugs. The admissions counselor said that he would "give me a chance, one semester to prove myself." I graduated and made the dean's list the entire time that I attended. My graduation was extra special because I graduated with two of my cousins. We were three Black males from public housing, in one family, graduating together.

After earning my master's degree in social work, I worked for Big Brothers Big Sisters coordinating their Children of Prisoners program. What an irony. As a convicted felon I am currently employed and working on my doctorate. But each move that I make in an effort to enhance my life, it is always "pending a criminal background check."

There is a saying that warns that, "People don't plan to fail, they fail to plan." When I was released on parole, I began to work the plan that I devised while I was incarcerated that I felt would lead to my success upon release. I felt that life outside of prison would move so quickly that without a plan in place to guide me, my chances of successful reintegration into society would decrease. Therefore, the first bit of advice that I would give any one is to plan your success. Planning your success is universal and is not just for those who have been incarcerated. I would strongly encourage brothers to use the internet as a research tool to cultivate, implement, and evaluate their plans.

My next advice is to get an education beyond high school. Whether it's college, vocational school, or some type of training program. Engaging in some sort of educational process is valuable and benefits us beyond the diplomas, certificates, or degrees. Being in a classroom and hearing words or concepts that we have never heard before, humbles us and helps us to expand beyond our socialization process. A more practical point is that people want to know "what we have done since our release." Getting more education provides us with an objective declaration that we are salvageable and that we have moved beyond whatever previous mistakes or missteps that we have made in our lives.

Finally, we can never ever lose hope. A person without hope is potentially the most dangerous person alive. This is because without hope, without believing that situations or circumstances that have driven us to a point of despair can improve, our mindset is altered and the potential for negative outcomes increases. So, we can never allow ourselves to be driven to hopelessness, no matter how bleak our situation is. Hope must always present possibility.

CHAPTER 46

AKOBEN

The Ancestors' Call

Mwalimu Donkor Issa Minors

Peace. May this writing reach you in good health and even better spirits! I begin by giving honor to the creator who has many names. I call him God. Thank you for every revitalizing breath that I may take for granted. Thank you for giving me the consciousness to enjoy this satisfying life. May I never underestimate the power of my loyalty to you. Ashe, is an African philosophical concept through which the Yoruba of Nigeria conceive the power to make things happen and produce change. To the *orishas* [other gods] (Elegua, Ochosi, Ogun, Oshun, King Chango, and Obatala), thank you for revealing yourselves to me, thank you for clearing the path, affirming my journey, and guiding my divine spirit. For my ancestors, whose blood runs through mine and those whom I seek refuge in their narrative, please continue to speak to me through the narratives and experiences you have sacrificially given in flesh and continue to provide indomitably through the spirit. To my great-great-great grandfather Baba Turner, to John Turner Sr., Carolyn Turner, Diane Carol Smith, and Roland Jones; Grandpa Ponda,

Aunty Linda. I pray that my decisions reveal through my actions that I put nothing before this holy union.

It is important for me to begin my narrative in ritual, in the same manner, that I make a strict effort to approach and live my life in an indigenous and neo-indigenous Afrikan-centered lifestyle. I was born in the 1980s prematurely on Cancerous July moonlit night in East Los Angeles. My mother was a 16 year-old LA Crip in so much love with a 22-year-old Jamaican immigrant stationed in California with the United States Marine Corp. My father was a successful, young entrepreneur and my mother was struggling in a emotionally wounded home, so together they provided one another a reciprocity. The story goes, my mother wanted to call me Da'mon but my father fought profusely because it sounded too much like a demon. After my entry into the world, my mother was in a really bad fight with a rival gang member to which, she triumphantly excited causing the girl that she was engaged in battle to return and proceed to shoot up the whole house. My mother says that there was a single bullet above my bassinet that made her make the most critical decision in all of our lives. We got in a car with nothing more than what could fit in the trunk. It was a small sedan and we drove 3,000 miles across this nation to secure a *better life*. My father, along with the other members of his Jamaican posse, stayed behind in hopes to use his passion for Jamaican culture to profit from the cultural exchange, only to eventually have to use his deployment tactics learned in the Marines to rob drug dealers then "conspire to launder money" for them. Along the way, my mother dropped me off in Pine Bluff, Arkansas to live the first 7 years of my life with my Nana, my grandmother. After my time in the pro-Black rural life of "The Bluff." I was then flown to live the rest of my life in the vibrant neighborhood of Roxbury (Boston), Massachusetts. Upon arrival in Boston, my mother had secured a small studio apartment in the basement of a large Muslim family's home.

All of my educational experiences were in Boston Public Schools, but I ended up at this private school in seventh grade in the suburbs where the only way to school was taking a $6 one-way commuter rail trip to become the token Negro at their private school. At this Catholic all-boy school, the church walls were marked in stain glass with white faces of their holy saints. The hallways were outfitted with Greek and Roman statues, armored with swords and crested shields. For 6 years, I pretended to be enjoying myself. Every day I struggled with getting money just to go to school. Some of my biggest arguments with my mother were a result of where I would get the money to get to school. During one English class, while reading the Odyssey, I wrote a paper about the dichotomy of moving 10 times in 1 year, paralleled it to Odysseus's underground experiences through Hades. My peers went home to million dollar homes on Newbury Street, and I went back to Dudley Square. My saving grace was the Nation of Gods and Earths, the Nation of Islam, and the street debates in front of Nubian Notions. I enjoyed the brass alpha-male bravado of watching strong Black men debate utilizing their intellectual prowess and ability to cite texts appropriately. Dudley was a ghetto geek's arena. I often skipped homework to hear the 5 Percenters debate the Black Israelites on their loud speakers. As part of my journey, I began to get my real education, the one I received on the street. Every Wednesday at school, I sat in Catholic mass; and on Sundays, I studied how to fight the United Nations to get reparations for all of the African diaspora in America. I survived private school with a great bond with brothers and techniques for surviving White privilege. All the 6 years that I attended private school, my mother was very clear: You are a Black man, you belong to Black people, and as you climb up you must reach back and bring another Black young man up with you. My 11th grade year she was arrested for a crime that four people admitted she could not have done; my father was arrested as well and later deported from this country the same year. I maintained a job and an 80% average.

Following that year, I attended an undergraduate college on an academic scholarship. I spent my holidays alone in my dorm to avoid returning to the hood because I was ashamed and depressed. I couldn't understand how life could be so tough: having the privilege of being in college but having to steal the books from the bookstore to pass class. Free and away from home, I took the values from my mother and my neighborhood, embodying the simple principles that kept one alive in the hood into the privileged spaces of a gated, predominantly old-money undergraduate college that sat at the highest peak of a working class city. I struggled to fight the Black Student Union and Latino Alliance Student Organization to think more strategically in order to be impactful on campus as well as the local community at large. They had very large budgets and the highlights were always annual fashion shows and quarterly parties. I was arguing for forums to discuss local issues, how to bring local youth from the housing projects to experience college, and to create a summer camp for youth. For 4½ years, I watched cultural death and mainstream assimilation only to arrive in the workforce to see the same death and cultural abandonment for a salary.

Upon my first salary position, as a substitute, I was excited to return to my middle school to teach creative writing. There I gained a wealth of knowledge around teaching and learning, but most importantly the need to be an advocate for young Kings (young men of color). Boys of color were always in detention, suspended, or involved in fights in and outside of the school. One year, there were four murders either with students from the school or directly in front of the school. That year I learned the meaning behind dead silent. In an effort to strengthen my writing course to heal the youth affected by the loss of their friends, I created journaling activities that challenged the young people to process how they internalized and processed the trauma caused by violence. Professionally, I felt like I had grown: I had received my first master's degree along with my teaching license. I grew courage enough to approach the administration to move up to become a core content eighth grade English teacher. I requested a meeting to discuss me becoming the eighth grade English teacher, and the principal laughed in my face and said I was too young; that I was too close to the age of the students to be effective in my instruction. I was disheartened and sunk into a slight depression because I knew that I could no longer be effective with my impact as a substitute.

I eventually left my former middle school because there was no more room for me to grow. Upon arriving at a new school with a new and stronger sense of purpose, I organized a young men's affinity group, I structured curricula that moved students through their personal contexts while developing their skills. I used my frustration from being blocked at the previous employer to impact the lives of the youth I was now in front. Eighty-five percent of my students scored proficient or higher on the state standardized tests, the basketball team that I coached for the school made it to the city finals, my young men's group received state and national recognition, and a colleague and I were able to provide our students opportunities that our colleagues felt they did not deserve. And despite all the success that I collaboratively worked to accomplish, many of my colleagues were threatened by the feats we were to overcome for Black and Latino poor, urban students. They began to use their knowledge of special education to further drive children that lived in my community into below grade level instruction. I did not know the terms that they were using so that I could advocate for my children, so I went back to school to receive a second master's degree to combat the social inequities and bias instruction occurring for the children whose families prayed that their children accomplish the unthinkable.

I lost that battle: My passion for social justice had not been able to defeat the American workplace social norms of *play along to get along*. I refused to play when children of color were involved. Children who lived below poverty line, in the projects, and a cycle of imprisonment. I could not allow myself to play fair when the lives of children who looked like me were involved. I knew what they'd become without a great education and a series of new opportunities: Their lives turned into the lives of my cousins, my sisters, my brothers, my uncles, and my aunts. So, ultimately, my advice is to develop a sense of core values, a set of principles that guide your mission in your work. Do not be so rigid that you cannot see small places to be flexible, it will lead to dissatisfaction and anger. Source your strength from the narratives of your ancestors (direct bloodline as well as historical). Lean on your faith, there are messages in even the smallest examples; do not let yourself have to be taught the same way twice. Learn your lessons as fast as you can, or you may be doomed to repeat the same mistakes over and over again. Strive for the highest level of influence that you are prepared to go; understand that every step along the way is preparing you for the next step. Remain humble. Remain faithful. Never settle for less than what you see or believe of yourself. And lastly, in the words of Kendrick Lamar remember "You got loyalty, got royalty inside your DNA." Go be unapologetically great!

SECTION V

SEXUAL AND SUBSTANCE ABUSE

In his recent book titled *Man-Not: Race, Class, Genre, and the Dilemmas of Black Manhood*, Curry (2017) suggests that Black men are often stereotypically constructed as dangerous, vile, and sexually abusive, especially towards Black women. This narrative, Curry proposes, has become a staple in most empirical studies on intimate partner violence (IPV) and maintains the racist construction of Black men through research studies conducted mostly by White scholars. However, Curry argues that what is often ignored in the extant literature on Black men are ways they too are victims of sexual violence and abuse (e.g., verbal and physical). While there is a growing body of work in Black masculinity studies which has begun to acknowledge the sexual victimization of Black men (Curry, 2017), we know little about the sexual victimization of other men of color.

Given the often unspoken, sexual trauma in the lives of men of color and the institutional oppression including unemployment, racial discrimination, and disproportionate criminal sentencing they face on a daily basis, some men of color turn to substance abuse including drugs and alcohol (Alexander, 2010; Curry, 2017). Excessive use of drugs and alcohol contributes to other social problems including the loss of employment and divorce that men of color face in society. In Section V, we introduce narratives of contributing authors who share their experiences primarily involving sexual abuse, drug and alcohol abuse, and physical and verbal abuse. Based on the aforementioned, the goal of this book is to regard men of color from a position of empowerment. However, we caution readers to not walk away with deficit framings and perspectives of these men of color who found the courage to be vulnerable in order to share abuse (verbal, physical, and sexual) downfalls, and struggles they experienced. Their stories serve as testimonies of how they overcame tragedies of life, which serve to uplift other men of color. Similarly, because of the sensitive nature of these experiences, we ask that readers read these narratives paying particular attention to the recommendations these men of color have provided at the end of their stories so that the reader can walk away with strategies to overcome verbal, physical, sexual, and alcohol abuse.

REFERENCES

Alexander, M. (2010). *The new Jim Crow: Mass incarceration in the age of colorblindness.* New York, NY: The New Press.

Curry, W. (2017). *Man-not: Race, class, genre and the dilemmas of Black manhood.* Philadelphia. Temple University Press.

CHAPTER 47

FORGED BY MY FOUNDATION

Michael A. Robinson

MY FOUNDATION

I grew up in St. Louis, Missouri. St. Louis has many reasons to consider it a proud city. Known as the gateway to the West, it is also home of the world-famous Arch, the world renown Anheuser-Busch Brewery, and the 11-time world champion St. Louis baseball Cardinals. Yet, there are aspects of my hometown I am ashamed and embarrassed to acknowledge. St. Louis is one of America's most segregated cities and was undoubtedly that way during the time I grew up. It is also the backdrop for the 2014 uprising in Ferguson, Missouri, after the murder of Michael Brown Jr.

However, with all its flaws and challenges, this is my place of birth. This town, with historical high Black unemployment, persistently underfunded schools, and limited career opportunities for people of color, is my beginning. I was born to a teenage mother in the historic Homer G. Phillips Hospital. I was the first of two children. My existence, my entrance into this world, represents the basic tenets of this book. I am both an example of an obstacle and a symbol of triumph.

My mother was the first born to my grandparents Virdell and Pauline Robinson. My mother had an older sibling, from a previous relationship my grandfather had before meeting my grandmother (or at least I think that is the case; I am honestly too afraid to ask). Uncle Sydney lived in Milwaukee and would visit on rare occasions. My mother had strong bonds with both her parents; she was named Virdell after her father. My mother was a daddy's girl. Their relationship was one of true love, respect, and admiration.

The relationship between my grandfather and my grandmother appeared void of any love, affection, and respect for one another. These early observations into the complexities of relationships would shape how I viewed personal interactions. They would serve as the foundation by which I would build lifelong friendships, find love at first sight, and overcome physical and emotional abuse.

THE HAPPY HOME

I loved living in my home; filled with love and laughter. A great deal of the warmth was due to my uncle Thomas, my mother's baby brother. My uncle represented a living contradiction for me as a child. He was complicated but also a simple person. He was treated like the baby of the family, and he did things and didn't do things I thought a man should do and should never do, but I knew he had my back. My uncle had a dark side; he was a drug user, dealer, and womanizer. He had a street reputation and was associated with sneaky and criminal minded characters. Irrespective of all his less than redeeming qualities, I loved my uncle.

Albeit flawed in many ways, my uncle was once a happily married man who provided a brief glimpse into the world of being young and in love with a beautiful woman. Uncle Thomas married the most beautiful woman I had seen in my life until I met my wife. I wanted to be like him in that way!

THE HAPPINESS OF A FAMILY

I was 3 years old when my sister Keli was born. I can recall the day when she came home from the hospital. My mom introduced her, I thought, she is pretty, but like any 3-year-old boy would do, I continued to play with my toys. I was a big brother! Not sure what that meant, but I understood, I was the oldest.

Being raised by a 22-year-old mother, who had yet to live her life, was not filled with challenges. My mom had the support of my grandmother, grandfather, her brother, and sister-in-law. We lived as one big happy family. This support allowed my mom to graduate from Hadley Tech High School with her class. She went on to earn a certificate as a radiology technician and landed a job working at the state hospital. One of my happiest moments came when as a young boy who was fanatical about St. Louis Cardinals baseball, I had the opportunity to go a 1968 World Series game. I could not believe it. I was going to the biggest event in St. Louis!

To see this once in a lifetime event, my mother and I would have to sleep outside Busch Stadium overnight to ensure we would be in line to purchase game tickets. It did not matter how cold it was; it did not matter if I had to eat cold sandwiches and sleep with a coat and blankets on the ground. The only thing that mattered to me that day was my mom was getting me (the family) tickets to the game to see my childhood heroes Lou Brock and Bob Gibson! I can recall little of the game or even the experience of sitting in the stadium, but the night I spent with my mother sleeping outside and waking up to purchase tickets will live with me forever and shape my thoughts on the impact of parents on and in a child's life.

THINGS CHANGE

Did I mention that I was a happy kid... My life seemed okay to me! But things would change dramatically. I am not sure exactly when the change came, but it seems like it happened overnight. My mother married my sister's father. I am not sure when they got married, I just know that from the first time he saw me, my stepfather hated me.

My stepfather never seemed happy to be part of the family. He fussed a lot, scowled a lot and criticized even more. My stepfather was a former military man. I am not sure if he retired or did not re-enlist. In either case, he made it known he had served in the armed forces. Attempting to unravel what was going on in my stepfather's head would come to be a painful waste of my time. Living in the same household would become a nightmarish experience for me. I relive many of those moments over and over in my mind, even more than 40 years later.

I cannot recall the very first moment of physical or mental abuse I received from my stepfather, but I know they often occurred unexpectedly or when I was alone, defenseless, or to add injury to embarrassment, in the presence of my friends. The irony of these experiences is that, at times, because I did not have a father who was active in my life, I saw him as my father. There were times I wanted to call him my father. How insane, as a young man, who was mistreated harshly and, in some cases, brutally by this man, I wanted to see him as a father.

My stepfather had a violent temper, but his verbal assaults were more profound as they were meant to pierce the soul and inflict a lifetime of damage. As I write this, memories I had forgotten are awakening, and my levels of anxiety are rising. I am finding myself tapping my left foot and gripping the computer mouse tighter. Fear has entered the room, which is precisely the way I felt as an 8- and 9-year-old child.

Being physically and mentally abused is numbing and often resulted in moments of self-doubt and self-hatred. My stepfather was not tall but was in excellent physical condition, and his presence was intimidating. He and I shared a living space on the third floor of the house. He worked a late shift at whatever security gig he could get. I never slept well, always listening for him to come home. My heart would race, and my anxiety rose with every step he took as he climbed the stairs. I never knew what mood he would be in, and I could never tell in what form or fashion he would seek to belittle me. Pretending to sleep was not a reprieve from his verbal assaults. He would say things to me when he believed I was sleeping. There were times when he would forcefully wake me, demanding that I perform some chore he never assigned. There was no escaping his presence. I did not want to tell my mother and create any more stress for her, nor did I want to leave my room, because, for the most part, it was my sanctuary. It was the one place I could go to find peace, until he came home.

One day, while outside on the front lawn with a few of my friends, my stepfather referred to me as a fat piece of shit. I was embarrassed. My friends laughed and snickered and eventually went home to surely share with their parents what just happened. The next day at school, I was teased as kids chanted "your father hates you." I tried to tell them he was not my father, but my stepfather; that only led them to tease me more. They focused on the fact I did not have a father. Over the years, neighborhood kids would refer to my never seen biological father as Ichabod Crane the Headless Father. Sometimes I would laugh at the joke, in hopes that would be the end of the roasting. Between the endless teasing, which at times came from anyone who needed a boost in their ego, to the physical and mental abuse by my stepfather, I considered suicide on many occasions. I thought of walking in front of cars as they sped up and down Grand Blvd., passing the Herbert Hoover Boys Club, which was on the ground of Sportsman's Park, the former home of the St. Louis baseball Cardinals.

I DIED TODAY

On one occasion, I asked my stepfather if he would take me to the circus. He refused with a resounding "No!" He emphatically told me I did not deserve to go. I was disappointed as all my friends had gone or were going. My disappointed did not last for long; my uncle who lived with us in the basement decided to take me. I did not ask him to take me because the wrath of my stepfather would be unbearable. When I told him why I could not go, he said not to worry, he would talk to my stepfather and let him know that it was his idea. I gladly went. I was sure everything was going to be alright and that I was going to have the time of my life. I did have a great time and was excited to have experienced this with my uncle, the closest person to a father I would ever know.

Upon returning home, my uncle dropped me off and continued out with his girlfriends. I was in the best mood any 9-year-old could imagine, but that feeling was abruptly and violently removed. When I opened the door, my stepfather snatched me by my neck. I felt as if I was struck by a car as the force jerked me back while simultaneously he pulled. He pulled me up what felt like a million stairs. I was stunned and not quite sure what was happening; I noticed the ceiling tiles were moving fast and my heels were knocking hard on each step. My stepfather was not saying a word, as his grip around my neck was getting tighter and tighter. When we reached the top of the stairs, he shoved me with such force; I landed in the family living room on my back.

I was stunned and fearful, but before I could get up, I saw my stepfather charging at me. He did not look like my stepfather. He appeared more like a werewolf or mad lion. He was very red in the face. He tackled me, causing my head to hit the hardwood floor. Then he straddled me, placing his knees on both arms. In this position, I could see his face clearly, and I knew, by the look on his face, I was going to die. I had angered him so much that he wanted me to die. I felt sorry for myself, because I did this to myself; to this day, there are moments when that time in my life and all the feelings associated with it reappears.

I could see his mouth moving, but I was not able to make out everything he was saying. My stepfather continued to punch me in the chest and slapped me across the face for good measure. But for a moment, he removed one of his knees from my arm, and I thought I could escape, get free, and run to my room and lock the door. That was a mistake because as I turned to break free, my stepfather placed his knee on my neck. I could not breathe, and he was applying more pressure. I was sure I was going to die. I began to say the Lord's Prayer. It was the only one I knew. I think I may have expired at that moment, but for reasons unknown to me, my stepfather removed his knee and stood up over me. I crawled from beneath him and ran to my room.

ONLY BY THE GRACE GOD

I remained in my room for what felt like years. I never shared this story with anyone in the family; but that moment forever changed my life. Over the years, my stepfather remained abusive, more verbal than physical. I was growing up, and he could see my fear of him was lessening. Then the moment came.

The evening of my favorite holiday, Thanksgiving, he and I had a physical altercation; this time, the outcome was different. As we fought from the hallway to the master bedroom, I was driving my stepfather as if he was a blocking dummy on the football field. I could see the window, and I knew if I could push him out of the second-floor window, then all my troubles would go away. I was driving and punching him at every step. I could hear my mother calling my name, begging me to stop. I could not stop, I had to banish this demon. I needed to rid our lives of the evil he represented, and as I had him hanging out of the window, my mother pulled me away and like the coward I later found out my stepfather indeed was, he ran to his room on the third-floor shouting he was going to get his gun to kill me. My mother ushered me downstairs to my grandmother's house and called my uncle upstairs to talk to my stepfather. When my mother returned, she asked if I would like to live with my grandmother. She wanted to keep the peace and keep me safe. By the grace of God, I was finally completely free of this menace; I was going to be safe.

TIME HEALS ALL WOUNDS... IT JUST MAY TAKE SOME TIME

Time went on, and eventually they divorced. My stepfather often said publicly and privately that I would not amount to much in life. He would visit neighbors and in the presence of my friends speak horribly of me, suggesting to anyone willing to listen, that I was too dumb to accomplish much in my life.

My stepfather was wrong by all accounts. I not only beat the odds, but I also thrived, despite his best efforts, I have become a man my mother and grandmother are proud to have raised. The relationship with my stepfather evolved to an ability to be in the same room. And he lived long enough to know of a few significant milestones in my life. He was aware that I graduated from college, married the girl of my dreams, earned a graduate degree, moved away from St. Louis, and became a proud father. He passed away shortly after the birth of my daughter. Overcoming the trauma he caused provided me with the resiliency that drives my accomplishments today.

I continue to struggle with the abuse I suffered, but through God, family, and friends, I am pushing back and moving forward. Those moments of violence fuel me to impact the lives of others. I am working to turn the moments of suffering and self-doubt into winning opportunities for those I help.

In 2008, I created a nation-wide initiative entitled National Men Make A Difference Day for Academic Success. In 2017, more than 147,000 fathers and father figures participated in this one day of engagement. The purpose of this initiative is to urge men to take an active role in the academic experiences of their children. When fathers are involved, children thrive but when they are absent, children have challenges associated with their lack of presence. I had those problems because my biological father was missing, and my stepfather was horrible.

I overcame my challenges, and I am proud to do whatever I can to support the lives of males of color to overcome their obstacles in life. Once we as men of color know what we can do, we will rise and take our rightful places in our churches, families, and communities. God Bless. Peace and Love!!!

CHAPTER 48

ALONE WAS MY SAFE PLACE

Raphael Crawford

It wasn't until after the last man had finished that the others stopped holding me on the ground. As I crawled out of the bushes, struggling to pull up my underwear and pants, no one said a word to me as they congratulated one another for what they had just done. Until that time, I had only known the J. C. Napier Housing Projects to be a safe community of hard working, church going families. I had never even heard the term gang rape, yet there I was, a young boy and a victim of gang rape. While I knew what had happened to me was wrong, especially because I was a boy, I was threatened with bodily harm if I ever told anyone. I would be sexually molested a couple of times more before my family moved to a new community. I lived with the guilt and shame of having been raped, while living in a community that I believed would never believe or support me.

As a child, I was left bewildered and devoid of any sense of self-worth because of what had happened to me. I was confused about people...about life. What I knew, but could not articulate at the time, was that my body had been violated and that I could never tell anyone. I don't remember which was worse, the physical pain caused by the young men or the intense fear and inability to process what had happened to me. In those moments while being held face down in the bushes, I lost both my innocence and the ability to trust. As a result, I kept my secret; but I would learn that some secrets eat away at your soul and rot you from the inside out. One doesn't overcome being raped, he simply learns to live with the guilt and shame it brings to his life.

I became somewhat of a recluse, an emotionally dead child. I was quiet and stayed to myself most of the time. I remember my parents forcing me to go outside and play with the other children. Games such as hide-and-seek, or when we were older, hide-and-go-get-it always caused extreme discomfort for me. I didn't like sports or anything that required that I be touched by other people. However, as I grew into adolescence, I became increasingly interested in sex. During my college and young adult years, I became extremely promiscuous. But, for me, sexual intercourse was only an act of pleasure without any emotional connection to the other person, just like those guys had been with me years prior.

My emotionally safe place was anywhere by myself. I created my own imaginary world where little Black boys like me were safe; however, I lived in a real world that devoured Black boys in many ways. To this day, I try never to be alone in a secluded place with men; and I cringe whenever I see men or older boys hug on little boys. Years passed before I could bring myself to trust men enough to form friendships and brotherly bonds.

During the time I isolated myself from other people, I became an avid reader and a strong writer. With outstanding academic grades, an unintended result of my tragedy was that I became a top student and would excel and receive academic scholarships and accolades. Despite my academic performance, I was a very sad and withdrawn child with few close friends. I lived my childhood and young adult years feeling isolated and lonely, but no one seemed to notice. No one ever really asked me why I stayed to myself or avoided groups of men. Instead, I was often forced to participate with groups of boys and men at school or work despite my opposition.

As the years rolled by, I experienced personal and professional accomplishments and pitfalls. I have been knocked down so many times by those I trusted, that I learned to keep getting back up stronger! Like every Black man I have ever known, I've experienced racial discrimination and stereotypes, racial profiling, microaggressions, and hostile environments. I tend to relate most of the bad things that happen to me to this childhood rape—either because the more current events stirred up some of the feelings from my past, or my response to the events were similar.

I remember working as a school principal in East Tennessee, when a White woman sexually harassed me; after I reported it to the school district, they retaliated against me and protected her, offering her the opportunity to resign. The violation of my personhood brought back unpleasant memories of being sexually exploited and knowing that no one would trust what I reported.

I spent my entire adulthood longing for affection and human touch; however, I struggled greatly with being caressed or touched by people, especially men. I tended to substitute school, work, and community affiliations for the love and affection I desired. I accepted public displays of gratitude from others as a sign of being wanted... and safe. However, I hurt emotionally because I had somehow become either incapable or unwilling to trust or love others intimately. Being a Black man doesn't mean I don't hurt!

In recent years I have learned that there were other Black men who were raped as young boys, and even adult Black men who were raped, and these men are slowly beginning to tell their stories. Funny, I spent my entire lifetime holding onto a "dirty secret," not knowing that other Black men were holding onto the same or very similar experience. Black boys and men... straight... gay... bisexual... poor... addicted... impoverished... incarcerated... effeminate... masculine... religious, despite the circumstances or environments, are perhaps the least discussed victims of rape.

Healing began when I decided that I was much stronger than my tragedy. I decided to accept what had happened to me and focus on how it shaped my life choices. I would no longer allow it to define me. To free myself from the bondage of my rapists, I stopped visualizing the little boy from my past. I learned to cry... for myself, to release the guilt and shame, and to talk about my experience. I aligned myself with groups who supported rape victims, and who spoke publicly about their experiences, though I was not ready to share my story.

None of these weakened my manhood; in fact, they made me more masculine, more powerful and more in tune with myself.

Despite my tough demeanor, in some ways I remained that naïve and vulnerable boy who was lured into the bushes and snatched from childhood to rape victim. I learned that I was not the blame for what had happened to me... but I had to release it. During my period of self-discovery, I wept for that little boy. I wept for the confusion, guilt, and shame with which I lived for so many years. I had earned the right to cry, and my tears moved me from sorrow to solution! Crying was cathartic and empowering. Crying and meditation would prove to become powerful tools in my recovery process.

Living with the emotional baggage and pain of being a male victim of gang rape resulted in a lot of damage. My young adulthood was marred by failed relationships (rejecting anyone who attempted to get too close to me), promiscuity, and reckless and unprotected sex—many times with strangers! Sexual intercourse was never about intimacy, it was only about an orgasm. I wanted love but settled for sex. I slowly began to talk to a couple of Black male friends, though it took a couple of years before I would open up completely and honestly. I found that many of my Black male counterparts had very conservative, homophobic, and narrow-minded views, which prolonged my decision to share my story with them. I finally did, and following their initial shock, I was encircled with unconditional acceptance and non-judgmental support. It was at that moment that I first began to feel more at ease with Black men. Imagine not trusting someone who looks like you.

I found a psychologist to help me. Most of the therapists in my area were White females or Black males who were also preachers, and I didn't want to chance feeling disconnected or judged. I found a Black female psychologist, and after a few sessions, I knew that I was on the road to recovery. She guided me through journaling, self-discovery, and visualization, which I still practice. Like many other Black men, I had never considered seeing a therapist, because I believed that I was in control of my emotional well-being. However, it was through therapy that I realized that I might have suffered unnecessarily for many years because I thought the internal pain would simply go away.

I have spent my entire life—as a Black boy, a Black man, a Black boy, a Black professional—trying to dispel negative images of Black males and to escape the bondage of Black male stereotypes. Yet, it was only during the past couple of years that I would turn my energies towards healing myself and freeing that little boy from his painful past. Given the systemic demonization of Black males, I would much more likely be portrayed as a violent rapist than as a victim of violent rape. I was always concerned and empathetic towards victims of rape, especially children. Yet, I never saw victims who mirrored me—little Black boys.

My journey to healing has been long, but empowering. Alone is still my safe place. My tears once flowed for the little hurting boy inside me, but now they flow for the little Black boys who are the faceless, nameless, and voiceless victims of child rape.

CHAPTER 49

WON'T HE DO IT...

From Challenges to Triumphs

Derek Irvin

"Little boy, you better go and use the bathroom before you go to bed. I don't want you to wet up my sheets!" my godmother yelled out to me from the kitchen. I went and "took care of my business." I then returned to my makeshift temporary bed on the living room floor. I and several other kids had been watching television—*Winnie the Pooh, Frosty the Snowman*—something, I do not recall what. My godparents had allowed us to stay up late that night. There was lots of family visiting, I recall. Lying on the floor, I feel asleep on my back.

When I awoke, he was laying on top of me. He was so heavy. I could not move. I could not breathe. I felt his breathe on my face. He was moving around on top of me. I tried to yell, but could not. I was petrified, defiled, and bewildered. Petrified because, I could not breathe, defiled because I knew what was happening was wrong, and bewildered because I did not think he cared much for me. As I child, you want the approval of the adults around you. He would always say, "You act too much like a girl."

When he finished, he left me there, alone, only his sweat and scent. I could not get it off me, no matter how much I washed. The dirt and oil from his skin was under my fingernails. I could not wash my body enough. For years afterwards, I did not really much care for playing outside, because I would hate to sweat. Not surprisingly, I thought this molestation and others were my fault—that I deserved it. In fact, I really do not recall him ever having anything good to say to me, except for when he wanted me to scratch his back. He always wanted me to scratch his back. Out of all the other kids, he would always ask me to do so. When I would finish, I remember dirt and oil under my fingernails. I thought that was the grossest thing ever. I could not finish fast enough so that I might wash.

Somewhere after all of this, the nightmares started. In the nightmares, it was just like when it first happened, I would always be on my back. And it would start with a bone-cold, chilling air on my neck, it felt like someone was breathing on my neck, instantly, I would go paralyzed. I would try to move and could not for the life of me. I could not breathe, but still attempted to yell out for help, but my mouth did not work. No one knew about this molestations nor the nightmares as I told not a soul. Shame, silence, and the blues became my companion.

Years later, I was at my biological mother's house. She had four or five additional children by this time and one was an infant. She gathered us around and she said to me, "I need to get something off my mind and you are probably the only one that will understand." I could clearly see that something was bothering her. She took a deep breath, lowered her head and said, "Mrs. Ruth died!"

Mrs. Ruth was my godmother. That was the most earth-shattering news I had ever received at my young tender age. I understood death but had not known someone that I so greatly loved and revered to just leave, so abruptly! It was as if someone had snatched out my heart, lungs, and soul. I was numb! My mother grabbed and hugged me. We both wept. For years, well into my 20s, I mourned privately and in silence. The nightmares did not cease, they increased.

For years afterward, through middle, junior, and high school, the nightmares continued. After high school, I joined the military and went through basic training and onto my first military assignment overseas. I had spent the night at the home of wonderful and loving friends, they were a couple. Their house was my home away from home. On this one night, I had again fallen asleep on my back. The nightmare or so I thought, happened again. It started with a man breathing cold and heavily on my neck. As I felt it happening, I wanted to punch him, but immediately was paralyzed. When I managed to open my eyes, I saw as clear as day, glowing in the dark and sitting atop of me a gigantic bear—a glowing cartoon like bear sitting on top of me. It was so huge and heavy, I could not move, nor speak. It was suffocating me. So, I closed my eyes and began to recite the 23rd psalm in my mind. I was around 20 to 21 years of age.

For years I wrestled internally with the meaning of these dreams, but too about my sexuality. Desperate for answers, a few times I reached out to spiritual advisers as I felt tormented. I felt victimized on the one hand that it was because of the molestation that I was gay. And I had fallen in love or had major crushes on at least three different soldiers—of course secretly. Those were the days of "don't ask, don't tell." I did not want to be gay. Depression was my constant companion, and I continued to mourn the loss of my godmother.

So, I fought the feelings and I prayed. I struggled, denied, and tried to "pray the gay away." Once, I remember praying so very fervently, so hard for God to "heal" me, to take away my pain, the hurt from the molestation, child abuse, and the death of my godmother. I was tired of having these feelings for the same sex. I wrestled with my same sex attraction to men in one moment and the subsequent rejection of those feelings in the next.

One Sunday, after church, I let God know that I was fed up. I prayed and prayed, but in a real sense ranted, saying, "God, I know you can do this, please do it! Take it away!" Then, I heard clear as day God say, "Derek, faith is not knowing that I can, but knowing that I will!" Then, a few weeks later, a traveling Christian bazaar, came and set up a marketplace of all sorts of Christian books, Bibles, trinkets, and so on. I came across and purchased a little magnet that read, "Faith is not knowing that God can, but knowing God will!" About this time, I believed that something very spiritual was happening to me. That my answers or healing was "on the way."

My third and final year on that base in Europe could not start and end quickly enough. It was not because of the base, but because of other personal challenges and triumphs that occurred that might be shared in another forum. My third and final year came and ended. I left Europe, but the nightmares followed me back stateside. I had just turned 22 years of age.

While on vacation, I visited my molester and his family. He acted as if I was a stranger. It was good to see his wife and kids, I still loved them, but he treated me so dryly. When I left their home, I left with a high sense of disregard and or disapproval—still. After I returned home to Phoenix, it was not very long after that word came to me that my molester was dead. It is my understanding he died of heart failure. I instantly felt liberated. My burden lifted. My nightmares ceased. The nightmares surrounding my deeply suppressed sexual molestation—died with him! It was as if a warm breeze came over me and I finally had peace.

Now, you must understand that I do not rejoice in my molester's demise. I offer this narrative here to demonstrate how I have come full circle being in the world as God, Spirit, the universe—whatever you would like to call it—have created me to be; I am Black, male, and gay! I served my country just short of 10 years in the Air Force. I have avoided prison, jail, drugs, and discarded depression and mourning as my constant companions. I am quickly moving into the ranks of what W.E.B. DuBois called, the "talented tenth." I will soon become Dr. Derek Irvin.

So, if there is one piece of advice that I could share with the reader is that you must believe in yourself. You have a right to be the very unique person that you were created. You fulfill the highest, most truthful, and unique expression of yourself. That, in spite of the number of deficit narratives regarding men of color: social, academic, economic, physical and sexual abuse, mass incarceration, and homophobia—you matter! You have a right to exist, so be you; prayer works; move through the challenges towards your triumphs; stand still and in doing so, you demonstrate resilience—grit. Faith is not knowing that God can, but knowing that God will come to your rescue. We ask the question today, "Won't He do it..." possibly more as a cliché. However, I am quite clear at this point on my life's journey. I do not have to ask, because I know He will!

CHAPTER 50

FROM VICTIM TO VICTOR

"I Don't Want to Play!"

Robert A. Massey

Often when people ask you how you achieved your success they are not prepared for you to uncover the darkest places of your life. The "secrets" that few people know that can still cause tears to fall when remembered. The secret to my success lies in the substratum of what was happening to me several times a week after school as a child between 3:30 and 5:00 p.m. prior to being picked up by my mom from the babysitter's house. My success is rooted in the helplessness of a little boy growing up in the urban community who was full of dreams and promise but dealing with the secret and shame of sexual abuse.

On a frigid winter night in February of 2017, I entered a dark AMC theater packed to full capacity to watch a movie entitled, *Moonlight*, directed by Barry Jenkins, based on Tarell Alvin McCraney's unpublished semi-autobiographical play entitled, *In Moonlight Black Boys Look Blue*. It stars Trevante Rhodes, Andre' Holland, Janelle Monae, Ashton Sanders, Jharrel Jerome, Naomie Harris, and Mahershala Ali. This film presented three distinct stages in the life of the main character, the first stage being: little (adolescents), the second stage "Chiron," which was his junior high school to high school years, and then the third and last stage as "Black," representing the maturing adult man he had become over his lifetime. It explored the difficulties that he faced not only with sexuality and identity but also what it meant to grow up under privileged in the 1980s and 1990s without a father figure and a mother who was addicted to crack cocaine narcotics. Midway through the movie, all I could see and hear was all the tears and sniffles as the movie played. I wiped the tears that formed in the corners of my eyes as I reminisced on my own childhood. I found myself identifying with the main character named "Little/Chiron/Black," three different names to describe the three different defining moments of his life. In all the different phase of his life from adolescents to adulthood I saw pieces of my own life. Unlike, the main character of the said movie I wasn't dealing with an absentee father, and/or a crack cocaine addicted mother. My parents were married, God-fearing, and were working hard to take care of our family. There was always enough food to eat and there was no question about where I was going to lay my head at night to sleep. But I was dealing with my secret of sexual abuse at the hands of my babysitter's son, human sexuality, bullying, and name calling which had me fighting in school during my adolescent years.

I can't recall the exact day the sexual abuse began, but I can describe the process. Often my babysitter would send me into her son's bedroom to be watched by him while she attended to the other children and took care of the affairs of her house. The babysitter's son would teach me how to fight by play-fighting and tickling me to the point of micturition. He would place me on the floor, face down on my stomach, and pin me down. Being older, bigger, and stronger than me; I was unable to move at which time he began to rub up against my rear end as I was pinned to the floor. He would dry-hump me through my clothes. I didn't know what was going on but he would always tell me that "how we played was our secret." This occurred at least several times a week after school until I finished the second grade. He would always buy me candy afterwards. I perceived it was just another game played by teenagers. Being so young, I was oblivious that I was experiencing sexual abuse. Vividly, I can recall the so surreal experience of my pants being pulled down around my ankles, my buttocks being spread, licked and humped upon. Although, my physical body had not been penetrated by him, my soul as a child was being pierced and swallowed up by his actions. I remember being in school and feeling confused, as I pondered what was going to happen at the babysitter's house today. My abuser was a strategist, in that he was the same guy that would teach me to speak up for myself, how to physically fight, and would defend me if others would call me derogatory names such as a "sissy" or a "faggot." I didn't know what a sissy or faggot was...Was I faggot...What's a sissy...I had no clue. However, once I began to understand that it was a "label" of disrespect for those who are perceived as homosexual. I began to fight back verbally and then physically. I was naturally a kind and loving child but my temperament was altered to survive. Unfortunately, for me the real damage was done, and so I began to fight. I learned to take a punch and to throw one as well. I fought until I became good enough to win over my bullies. My name was Robert and I was going to be respected!

After realizing this behavior was wrong! I made it clear, "I don't want to play," and I threatened my abuser that I was going to tell my parents if he did not stop touching me. In the fear of being exposed he stopped making advances towards me. I was about to enter the third grade when my family moved away from that neighborhood. I was officially a latchkey kid and safely tucked away in my own bedroom at home after school far away from the sexual abuse.

As I began to mature, it become painfully clear to me that I had to get a good education, a good job, and get the hell out of the ghetto! My parents had it etched into my mind and I was determined to follow the blueprint. As a result of the sexual abuse, I withdrew mentally and kept my head down, my mouth shut, and my secret hidden from all until I became an adult. I threw myself into education and the Christian church.

Fast forward, I must admit the majority of my junior high and high school years were enjoyable for the most part. I focused on the arts such as acting, singing, learning music, and playing sports. I even picked up a few girlfriends along the way. I graduated from Newtown High School with honors and was accepted into Bernard M. Baruch College The City University of New York.

Over time, I learned that elements of my success was because people saw that I was trying to better myself and stretched out to help me. I also knew how to be humble and receive the help that others extended towards me. I realized that another key to my personal success was found in the power of prayer. I firmly believe that prayer changes things. However, it wasn't just prayer, but prayer and faith-in-action working together. Most people seemed to like that I had boot-strapped up from "the hood," attained a bachelor's degree, a master's degree from New York Theological Seminary, had become a law instructor, a husband, a father, and a taxpayer. But the backdrop that others couldn't see was I was determined to fight daily, and not live underneath the shame and emotional pain of having my innocence snatched at an early age.

Success does not happen just because we want it to but because we set ourselves in position to be successful. Meaning, you can have all the talent and gifts in the world; but if no one sees them, hears them, or knows that you possess them then they go unnoticed. Therefore, it's *gift* + *talent* (working at the gift) + *opportunity* = *success*. I realized that each one of these components is necessary for success to occur. For example, even if you have a natural gift to cook or sing you will become better and sharper at it underneath the right teacher. My success has been steeped in pain, forgiveness, loss, and overcoming the issues of life. Unfortunately, at times it meant failing until I was able to get it right. I was unwilling to settle for what others thought was good enough for me. I was willing to "do the work" to learn and earn what I needed in order to ensure success. I learned there are no shortcuts on the road to success but long days and nights filled with hard work and perseverance.

After instructing at the NYC Police Academy for over twelve years as a master instructor, I transferred to the Internal Affairs Bureau and was promoted to the rank of detective investigator. I continued in my pursuit of education and was accepted on paper to attend Princeton University to pursue a doctoral degree in biblical studies pending GRE's. A colleague asked, if I would consider an honorary Doctor of Ministry degree, from Anointed by God Alliance Seminary because he had already submitted my name for consideration. Initially, I struggled with accepting the honor because I was not looking for an easy way to receive a doctorate. I was assigned a doctoral mentor, who insisted that I write a paper and submit several samples of my writings along with my college and graduate school transcripts, to which, I did comply. On May 2, 2015, I was conferred, hooded, and I received the Doctor of Ministry degree. Having received this honor, it continues to open the door to innumerable opportunities all over the world. Currently, I am a professor at Mantle Christian College, which is located in Middleton, Delaware and I lecture in the field of chaplaincy and hospice. As a master instructor for the Division of Criminal Justice Services State of New York, I lecture for the ALM Group Security Guard Law Enforcement Training Academy located in Brooklyn, New York, teaching the instructor development course. I humbly serve as clergy in my church, and I work in my passion as an HIV/AIDS awareness activist, as the founder/CEO of Xtra Mile Mindset, LLC.

Lastly, I believe through faith, prayer, and the right support system you can overcome anything you go through in life. I've heard it said, "What doesn't kill you can and will make you stronger." I know I have been able to accomplish what I have today due to the love of my family, friends, and the power of prayer.

REFERENCE

Romanski, A. (Producer), Gardner, D. (Producer), Kleiner, J. (Producer) & Jenkins, B. (Director). (2016). *Moonlight* [Motion Picture]. United States: A24.

CHAPTER 51

LEARNING TO OVERCOME EXCESSIVE DRINKING

Charles Brown III

I grew up in Flint, Michigan from 1977 to 1996. I lived with my mother who worked a full time and a part time job to make ends meet. My mother made many personal sacrifices to provide for both my older sister and me. At a young age, my father moved out of our house to pursue a relationship with a younger woman. After my father left our home, he did not talk to me for approximately 5 years. My father resurfaced in my life when I turned 13 years old. In my teenage years, I realized that it would be difficult to establish a father–son relationship due to my father's inconsistent presence in my life. While spending time with my father, I started noticing that he consumed alcohol regularly. I had nothing against my father drinking alcohol when we were together; however, I felt that it would be hard to build a strong connection with my father when he was drinking alcohol excessively.

In 1996, I moved away from my home to go to college. As a college student, I started drinking alcohol regularly too. On a weekly basis: I liked drinking alcohol at social events, when watching sports on television, and coping with stress and anxiety in my life.

After years of excessive alcohol use, I begin to feel like something wasn't right. My ability to function on a daily basis felt different. I had a hard time with maintaining close relationships, achieving academic goals, and managing my finances. I suspected I had a problem with drinking alcohol excessively since both my father and grandfather consumed alcohol regularly.

On several occasions, when I would travel home to see my family, I can remember that I would drink alcohol excessively with my father and grandfather to make it easier to socialize. I wanted to connect socially with my father and grandfather, so I thought it would be good to develop a high tolerance level for alcohol. For a long time, I thought my drinking habits helped me to socialize and connect with various family members. When drinking alcohol with my father and grandfather, it seemed like I was able to get past my father's shortcomings from my childhood. Nevertheless, during the times when I wasn't drinking, the old wounds and unresolved issues seemed to come up when I had heated conversations with my father.

Consequently, until the age of 23, it seemed like heavy drinking played a significant role in my life. The heavy drinking led to social, environmental, and academic problems. Throughout these years, I also had a lot of issues with various friends, family members, and dating my girlfriend.

My interactions with various friends were very moody and short-tempered. For example, I was living with a friend, and we would get into arguments because the person would borrow my clothes without asking. We would try to sit down and talk to resolve the issue; however, the situation would get a whole lot worse because we were drinking alcohol during our conversation which added fuel to the fire.

After a while, my heavy drinking started to take a toll on my relationship with my girlfriend. I had a habit of breaking personal commitments because of my drinking habits. On some days, I couldn't function normally and interact with my girlfriend due to a hangover. I initially thought that my girlfriend would understand my drinking habits, but she shared with me that this behavior wasn't healthy for our relationship. I was surprised to hear my girlfriend say that she thought I had a drinking problem, and it would be best for us to separate. This moment made me even more aware of my drinking problem.

Despite my continued social struggles and challenges as a college student, I managed to stay enrolled in school. During my freshman year of college, I had a 1.9 (GPA), and the committee on academic affairs placed me on academic probation. The next two years as a sophomore and junior in college, my GPA fluctuated each semester. It was difficult to go to class because I had a hangover or I had been up all night. I knew that I could succeed as a college student if I took the time out to address my drinking issues.

Another significant issue that emerged in my life during this time was the inability to manage my finances. As a young adult, I didn't see the need to plan and manage my money wisely. On numerous occasions, I would spend a lot of money buying alcohol rather than paying my car note and credit card bills. For many years, it seemed like my financial situation was getting worse and worse. Eventually, the stress of my financial hardship began to impact other areas of my life.

After going a long time without addressing the numerous issues mentioned previously, it became apparent that my life had snowballed out of control. In retrospect, I believe my life turned around when I started to become interested in the role of spirituality in my life and take my walk with Jesus Christ more seriously. As a Christian, I learned that it is essential to take care of your body. In my family, excessive drinking has caused several illnesses such as liver damage, diabetes, and nerve damage that led to amputation. After thinking about the way that excessive drinking can affect one's physical health, I accepted the need to address my excessive drinking issues. Also, I didn't want the problems that I was experiencing with drinking alcohol excessively to prevent me from developing socially, succeeding academically, and establishing good financial habits.

During my senior year in college, I also started surrounding myself with positive people who consumed less alcohol to resist the urge to drink excessively. Surprisingly, at the beginning of my senior year, I was placed in an apartment dorm room with a roommate who had good studying skills and safe drinking habits. I honestly think this new environment helped me change my life.

Furthermore, I reconnected with my former girlfriend to see if we could rekindle our relationship. I felt convinced that we could keep our relationship healthy because I took the necessary steps towards changing my life and reducing my alcohol consumption. After several conversations with my girlfriend, we gradually started to date again. Over time, I learned to be more open with my girlfriend while dealing with stress and financial problems. My girlfriend supported me in so many ways and gave me some good advice on how to manage my finances. In fact, we talked about setting spending limits, keeping track of expenses by monitoring receipts, and balancing my checkbook each month. After 3 years of dating, my girlfriend and I agreed to get married. We have now been married for 14 years. I can genuinely say that my wife has helped me put life into perspective.

I knew at an early age that I wanted to spend the rest of my life helping people reduce and eliminate unhealthy behaviors related to alcohol misuse. To carry out my goal of helping people, I decided to pursue a career in the public health field. Over a period of 10 years, I was able to achieve my goals of obtaining a bachelor's degree, a master's degree, and a doctoral degree in the area of health. One aspect of my work in the health field involves developing and implementing substance abuse prevention and treatment programs for youth and young adults. For several years now, I have collaborated with individuals in community-based organizations, P–12 public school systems, and higher education institutions to develop and implement substance abuse prevention and treatment programs. It is rewarding to know that I contributed to several substance abuse programs that were highly successful in helping people to change their lives.

At this point, I have realized that I want my life to be a beacon of change. Sometimes it's hard to believe that I have overcome the issues related to excessive drinking in my life. Once unable to interact with my family without drinking, I now socialize with my family, and I don't feel the urge to drink alcohol. Once unable to achieve my academic goals, I graduated with a doctoral degree in the area of public health. Once irresponsible with my finances, I now manage my budget effectively.

For people with similar challenges, I encourage you to grow spiritually, surround yourself with positive people, and refrain from social environments that may involve people drinking alcohol excessively. I am a firm believer that it is never too late to change your life. You can overcome this issue, if you take the necessary steps to make a change. Although I had to sacrifice a lot to turn my life around, I am grateful that I have made a change and it has all been worth it. I feel truly blessed to reflect on my experience with drinking alcohol excessively and sharing the steps that were used to help me overcome excessive alcohol drinking.

SECTION VI

EXPERIENCES IN HIGHER EDUCATION

For men of color, higher educational institutions are not often welcoming spaces, particularly predominantly White institutions (PWIs). Like broader American society, men of color face a plethora of challenges including racial discrimination, microaggressions, and profiling, which often impede their academic success at PWIs (Harper, 2015; Johnson, 2013) However, at historically Black colleges and universities (HBCUs), men of color are culturally-affirmed and in most cases are able to develop a sense of belonging, which often increase the likelihood of successful matriculation from HBCUs. In other words, despite low college degree attainment in general, men of color, particularly Black men, are far more likely to graduate from HBCUs than from PWIs that uphold institutional inequities—many of which will be discussed later in this section of the book.

In Section VI, many of the authors share higher educational experiences at either HBCUs or PWIs and how they overcame and navigated situations that were designed to ensure their failure. At the end of each narrative, male collegians of color share stories of wisdom to younger men of color who may consider attending HBCUs and PWIs.

REFERENCES

Harper, S. (2015). Black male college achievers and resistant responses to racist stereotypes at predominantly White colleges and universities. *Harvard Educational Review*, 85(4), 646–674.

Johnson, R. (2013). Black and male on campus: An autoethnographic account. *Journal of African American Males in Education*, 4(2), 103–123.

CHAPTER 52

HOW SPIRIT AND SOUL LED ME TO A LIFE AS A PSYCHOLOGICAL SCIENTIST

Brandon E. Gamble

INTRO-GRANDPA'S VISION

As a little boy, my grandfather, my mother's father, would tell me fantastic stories about how his grandmother who raised him would heal people. In rural East Texas, his grandmother of mixed White, Native American, and African heritage was sought out for her ability to heal various maladies. She would also have visions about life, and my grandfather told me he had similar visions.

I was often sent to the principal's office for my behavior. I wanted adults to understand me better and wished someone was there to explain to the adults how to better interact with me. I was one of only two Black children in every class I attended from preschool through high school and often felt misunderstood. When I was 10 years old, I had visions too, which did not scare me but gave me a sense of hope. The visions I had, even while daydreaming in the principal's office, were of me as a grown man. I was working at a school but I was not a teacher. I explained things to adults for other kids who were struggling in school. I realized now that I always wanted to be a school psychologist even though I did not know what an actual school psychologist was until I applied to graduate school.

ABOUT A GIRL

High school was a time when I finally officially learned about educational or school psychology, thanks to heartache. During my sophomore and junior years at my boarding high school, I dated someone who was a grade ahead of me. We spent very little time apart and wanted a way to spend more time together, so we took an elective psychology course. It was great! I learned about various types of psychologists. When I learned about an educational psychologist, I said to myself, "This is a profession that will allow me to live up to my vision." I could feel in my soul that becoming a school or educational psychologist would provide the training I needed to become a person who explains to adults what kids in trouble need. Unfortunately, just as I came into this awareness, my girlfriend broke up with me. I was devastated, but many of the strategies we learned in class for self-reflection, awareness, and overcoming grief helped me to move on from that heartache.

CAN I KICK IT...

As I started my freshman year of community college, I declared myself a psychology major. Although I had a good experience in my high school psychology course, my challenges as a little boy still plagued me. Doubt about my academic capability, as well as trusting my vision crept in. Community college helped me build my confidence because I earned an A grade in my first psychology 100 course! That A grade calmed my deepest fears about even my fitness for college. When it came time to transfer to a 4-year institution, because I had been the only Black child in my classes, I wanted to attend a historically black college or university (HBCU). There was as television show called *A Different World* (Carsey, Werner, Mandabach, & Fales, 1987–1993) that inspired many young people in my generation to attend an HBCU. My mother who had grown up in the South agreed. My father was unsure, but was content I had proved I could work, pay for school, and earn passing grades during my years at community college. So off I went to an HBCU.

MAMA KNOWS BEST

My mother, who never told me about visions but who did tell me about her expectations for me, had saved money for me to attend school. I had wanted to attend a school in the big city—Howard University. However, my good friend who grew up in the same small town I did had flunked out due to being overwhelmed, and what we would later discover was a learning disability. My mother, mindful of my challenges in school, recommended a small college in Huntsville, Alabama—Oakwood University. Twenty-five years later as I write this, I am hit with a flood of emotions as I think about the year I left for Oakwood. That year my mother had been diagnosed with breast cancer. She had several surgeries and treatments that left her so sick that she could not care for herself. Yet, she had taken time to make sure I was ready for school. She sent me to this small town with her blessing although I did not know if she would be alright. This town was so backwards in my mind: They did not have a bus system, yet they had four colleges! Leaving from suburban California to mostly rural Alabama was indeed a culture shock for me. That said, what Alabama lacked in resource, they made up for in people. The strong faith of the people at the school, the amazingly smart and beautiful women, and the comradery of my fraternity brothers embraced me as I hit that campus sad and scared.

THE EMBRACE OF AN HBCU

Oakwood College is now a university with master's degree programs. However, 25 years ago, this small college did not have proper printers or funding for students to conduct research. Despite these things, their teachers could and can still teach! Dr. Melvin Davis, my experimental psychology teacher, told me and my classmates to "wake-up" because the boiler had overheated and caused us to go to sleep in a basement classroom. I woke up to an admonishment by Dr. Davis who was wide awake, telling us to pay attention because people, other than Black people, were often influencing policy with large scale evaluations. We needed to know policy. Dr. Belvia Matthews, told me she saw potential in me after I scored high on a departmental psychology exam and she took me to my first professional conference. She was the first to tell me to I must earn a doctoral degree. I also started a math tutoring program with my fraternity brothers. We helped Black boys in middle school with remedial work and eventually algebra. I graduated from Oakwood in the Fall of 1994 and spent the Spring of 1995 working as a substitute teacher and unloading the truck on the night shift at a department store in the Alabama heat. During my breaks, which were few, I completed my graduate school applications. I was accepted to two school counseling programs but my mother, who had survived cancer treatment, encouraged me to apply to her and my father's alma mater, San Diego State University (SDSU).

GRADUATE SCHOOL BLESSINGS

Early in the Summer of 1995, two weeks after I got married to my wife Kia, SDSU's graduate assistant called me to inform me that they liked my application but it was not complete. I had filled out the university application but because the internet was fairly new to my small college and to me in general, I did not see that there was a program application. Being naïve, I asked them to fax me the program application, which included seven essay questions! The only challenge was that Oakwood was closed during the summer. I had to go to Kinko's to rent a computer and fax time. I wrote my essay and my wife helped me to fax each page. It cost $56.63 for me to send all of that information. Fortunately, it paid off. A professor from SDSU called me and said, "We want you to come for an interview!" I said in my mind, "Thank you God!" Then I got a little testy with God. I said again in my mind, "You know I don't have money to fly out there!" Then I said it out loud on the phone. Without missing a beat, the professor who was not a believer in any religious faith said, "You don't understand, we have a plane ticket for you." I said, not believing or accepting this offer, "No, I have to work the night shift." She got a little testy with me and said, well your loss then." Then it hit me. I was flying to San Diego! I called my grandfather who had already been talking to the Creator and he said, "Yep, God already told me you'd be back to California." I do not remember much about the interview other than I was not nervous at all but excited to be living my purpose. I actually told the interviewers at SDSU, "It does not matter if I get accepted here or somewhere else, but I am going to be that man who works for Black boys and any other youth who needs help." Despite my bravado, SDSU accepted me.

FULL CIRCLE

Now, remember I had no money; but what I did not know is that they offered me full tuition assistance as well as money each month to help me buy books and my new wife and I pay rent. I attended two professional conferences a month presenting papers on Black psychology and school psychology topics in general. One thing I learned from Black psychology is that beyond simply explaining and classifying behavior, which all good scientific psychologist must do, psychology is the study of the soul. The soul should be illuminated and enlivened not merely measured and classified. My soul itself was enlivened due to my faith and hope being rewarded. If that was not enough for my first year in graduate school, I had a job that paid more than my truck unloading job and my substitute teacher job. It was as an "counseling intern." My job, just as my vision had showed me, entailed, "working at a school but I was not a teacher. I explained things to adults for other kids who were struggling in school."

CONCLUSION—BELIEF REWARDED

Today, in my humble career, the boy with visions in the principal's office has grown up to be awarded "school psychologist of the year" at the local and state level and the president of the California Association of School Psychologists. I got my temper under control, well most days, as a Black belt in karate and jujutsu. I worked with my friend from Howard to earn a doctorate. My friend is now a medical doctor and psychiatrist at Johns Hopkins University. After working for 10 years as a school psychologist in Long Beach Unified School District in California, I teach full time as a college professor at Cal State University, Long Beach. I teach my students how to speak up for young people in trouble. I have had a great career but none of it would not be possible without my belief in Spirit, amazing women in my life, especially my mother and wife, and staying true to the power of the soul. Believe in yourself, your people, and in ultimate hope. Finally, serve somebody, and you will be rewarded.

REFERENCE

Carsey, M., Werner, T., Mandabach, C., & Fales, S. (1987–1993). A different world [Television Series]. Universal City, CA: NBC.

CHAPTER 53

DO NOT APPLY TO COLLEGE

Eugene Pitchford III

I remember like it was yesterday. Hearing those words from my high school counselor was something I would never forget. It still haunts me to this day. My counselor told me, "Do not apply to college." That was a knockout punch a high school senior did not want to hear. I went down for the count, but my high school counselor delivered one more body blow. She told me the only way I would make something of myself would be if I joined the armed forces.

I did my best to hold it together. As soon as I walked out of her office, my tears began to flow and didn't stop until I crossed paths with a classmate. I played it cool for the remainder of the school day, but at the same time I could not tell anyone the devastating message I had received.

Riding the city bus home that afternoon was really difficult. I kept replaying the conversation in my head. The following words were getting louder and louder: *You are not smart enough to go to college.* I could hear, see, taste, and smell those words. It was the worst feeling in my life. Imagine a school official telling you not to apply to college. Wasn't the job of a high school counselor to help build dreams, not to destroy dreams... I was devastated, but there was one more level to this day that quickly spiraled out of control. How would I tell my parents that I was not smart enough for college... My high school counselor told me I was not smart enough for college which meant there was no need to apply to college. I believed her since she was the school authority. I could not tell my parents. College was the expectation and, based on my conversation with my high school counselor I was too "stupid" for college. The only way I could tell my parents was to stop applying for college and find a factory job. The armed forces would not work for me because I was too scared. At 18 years old I felt like I was running out of options to be successful. I just wanted to be average and fly under the radar and hopefully nobody would recognize I was too stupid for college. In the defense of my high school counselor my grades weren't the best, and my effort in class was lackluster. Did that equal not applying to college...

Two life changing events occurred that summer. First, I had to take the Air Force exam. I knew I did not want to join the Air Force, so let's just say I did not put much effort into passing that particular exam. Second, my church at the time had a scholarship banquet. The program highlighted each candidate and the school in which they planned to attend. By my name Jackson State University was listed, but I knew I wasn't going there. Why did Jackson State accept me if I was stupid... Why would I waste my time going to college if I was stupid... The scholarship banquet date was also my personal timeline for informing my parents that I would not be attending college because I was stupid.

As you can guess, that conversation did not go well. I felt even worse after revealing my decision. I felt I let a lot of people down. I also did not want to waste money dedicated for me to attend college. I did not have the necessary skills at 18 to start my professional career. I could not find a job, which made me feel stupid again. The Air Force was already off my list, but I added the streets to that list. I was too scared to sell drugs, though. My senses were telling me the end result would be getting robbed, shot, or killed. I was basically stuck with no legitimate options for college.

A strange thing happened during the second week of August. This was about the time my peers were leaving to go to college. I got a call from the local community college asking me to come to their admissions college to complete my application. This was strange since I had never applied to their school. I informed the person on the phone that this had to be a mistake and they had the wrong number. The person on the phone knew my full name, social security number, and where I lived.

My aunt who worked at this local community college went behind my back and enrolled me for the fall semester. I did not want to go to college there, plus I was *stupid*. This would definitely impede on the job I did not have. I politely declined. I reflected for several days and out of desperation, I met with the admission counselor.

I was officially in college, but I was not confident. The classes were easy, but I hated every aspect of attending this local community college. I felt out of place and most of my classmates were my parent's age. My experiences were totally different from my peers that went away to college. I was unhappy, felt worthless, and going through the motions of life.

During midterms I had a conversation with a classmate that totally changed my life. This classmate was a White man, who was probably in his mid-40s. He asked me why I was attending the local community college. I told him I was not smart and that a family member had signed me up to attend. The classmate asked me to look around the classroom. He stated that everyone in the room had made major life mistakes and was attempting to get their life back on track. He also told me that I was the smartest in the room and should not be mixed up with people that had real challenges in life.

The light bulb went off. While riding the city bus home I kept saying to myself, *"I am not stupid."* That evening, I informed my parents that I needed to go to a traditional college. I did not care if it was in or out of state. I selected Mississippi Valley State, and by January I was starting my first semester there. During my time at MVSU, I decided to understand my worth and embrace the skills that I had. From that point, I maintained a 3.0 or higher throughout undergraduate studies, master's degree program, and doctoral studies.

I have worked in education my entire professional career. I am in no position to tell any student do not apply to college. I am honest about barriers and immediate challenges, but I also provide strategies on how to overcome those barriers and challenges. So many educators kill the dreams of students. We use our influence in the wrong way then wonder why students do not respect us. What hurts me the most is the fact that many educators of color are guilty of killing the dreams of youth.

I would love to have a meeting with my former high school counselor. It would not be to get back at her for killing my dream. It would not be to say I told you so. It would not be to share my success in life. I want to meet with her to share how powerful our words can be and how we can be the one person to change the life of a young person. I am convinced this high school counselor was not being rude or racist when she told me not to apply to college. However, I am certain she had low expectations for me. I also do not think she understood the power of her words. Based on our conversation, I thought I was dumb. There are many African American students that do not have a family member telling them to chase their dreams.

Someone reading this book might have the same experience as I did. It hurts when people believe you are not smart enough for college, although it does not mean they are correct. Please use the following as a guide if you are struggling to determine if you are smart enough for college. First, believe in yourself. There will be times when your parents, family, friends, and school counselors will not believe in you. It is important for you to know you can attend and complete college. If you do not believe in yourself, nobody else will. Second, you need to believe that college is for you. It is possible to make it without a college degree, but it is a lot harder. Make attending college your number one goal. By embracing the goal of making it to college, it will force you to take the necessary steps to be successful in high school. Third, understand your strengths and weaknesses. You need to research which colleges have the major you are interested in studying. If your grades are shaky, Harvard University probably should not be on your list. There is a college out there for everyone. Research to determine a college that you would have a great chance of being accepted to based on your grades and interested area of study. Don't rule out starting at a technical or community college and transferring to a 4-year college. Fourth, always do your best. If you have a goal you must work extra hard to meet the goal. If attending college is your goal, are you doing the best you possibly can in high school… If you are doing your best, maintain that effort and do better. If you aren't doing your best, the time is right now to improve. Do not wait for your teachers to tell you to improve; you should always know your strengths and weaknesses. You can do it. If you follow the four tips in this paragraph you will master the steps needed for college readiness. If you have nobody telling you that can make it, please understand that I support you on your journey to college.

CHAPTER 54

CHALLENGING TRANSITIONS
Reflecting Back, Projecting Forward

Brian A. Burt

I do not have the magic formula for succeeding in college or graduate school, but as I reflect on my academic experiences, some commonalities cut across my journey: engaging in meaningful mentoring relationships, participating in key opportunities, and taking advantage of leadership experiences. In the following pages, I tell the story of an ambitious man with dreams of positively impacting the field of education.

MY ACADEMIC JOURNEY

My academic journey began as I left my hometown of Grand Rapids, Michigan, to pursue college in what seemed a faraway land—Indiana University—Bloomington, 6 hours away. As an out-of-state student, I encountered differences in everything I had grown to know. Not only did I feel different, I was told I was different: I did not have an Indiana accent, did not come from the state, and did not participate in the school's storied summer bridge program for talented underrepresented students. Although I was previously involved in cocurricular experiences in high school, during my first year in college, feeling different led me to become so overwhelmed and demoralized that all I wanted to do was sleep. Ultimately, I felt like I did not belong and had made the wrong choice for college—an overwhelming feeling for a young Black man attending a predominately White institution located out-of-state.

Despite being unhappy, I never let go of the idea that I could make it if I just held on. Fortunately, holding on helped. In addition to leaving my room to attend classes, I occasionally attended affinity-based campus programs. There, I began meeting other Black academic achievers, Black graduate students, and Black professionals on campus. I slowly became comfortable sharing with them how I was socially struggling. Almost serendipitously, several individuals offered to serve as mentors for me. Some held formal mentoring roles (whereby the university facilitated agreements about what the mentoring relationship would entail); for most others, however, the informal mentoring organically evolved, from occasional lunches and dinners, to hanging out. Recognizing my potential for leadership, they *all* encouraged me to become more involved on campus. Taking their advice, I became involved and began to feel connected to the university as I built my own community. When I was around the graduate students, I witnessed their joyful and challenging experiences, and began seeing myself as a future graduate student. I learned by observing them that graduate school would not be easy—that I, too, would face challenges, but that those challenges would make me stronger—and that I, too, could succeed in graduate school. Reflecting back, engaging in mentoring and involvement on campus was the turning point that led me from being uninvolved and unhappy to being a campus leader engaged in selective and prestigious organizations.

Through my sustained connection with mentors, my career goals evolved. I decided I was interested in helping students like me; I decided to pursue a master's degree in higher education at the University of Maryland, College Park. Although I knew from observing my mentors that graduate school would be challenging, the first year was a struggle. I again felt different, isolated, and in search of a new supportive community, and I needed to understand and master more intense academic expectations (e.g., reading load, field-specific jargon). I believed that everyone was smarter than me, that perhaps I had again made the wrong choice.

Things changed once I became involved in a key opportunity. One of my graduate school professors, Dr. Sharon Fries-Britt, invited me to join her research team. I was terrified of the opportunity to work with someone I respected so much and nervous that my minimal experience doing research would be detrimental to the group. Perhaps even scarier, I was concerned that Dr. Fries-Britt would realize how much I did not know and ask me to leave. None of those things happened. She provided the right balance of challenge and encouragement and helped me understand how my contributions to the team—no matter how minor I thought they were—benefited her assembled community of scholars. That experience improved my sense of my academic self and being in the research group improved my understanding of doing graduate level research while giving me a glimpse of what was expected at the doctoral level. It also planted the seeds of a future faculty career and research agenda.

After completing my master's degree and working full time for a couple of years, I began my doctoral studies at the University of Michigan. Like many other students, I experienced challenges that impacted my academic work. It took several years to understand how I fit into my new department, particularly as one of only a handful of Black men in the entire school of education (students and faculty combined). I dealt with imposter syndrome—meaning I was not sure I really belonged at Michigan—with the need to prove my worth in the doctoral program, and with consistent critiques that I needed to improve my writing. Learning from my previous experiences with mentoring, I sought out wisdom from my Black male and non-Black professors (at my institution and others) to guide me through this terrain. Words from them, such as "those of us who can, must!" and "The PhD is not given to those who are the smartest, it is earned by those who persevere to the end," reminded me that my doctoral journey would be an exercise in endurance, but seeing it through would make me a stronger scholar, mentor, and man.

In addition to gaining support from faculty, I developed an unbreakable bond with my fellow Black male colleagues. Together we cultivated a well-oiled support system where we routinely proofread each other's writing, collaborated in leadership experiences, and encouraged one another. We promised each other that we would not leave without earning our degrees, together. For the first time in my academic journey, I allowed myself to be vulnerable and accountable to people other than myself.

As my doctoral career evolved, I took advantage of opportunities that eventually led to my current career. For example, I determined that I could help make a difference as the graduate representative on the board of directors of my field's premiere professional organization, the Association for the Study of Higher Education. I applied and was elected. During my 2-year term, I voted on the future direction of the association, planned programs for the graduate population at our annual conference, and created infrastructure for future elected representatives holding that post. I learned about the needs of graduate students, which informs how I currently think about advising and teaching. Also, having gained access to the top scholars in my field, I had the opportunity to observe how leadership takes place at the association level, and how to balance my academic responsibilities with service to the field. Most germane to this chapter, this invaluable experience not only helped retain me but also propelled me to the next level: in the Fall of 2014 my dreams came true as I began an assistant professorship in the higher education program at Iowa State University.

REFLECTING BACK, PROJECTING FORWARD

As I think about my future and the limitless possibilities to come, I am reminded how I got to this point, and this leads me to make the following recommendations to others:

- *Engage in meaningful mentoring relationships.* I did not get here on my own. I sought mentorship from people in positions I aspired to hold. They shared their journeys of tenacity and perseverance, which made my path a little clearer. Similarly, you should realize that you, too, need help to succeed, and that needing help is normal. Ask friends, family members, professors or staff members (to name some examples) for suggestions of those who might be good mentors. In some circumstances, you may need to be fearless and ask someone to be your mentor; in others, someone might identify you as one who might benefit from mentoring. Remember that peers can be outstanding mentors as well. Once you connect with a mentor, nurture the relationship. Do not let your mentor do all of the work. Meet that person half way; this will ensure that it is a mutually beneficial relationship, rather than a one-sided exchange.
- *Take advantage of leadership experiences.* Participating in leadership experiences made the difference between feeling isolated and feeling a part of college. Serving in leadership roles allowed me to learn my leadership style, test out new styles, appreciate my unique contributions, and share my talents with my institutional and city communities. Joining an organization on campus or in your local community may similarly make you feel more connected. In addition, participating in leadership experiences will help make the campus community smaller. Seek out opportunities to share your unique skills.
- *Participate in key opportunities.* I was fortunate to participate in research at the undergraduate and graduate levels. These experiences were formative and invaluable; they provided me with foreshadowing of the researcher and scholar I am today. I was reluctant to participate at first because I did not feel ready. For you, the key opportunity may not be research, but something else for which you may not feel smart enough or prepared enough. Try to silence your

inner critic and take advantage of the opportunity. You are likely to learn more about yourself and develop new skills. Additionally, you, too, may be exposed to new professional interests you had not previously considered. Prepare yourself to accept invitations to key opportunities so that you will be ready to say "yes" when they arise.

I am honored to continue this chain connecting Black male educators in the academy. I use this chapter to recommit myself to the important work I have begun on Black male achievement. This work of giving voice to Black men who are often unheard, overlooked, and misunderstood is inextricably linked to my own experiences as a Black male in the academy who struggled at every turn. In sharing my story, I hope to inspire someone, just as I was and continue to be inspired by the men in this volume, and our ancestors before us.

EPILOGUE

He's misunderstood, some say that He's up to no good around the neighborhood
Well, for your information Alot of my brotha's got education
Now check it
You got your wall street brotha, Your blue collar brotha,
Your down-for-whatever-chillin'-on-the-corner brotha
Your talented brotha, and to everyone of ya'll behind bars
You know that Angie loves ya, my my

—Stone, Saadiq, Lilly, Standridge, and Ozuna (2001)

The lyrics to the song "Brotha" sung by Angie Stone, specifically the verse above, is used to frame, describe, and explain the diverse lived experiences of males of color in society. Despite persistently negative stereotypes that suggest, *"He's up to no good around the neighborhood,"* the individual and collective chapters in this book give different voices to the trials, tribulations, and triumphs of men of color who have overcome many odds to achieve a measure of success. The collection of stories, meditations, affirmations, and inspirations shared by the authors, lined up together, offers a robust and compelling counter-narrative to the dominant-narrative to boldly echo Angie Stone's sentiment that *"for your information, a lot of my brotha's got education."* Evidence of education is found in the diverse narratives of the men of color in this book who have earned baccalaureate, master, and doctoral degrees in a variety of fields and disciplines—most, ironically, are in the field of education, where, nationally, men of color constitute 2% of the P–12 teaching force. Their stories are just one of the myriad ways in which the men of color have in the past and presented defied society's often negative view of them as simply "problems" and "pathologies."

Each of these stories end in promise, potential, and possibility to encourage other men of color as early as high school to recognize that value and resiliency in the face of challenging circumstances and situations. These stories aim to provide educational and social uplift to men of color who share similar struggles. As stated in the introduction, sharing our stories herein collectively, is our way of pushing back against the primary ways in which the lives and experiences of men of color are framed—leaving them "broken," while ignoring the myriad existing institutional and structural factors that negatively shape our lives. While this edited book focuses on the critical academic, social, and environmental issues men of color face, it is important to emphasize the different paths taken by each man of color on his journey to circumvent institutional inequities and to achieve success.

The six themes: (a) Familial Impact on Education; (b) Intersections of Race, Gender, and Sexuality; (c) Racial Discrimination; (d) Overcoming Narrative of Failure; (e) Sexual and Substance Abuse; and (f) Experiences in Higher Education that comprise this book are a reminder that despite the many harsh and ominous societal realities and injustices experienced, they are resilient. This resolve to live on the part of these men of color is an analogous to an essay entitled, "Are You Hunting for Jews..." appearing in *Some of Us Did Not Die: New and Selected Essays of June Jordan* (Jordan, 2002). The question that the essay invokes can be asked of society when consideration is given to the countless men of color, especially Black men, who have been murdered at the hands of police officers, security guards, and self-appointed vigilantes. The names of Black men, Sean Bell (23 years old), Rumain Brisbon (34 years old), Kalief Browder (22 years old), Michael Brown (18 years old), Philando Castile (32 years old), John Crawford II (22 years old), Terence Crutcher (40 years old), Jordan Davis (17 years old), Ezell Ford (25 years old), Eric Garner (43 years old), Oscar Grant (22 years old), Freddie Gray (25 years old), Akai Gurley (28 years old), Dontre Hamilton (31 years old), Eric Harris (44 years old), Ernest Hoskins (21 years old), Tyre King (13 years old), Trayvon Martin (17 years old), Alfred Olango (38 years old), Dante Park (36 years old), Jerame Reid (36 years old), Tony Robinson (19 years old), Tamir Rice (12 years old), Keith Scott (43 years old), Walter Scott (50 years old), Phillip White (32 years old), and countless others, begs a similar question, *"Are You Hunting for Black Men...?"* The distinct pattern is of the countless number of men of color in general, especially Black men, whom we have watched up close and afar, as they were sent to their deaths—figuratively and literally.

As fate would have it, the Auschwitz survivor was sent to a concentration camp, and to slave labor, forced upon her like thousands of other Jews. The Auschwitz survivor sums up her survival to this time in one short phrase very succinctly, *"I guess it was my destiny to live."*

To live is not just a given: To live means you owe something big to those whose lives are taken away from them (pp. 12–13)...And two things happened for me [after hearing the voice of courage, strength, and determination] I realized that regardless of the tragedy, regardless of the grief, regardless of the monstrous challenge, Some of us Have Not Died. (Jordan, 2002, p. 13)

These words epitomize the survival against unfortunate fates that have befallen so many men of color, many of whom are in the pages of this book. Therefore, it too was their destiny to live. Despite the many struggles and challenges documented herein, the authors have endured to share their story with you—which is a true measure of the human spirit and their will to live! Their stories have resulted in their personal evolution from that of an observer, to a victim at times, to their present status as agents of social change who challenge themselves and others to recognize, value, encourage, and cultivate the many gifts, talents, and resiliency of men of color whose "secret recipe" lies in their individual and collective *"Gumbo for the Soul."*

REFERENCES

Jordan, J. (2002). Some of us did not die: *New and Selected Essays of June Jordan.* New York, NY: Basic/Civitas Books.

Stone, A., Saadiq, R., Lilly, H., Standridge, G., & Ozuna, R.C. (2001). *Brotha* [Recorded by Angie Stone]. On Mahogany Soul. New York, NY: J Records LLC.

ABOUT THE EDITORS

Brian L. Wright, PhD, is program coordinator and associate professor of early childhood education at the University of Memphis. Brian's research focuses on high-achieving African American boys/males in urban schools pre-K–12, racial-ethnic identity development of boys and young men of color, African American males as early childhood teachers, and teacher identity development. Brian is the author of *The Brilliance of Black Boys: Cultivating School Success in the Early Grades*, an award-winning book (2018 Philip C. Chinn Book Award–National Association for Multicultural Education—NAME).

Nathaniel Bryan, EdD, PhD, is assistant professor at Miami University in Oxford, Ohio. His teaching and scholarship explores issues of equity and diversity, critical race theory, culturally relevant teaching, urban education, and Black education. Though he studies broadly these theories and frameworks, he is particularly interested in the constructed identities and pedagogical styles of Black male teachers in early childhood education and the schooling and childhood play experiences of Black boys, particularly those boys who defy hegemonic and Black masculine play norms and expectations in early childhood classrooms and urban communities.

Christopher J.P. Sewell, EdD, is an associate dean at Williams College. His current scholarship focuses on studying the experiences of gifted students of color and how schooling and policies around gifted and talented education affect their long-term experiences and the ways in which LGBTQ+ gifted students negotiate their academic, racial, and sexual identities.

Lucian Yates, III, PhD, is an interim provost and vice president for academic affairs at Kentucky State University. Prior to KSU, Lucian served as the graduate school dean and professor of curriculum and instruction at Tennessee State University. He also served as the dean of education and a professor of educational leadership at Prairie View A&M University in Texas (2008–2016). Lucian is an award-winning teacher, assistant principal, principal, assistant superintendent, superintendent, and a directorship at KDE.

Michael A. Robinson, EdD, is founder/CO-CEO of Forest of the Rain Productions, and the host of Parent Talk Live and Educational Gateway radio shows on the Journey Begins, Internet Radio for the Engaged Parent and Dedicated Educator. Michael is creator of *Men Make a Difference Day*. The implementation of the program resulted in over 10,000 fathers and significant male role models engaging with their children's schools on a single day.

Kianga Thomas, EdD is an assistant professor of Elementary Education at Norfolk State University. He also serves as the assessment coordinator in the School of Education. Kianga teaches courses in elementary education, diversity, and monitors the assessment system for the School of Education. His research interests are gifted African American students, Science, Technology, Engineering, and Mathematics (STEM), and teacher efficacy. Some of his published works include problem-based learning with pre-service teachers, STEM development with pre-service and in-service teachers, and psychological factors towards academic success among high-achieving African American students. Kianga earned his EdD from the College of William and Mary and prior to joining higher education, taught elementary school in Virginia.

ABOUT THE CONTRIBUTORS

Raymond Adams, MSW, is an assistant professor of social work in the College of Liberal and Performing Arts in the Department of Social Work at Southern Arkansas University. Raymond's research focuses on the intersection of spirituality and prostate cancer survivorship among rural Black Americans.

Charles A. Barrett, PhD, serves students, families, schools, and communities as a school psychologist in Northern Virginia. Charles is also an adjunct professor in the Graduate School of Education at Howard University and holds various leadership positions in state and national associations. Charles' research and professional practice are anchored by promoting equitable policies for all students, especially those who have been marginalized by systemic injustice.

Joel Bratton Jr., EdD, is an educational specialist II for Baltimore City Public Schools. Joel's research focuses on urban education and the achievement gap in African-American male student success in K–20 and the achievement gap in the community college.

Charles Brown, PhD, is an assistant professor in the Department of Public Health, Health Administration, and Health Sciences at Tennessee State University. Charles's research involves designing, implementing, and evaluating behavioral health programs in the areas of alcohol and drug addiction treatment, HIV/AIDS prevention, and mental health services. He has worked collaboratively with local school systems, after-school programs, higher education institutions, government agencies, churches, community-based behavioral health care organizations, primary care clinics, and the Army National Guard to conduct research and grant activities.

Brian A. Burt, PhD, is an assistant professor of higher education at Iowa State University, a National Academy of Education/Spencer Postdoctoral Fellow, and a National Science Foundation Early CAREER award recipient. He researches graduate students in STEM and their participation in research experiences (i.e., the science of team science).

Raphael Crawford, EdD, is the chief consultant in educational reform and organizational leadership with The Crawford Group, LLC. Formerly a highly effective school principal and district administrator, Raphael researches the criminalization of students of color, nontraditional families, mirror neurons and ethical leadership, and urban school leadership.

Verontae Deams, EdD, is the associate registrar and adjunct professor at Tennessee State University in Nashville, Tennessee. Dr. Deams' research focuses on minorities in higher education and academic success.

Antonio L. Ellis, EdD, is an adjunct professor of educational leadership and policy studies at Howard University. In addition, Antonio is the director of specialized instruction at Stanton Elementary School in Washington, DC. His research focuses on critical race theory in special education specifically African American male students who are speech impaired.

Brandon E. Gamble, EdD, is an associate professor and dean of student success at Oakwood University. Brandon's research focuses on African American students and their college readiness, access, retention, as well as positive educational outcomes in K–16.

Dwight E. Gordon, II., MBA, is pursuing an EdD in higher education. Dwight is proficient in all things concerning being an educated, conscious Black male.

Darreon Greer, Sr., MS, is a doctoral candidate in the counseling psychology program at Tennessee State University. Darreon's research focuses on the college-age student population, youth in the juvenile justice system, and STEM as it relates to underrepresented students of color. Darreon is a social justice advocate for communities of color to increase their upward social mobility.

Wil Greer, PhD, is an assistant professor of educational leadership at California State University, San Bernardino. Wil's research focuses on implementing and sustaining culturally responsive school leadership in P–12.

LaMarcus Hall, is a doctoral student in the curriculum and instruction program at Purdue University. LaMarcus is a center director for Family Development Services, researcher, and motivational speaker. He's also a graduate board member for RM.

Tyrone Hamler, MSW, LSW, is a doctoral candidate in social welfare at Case Western Reserve University. Tyrone's research focuses on kidney disease, health equity, and medical social work practice.

David Hughes, MEd, is a doctoral candidate at Prairie View A&M University and a graduate of Morehouse College. David's research focuses on collegiate selection, HBCU athletics, and Black athletes' social issues.

Derek O. Irvin, is a PhD candidate and a program manager in the corrections program at Houston Community College. Derek's research focuses on school-to-prison pipeline, correctional education, criminal justice reform, critical race theory, critical spirituality, social justice, and queer and quare theories.

Jajuan Johnson, is a doctoral candidate in heritage studies at Arkansas State University. Jajuan is an oral historian and scholar whose work focuses on African American material culture in the South. He is the founder of Speaking History, an oral history initiative; and The Forum of Black Gay Men in Arkansas which focuses on empowering Black gay men through interactive dialogue.

C. Emmanuel Little, is an EdD candidate in the institute of higher education at the University of Georgia. Emmanuel's research and practice focus on Black male experiences in both K–12 classrooms and higher education, as well as diversity and inclusion initiatives. Emmanuel currently works as an administrator in the College of Education at Georgia College.

John David Marshall, EdD, is the chief equity officer for Jefferson County Public Schools in Louisville, Kentucky. Dr. Marshall's research, work, and interests focus on diversity, inclusion, and systemic practices that improve or weaken life outcomes for students of color.

Robert A. Massey, DMin, is an assistant professor of chaplain practitioner and hospice at the School of Theology at Mantle Christian College. Robert's research focuses on pneumatic theology (Gnosticism), psychoneuroimmunology, and bereavement and grief counseling.

Joseph Mathews, MA, MEd, is a doctoral candidate at Teachers College Columbia University and an adjunct professor at Hunter College. Joseph's research focuses on Black male academic achievement, school-to-prison pipeline prevention, and best practices for engaging disengaged students.

Robert Akeem Mays, is a PhD candidate in the School of Social Work at Morgan State University. Robert is a licensed independent clinical social worker. His research interests are mental health disparities, Black adolescents and young adults, race, culture, identity, and psychological well-being.

N. Jamel Miller, PhD, is a high school counselor working in the Augusta-Richmond County School System. Jamel's research focuses on critical race theory, counter storytelling and effective counseling techniques for Black boys.

Burgess Mitchell, MEd, is an assistant dean for student services in the School of Engineering at Vanderbilt University. Burgess is a doctoral candidate at Tennessee State University in the Educational Leadership program with a research focus on diversity, STEM, and online student services.

Mwalimu Donkor Issa Minors, MEd, is a program coordinator of Boston Public Schools in Roxbury, Massachusetts. His work focuses on holistic healing modalities, decolonizing curricula, and developing youth leaders dedicated to social justice. Donkor's initiative is rooted in rites of passage traditions modified to fit the school context, offering a character-based curriculum model to improve students' academic performance while working to reshape their life trajectory.

Zaccheus L. Moss, is a social entrepreneur and minister and managing member of Moss Consulting, LLC that understands that service to others is the currency required for a community to thrive and be successful.

Nickolaus Alexander Ortiz, PhD, is a graduate of Texas A&M University in mathematics education and a post-doctoral research associate at Michigan State University in East Lansing, MI. Originally from Atlanta, GA., Nickolaus taught mathematics for 3 years in their public schools where he also teaches each summer with the Upward Bound Program at Morehouse College. Nickolaus's primary research interests focus on Black students and the impact that their teachers have on their performance and appreciation for mathematics.

Michael T. Owens, is a college professor, author, and motivational speaker. His latest book is entitled *Burned: Conversations With a Black WWII Veteran*.

Oscar Espinoza-Parra, PhD, is dean of enrollment services at the College of the Desert. He enjoys playing softball, snowboarding, attending music festivals, and working out. Additionally, he is an avid reader, loves to listen to music, and a strong advocate of the powerful positive effects of pursuing a college education.

MarQo D. Patton, EdD, is an artist and creative consultant, serving as a founding music business instructor at Pearl-Cohn Entertainment Magnet High School. MarQo is the CEO of Jusreall Music Group Global, LLC (JMGG), a creative consultancy. For more information, visit www.jmgroupglobal.com.

Dante Pelzer, PhD, is an assistant professor in the academic affairs faculty and the assistant director for student diversity at the Medical University of South Carolina. Dante's research focuses on Black male college achievement and the experiences of underrepresented student populations at academic health centers.

Eugene Pitchford, is an assistant professor of education at Concordia University Wisconsin. Eugene's research focuses on successful learning environments for urban education settings, creating pipelines to increase college readiness for students of color, and ways to motivate young learners to become proficient readers. Eugene is also the co-author of the book *Superhero Educator* and frequently presents at local schools to help improve learning outcomes.

Victor L. Powell, MAE, is the principal of Matthew Maury Elementary School in Alexandria City Public Schools in Alexandria, VA. Victor is invested in inspiring, connecting, and educating (I.C.E) youth in the Washington, DC metro area. Victor's work focuses on achieving high school readiness, higher education readiness, and the development of life skills that will assist the growth of young people within their communities. Victor is also a young adult Sunday school teacher at Third Street Church of God.

Stuart Rhoden, PhD is an instructor at University College at Arizona State University. Stuart's research is interdisciplinary focusing on academic achievement, education policy, sociology of education, and Black male achievement and resilience.

Jason Rivera, PhD, is vice chancellor for student academic success at Rutgers University-Camden. His research explores college completion for Latino and African American male students as well as the ways care, capital, and community cultural wealth influence student outcomes.

Derrick Robinson, PhD, is an assistant professor of educational leadership in the college of education at the University of Memphis. Derrick's research focuses on P–20 school culture and climate, leadership effectiveness, and teacher effectiveness.

Lawrence Scott, PhD, is an assistant professor of educational leadership at Texas A&M University San Antonio. He is also the executive director of the community for life foundation. Lawrence's research interests include noncognitive factors influencing academic success of underrepresented populations, leadership development, and teacher efficacy and retention.

Alex Sekwat, PhD, is a professor of public administration and associate dean of the School of Graduate and Professional Studies at Tennessee State University. His research interests are in the areas of public management, public budgeting, financial management, and economic development.

Oscar Fabian Soto, is a graduate student of sociology at the University of California-Santa Barbara. As a formerly incarcerated student, Oscar's research focuses on the mechanisms of oppression of prison reentry and global political economy. He is also a strong advocate for prison abolition.

Nathan Stephens, MSW, is a doctoral candidate in the educational leadership and policy analysis program at the University of Missouri-Columbia. Nathan's research focuses on racial trauma and Black males in higher education. Nathan also serves as the director of the Bruce D. Nesbitt African American Cultural Center at the University of Illinois at Urbana-Champaign.

George E. Stewart, II., is an educator, author, and ordained minister. The focus of his work consists of the academic, social/emotional, and spiritual development of youth and families.

George Suttles, MPA, MA, is a program officer at the John A. Hartford Foundation, a national healthcare philanthropy working to improve the care of older adults and provide supports for family caregivers.

Jeremiah N. Taylor, MEd, is a doctoral candidate in executive educational leadership at Houston Baptist University. Jeremiah is a secondary teacher, educational diagnostician, and consultant in Galveston County. Jeremiah's research focuses on students with disabilities in postsecondary educational institution.

Solomon Tention, EdD, serves as a director for student engagement/Title IX coordinator at South Louisiana Community College. Solomon's research focuses on student affairs, cultural competency, diversity and inclusion, community colleges, and student success.

Eddie Vanderhorst, is a doctoral student at Capella University in the School of Education. Eddie's research focuses on mass incarceration among minorities and the overrepresentation of African American males in special education.

Brandon C. S. Wallace, an award-winning educator, instructs coursework in English, reading, and special education at Prince George's Community College, Montgomery College, and the Johns Hopkins University, respectively. He serves on two national assessments committees, specifically as an English language arts (ELA) and accessibility, accommodations, and fairness (AAF) consultant for the Partnership for Assessment of Readiness for College and Careers (PARCC) and standing reading committee member for the National Assessment of Educational Progress (NAEP). Brandon is a curricula writer, public speaker, presenter, and author, who originally taught in the middle and high school level in Baltimore City Public Schools.

Larry J. Walker, EdD, is an independent researcher. Previously, Dr. Walker served as a Congressional fellow with the Congressional Black Caucus Foundation and legislative director for Congressman Major R. Owens. His research focuses on HBCUs, race, politics, teacher education and mental health.

Gregory Washington, PhD, is a professor in the Department of Social Work and coordinator of the Hooks African-American Male Initiative (HAAMI) of the Benjamin L. Hooks Institute for Social Change at the University of Memphis. A major goal of Gregory's research is to identify and promote the use of innovative culturally-centered group interventions that reduce risk for disparities in behavioral health and incarceration outcomes among young African Americans.

Michael S. Washington, MHR, a 20-year veteran in human resources and higher education, is currently pursuing doctoral studies at the University of Illinois at Urbana-Champaign. He is also a career coach and motivational speaker who enjoys inspiring individuals and groups to succeed despite personal challenges. Possessing enhanced awareness of what it means to live in a pluralistic society, Michael offers expert insights to organizations who desire to create more diverse and inclusive work and learning environments.

Brian K. Williams, PhD, is an assistant professor of education at North Carolina A&T State University. His research focuses on literacy, teacher preparation, urban education, and culturally sustaining pedagogy.

C. Sheldon Woods, PhD, is an associate professor of science education in the College of education at Northern Illinois University. His research focuses on elementary science education, service learning, and HIV/AIDS education.

www.ingramcontent.com/pod-product-compliance
Lightning Source LLC
Chambersburg PA
CBHW050620300426
44112CB00012B/1588